THE MARYLAND
ONE-DAY TRIP BOOK

To my good friends: Marian Bellama,
Pat Richards and Barbara Rollin.

THE MARYLAND ONE-DAY TRIP BOOK

190 DAY-LONG EXCURSIONS IN THE LAND OF PLEASANT LIVING

Jane Ockershausen Smith

EPM
Publications, Inc.
McLean, Virginia 22101

Library of Congress Cataloging in Publication Data

Smith, Jane Ockershausen.
  The Maryland one-day trip book: 190 day-long excursions in
the land of pleasant living/Jane Ockershausen Smith.
    p. cm.

  Includes index.
  ISBN 0-939009-06-4
  1. Maryland–Description and travel–1981—Guide-books.
I. Title. II. Title: Maryland 1-day trip book.
F179.3.S65 1988
917.52′0443–dc19 87-37953 CIP

EPM Publications, Inc., 1003 Turkey Run Road,
  McLean, Virginia 22101

Printed in the United States of America

Cover photograph by Everett C. Johnson
Cover and book design by Tom Huestis

Grateful acknowledgment is made to the Office of Tourist
Development, Maryland Department of Economic &
Community Development, for the use of its photographs.
Photos from other sources are individually credited.

Contents

THE MARYLAND ONE-DAY TRIP BOOK

================MARYLAND'S CAPITAL DIVERSION================

MONTGOMERY COUNTY

PRINCE GEORGE'S COUNTY

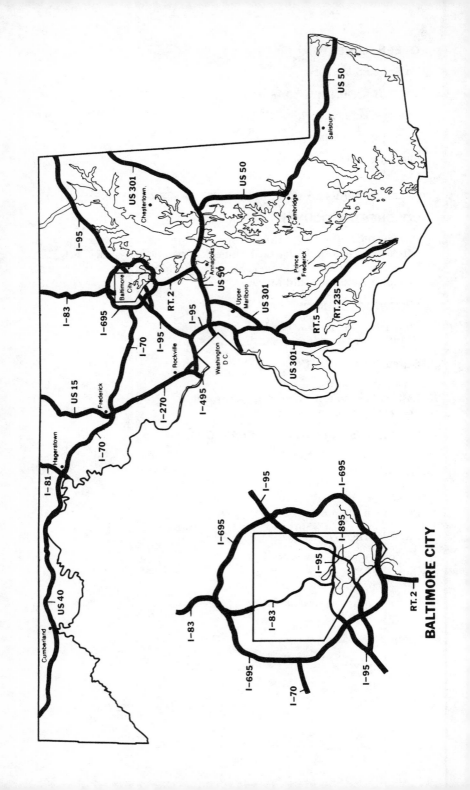

BALTIMORE CITY

WHERE TO OBTAIN A FULL-SIZE MAP:

For a free state highway map of Maryland, write to:

MARYLAND TOURISM
Room 269
45 Calvert Street
Annapolis, MD 21401

Or go in person to any of the following Visitor Information Centers:

YOUGHIOGHENY OVERLOOK
YOUGHIOGHENY OVERLOOK
  INFORMATION CENTER
US 48 Eastbound Lane
Friendsville, MD 21531
(301)746-5979

I-70 WEST (SOUTH MOUNTAIN)
I-70 WEST INFORMATION
  CENTER
Interstate 70 Westbound Lane
  Rest Area
Frederick County, MD 21773
(301)293-4161

I-70 EAST (SOUTH MOUNTAIN)
I-70 EAST INFORMATION
  CENTER
Interstate 70 Eastbound Lane
  Rest Area
Frederick County, MD 21773
(301)293-2526

US 15 SOUTH
US 15 SOUTH INFORMATION
  CENTER
US 15 Southbound Lane
  Rest Area
Frederick County, MD 21727
(301)447-2553

CORRIDOR INFORMATION CENTERS, INC.
I-95 NORTHBOUND TOURIST
  INFORMATION CENTER
I-95 Northbound Rest Area
  between Exits 35 & 38
Savage, MD 20763
(301)490-1333 I-95 N
(301)490-2444 I-95 S

CHESAPEAKE HOUSE
CHESAPEAKE HOUSE
  INFORMATION
  CENTER, I-95
North East, MD 21901
(301)287-2313

STATE HOUSE
VISITORS CENTER, Lobby
Maryland State House
State Circle
Annapolis, MD 21401
(301)974-3400

US 13 NORTH
US 13 NORTH INFORMATION
  CENTER
US 13 Northbound
  Rest Area
Pocomoke City, MD 21851
(301)957-2484

County Tourism Contacts for Maryland

(All Maryland phone numbers have a 301 Area Code.)

ALLEGANY COUNTY
TOURISM & PUBLIC RELATIONS
3 Pershing Street
County Office Bldg.
Cumberland, MD 21502
77-5905

ANNAPOLIS
PUBLIC INFORMATION AND
   TOURISM OFFICE
City Hall
160 Duke of Gloucester Street
Annapolis, MD 21401
263-7940

**ANNAPOLIS & ANNE
ARUNDEL COUNTY**
TOURISM COUNCIL
152 Main Street
Annapolis, MD 21401
268-7676

ANNE ARUNDEL COUNTY
OFFICE OF ECONOMIC
   DEVELOPMENT
Arundel Center
Annapolis, MD 21404
263-7940

BALTIMORE
OFFICE OF PROMOTION &
   TOURISM
34 Market Place, Suite 310
Baltimore, MD 21202
752-8632

BALTIMORE COUNTY
OFFICE OF ECONOMIC
   DEVELOPMENT
111 W. Chesapeake Avenue
Towson, MD 21204
494-3648

CALVERT COUNTY
DEPT. OF ECONOMIC
   DEVELOPMENT
Calvert County Court House
Prince Frederick, MD 21204
494-3648

**CALVERT, CHARLES & ST.
MARY'S COUNTIES**
TRI-COUNTY COUNCIL FOR
   SOUTHERN MARYLAND
P.O. Box 1634
Charlotte Hall, MD 20622
884-2144 or 870-2520 (D.C.)

**CAROLINE & QUEEN ANNE'S
COUNTIES**
TOURISM
County Office Building
208 North Commerce Street
Centreville, MD 21617

CARROLL COUNTY
OFFICE OF INFORMATION,
   PROMOTION & TOURISM
County Office Building, Room 109
225 North Center Street
Westminster, MD 21157
848-4500 Ext. 2231 or 876-2085
   Ext. 2231 (Balt.)

CECIL COUNTY
OFFICE OF PLANNING &
   ECONOMIC DEVELOPMENT
County Office Building, Room 300
Elkton, MD 21921
398-0200 Ext. 144

CHARLES COUNTY
PUBLIC INFORMATION
   ASSISTANT
Courthouse
P.O. Box B
LaPlata, MD 20646
645-0559 or 870-3000 Ext. 559
   (D.C.)

DORCHESTER COUNTY
TOURISM
P.O. Box 307
Cambridge, MD 21613
228-3234

FREDERICK COUNTY
TOURISM COUNCIL OF
  FREDERICK COUNTY, INC.
19 E. Church Street
Frederick, MD 21701
663-8687

GARRETT COUNTY
PROMOTION COUNCIL
Garrett County Court House
Oakland, MD 21550
334-1948

HARFORD COUNTY
OFFICE OF ECONOMIC
  DEVELOPMENT
29 W. Courtland Street
Bel Air, MD 21014
879-2000 Ext. 339 (Balt.) or 838-
  6000 Ext. 339

HOWARD COUNTY
ECONOMIC DEVELOPMENT
  OFFICE
3430 Court House Drive
Ellicott City, MD 21043
992-2344

HOWARD COUNTY
TOURISM COUNCIL
c/o Columbia Hilton
5485 Twin Knolls Road
Columbia, MD 21045
730-7817

KENT COUNTY
CHAMBER OF COMMERCE
P.O. Box 146
118 N. Cross Street
Chestertown, MD 21620
778-0416

MONTGOMERY COUNTY
MARYLAND TRAVEL COUNCIL,
  INC.
Red Brick Courthouse
29 Courthouse Square
Rockville, MD 20850
588-8687

OCEAN CITY
VISITORS & CONVENTIONS
  BUREAU, INC.
P.O. Box 116
Ocean City, MD 21842
289-2800

OCEAN CITY, TOWN OF
PUBLIC RELATIONS DIRECTOR
P.O. Box 158
Ocean City, MD 21842
289-2800

PRINCE GEORGE'S
TRAVEL PROMOTION COUNCIL,
  INC.
6600 Kenilworth Avenue
Riverdale, MD 20737
927-0700

ST. MARY'S COUNTY
CHAMBER OF COMMERCE
Tourism Development
Route 5, Box 41A
Mechanicsville, MD 20659
884-5555

SOMERSET COUNTY
TOURISM COMMISSION
P.O. Box 243
Princess Anne, MD 21853
651-2968

TALBOT COUNTY
CHAMBER OF COMMERCE
P.O. Box 1366
Easton, MD 21601
822-4606

WASHINGTON COUNTY
TOURISM DIVISION
Court House Annex
Hagerstown, MD 21740
791-3130

WICOMICO COUNTY
CONVENTION & VISITORS
  BUREAU
Wicomico Youth & Civic Center
Glen Avenue Extended
Salisbury, MD 21801
548-4914

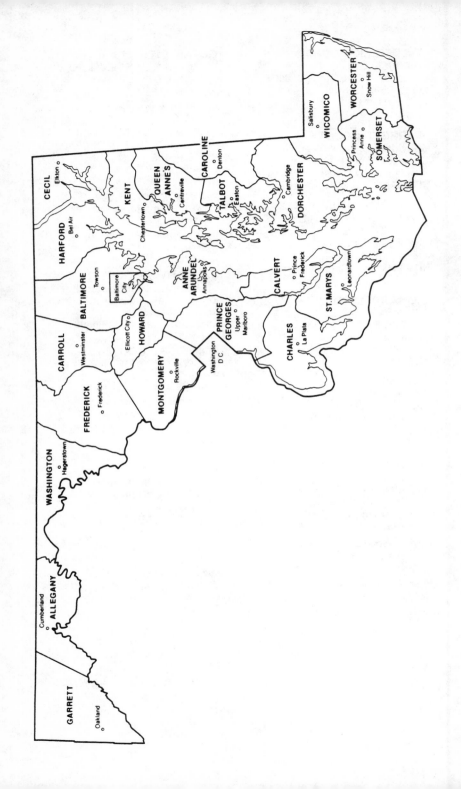

Maryland,
My Maryland

Maryland is my home. I grew up, was educated, taught school and reared a family here. It was a labor of love to spend 18 months exploring my home state. As I traveled from its western mountains to its eastern waters, I discovered that Irving Berlin's "America, the Beautiful" just as aptly describes Maryland, often called America in miniature.

Maryland offers an amazing diversity of hidden pleasures and treasures both urban and rural. There is, without doubt, something for everyone. *The Maryland One-Day Trip Book* groups almost 200 sites by county, covering the state's 23 counties, and also by its major cities.

This geographic focus encourages you to plan a one-day outing that includes several nearby sites. I suggest you read all the selections in the city or geographic region you're planning to visit. Keep in mind the total distance you'll be traveling—a daytrip from one end of the state to another may not be practical, especially with small children. Nearly every site described in the book lies within a day's drive—out and back—from Baltimore. That is why all directions to the sites are given from there. Readers in other areas of the state will have to consult their maps to gauge distances and driving time from wherever they are located. I urge you to consult the book's Calendar of Events as well; it will help you choose the attractions best suited to the time of year and to your personal interests.

Where to go and what to see are important considerations, but you also need to know when to go. The Calendar of Events alerts you to festivals and celebrations throughout Maryland. There are travelers who enjoy the excitement of these special days; others prefer quieter times. Timing is especially important at many nature and garden sites. Spring transforms the slopes of the London Town Garden along the South River into a blooming treat—first with bright yellow banks of daffodils and then the pastel hues of azaleas. Summer is the time to meander along the poolside paths at Lilypons Water Gardens, and Woodend trails are a delight when autumn tints the leaves. You can escape the chill of winter weather with a visit to the Brookside Gardens Conservatory. Birds too follow a natural calendar. Wildlife sanctuaries are best visited during the birds' annual spring and fall migrations.

Read through each selection when you develop your day's itinerary to be sure sites are open when you plan to visit. If you are scheduling your trip to coincide with a specific event, call ahead, because event times and dates may change from year to year.

Don't limit yourself to an annual two-week holiday. One-day vacations can provide escapes all year long. These short trips can broaden your horizons, introduce you to new ideas and interests and delight your senses. Many of these gardens, parks, wildlife sanctuaries, artists communities and even museums do not charge admission, so you can enjoy them with very little strain on your checkbook.

I invite you to explore my state. Maryland, my Maryland, God did shed His grace on thee!

J.O.S.

══Western Maryland══

GARRETT COUNTY

Bear Creek Trout Rearing Station

Small Fry Fascination

And now here's more of the story. . .roughly 60,000 to 80,000 of the rainbow and brown trout fingerlings hatched at the Albert Powell facility in Washington County (see selection) are shipped to the **Bear Creek Trout Rearing Station** in Accident.

The two- to three-inch fingerlings stay in eight holding ponds until full-grown. The adult trout are then used to stock the streams, rivers, ponds and lakes of Allegany and Garrett Counties. One of the eight rearing ponds holds trout, weighing 1½ to 2 pounds, that during stocking are mixed with the younger fish in a ratio of 15 big trout to 1,000 smaller.

Nearby Bear Creek is stocked by this hatchery five or six times a year, starting around the first of March. There is no season for trout, but fishing is best in Maryland's freshwaters from late March to mid-November. Anglers need both a fishing license and a trout stamp to go after the brook, brown and rainbow trout. Fishing regulations restrict the catch to five trout per fisherman; there is no minimum size per fish.

Bear Creek Trout Rearing Station does not provide a guided tour, nor is there a brochure for the low-key operation. Visitors are welcome to wander around this tree-shaded glade any time from 9:00 A.M. to 4:00 P.M. daily. If there are young children along, be sure to walk down to the lower holding pond and watch the fingerlings try to leap upstream against the water spilling from a large pipe. The hatchery staff had to add a wooden barrier to keep the young fish in the pond. The fish continually throw themselves against this barrier, instinctive behavior that's fascinating to watch. Children also like watching the staff feed the fish, but there is no set schedule for the three daily feedings.

Directions: Bear Creek Trout Rearing Station is approximately 165 miles west of Baltimore. From Baltimore take I-70 west to Hancock. At Hancock take Route 40 west to Cumberland. At Cumberland take Route 40/48 west to Exit 14 at Keysers Ridge. Proceed south on Route 219 to Accident. Turn right on Accident—Bear Creek Road and then take the next right on Fish Hatchery Road for the well-marked facility.

Casselman Bridge State Park and Grantsville

Little Crossing Links National Road

In 1775 Colonel George Washington, aide-de-camp to British General Edward Braddock during the French and Indian War, blazed a trail along the old Nemacolin Indian path. The trail Washington marked led the British into Pennsylvania; where it crossed the Casselman River he named it Little Crossing.

When the French empire in North America ended after the fall of Quebec in 1759, British settlers moved into western territory formerly controlled by the French and their Indian allies. One of the areas that attracted the British was Little Crossing. In the early 1760s Joseph Tomlison built an inn just a few miles east of Little Crossing. A ford and road followed, and this became a major thoroughfare for westward travelers.

In 1813 a single arch stone bridge, the largest of its type in the country, was built over the river as part of the National Road linking Cumberland with Wheeling, West Virginia. When the workmen removed the timbers supporting the 80-foot span, onlookers expected the bridge to fall. It stands to this day. In 1933 a new steel bridge on Route 40 replaced the stone arch, but the bridge remains a scenic focus at **Casselman River State Park**.

One of the stagecoach inns built in 1818 beside the river crossing has been remodeled. It's now Penn Alps Restaurant and Craft Shops. Four dining rooms serve Pennsylvania Dutch specialties, and the gift shop is filled with handcrafted creations. Across the parking lot is an artisan's village with studios for potters, weavers, sculptors, stained-glass workers and a world-renowned bird carver, Gary Yoder. One of these log cabin studios dates back to Revolutionary days, another was built in 1820 and a third in the middle of the 1800s. Just footsteps away is Stanton's Mill, the county's oldest operating mill. The original grinding stones from the 1797 mill are on display.

Yet another old hostelry, the Casselman Hotel, is still operating in **Grantsville**. Built in 1824 for travelers on the National Road, it has nine bedrooms, each furnished with Early American pieces (as are the rooms in the adjacent motor court). All the rooms on the first and second floor of the old inn have fireplaces. The restaurant serves wholesome country cooking using favorite Amish recipes. The Casselman makes all its own breads, cakes and pies in a downstairs bakery you can visit. There is a gift shop next to the bakery.

You'll also find bakery departments at two Grantsville markets that sell country produce and homemade wares. The Hill Top Fruit Market on U.S. Route 40, three miles east of Grantsville,

Casselman Hotel, built in 1824 for travelers on the National Road (US 40), still provides accommodations and country cooking, also baked goods made in a bakery you may visit.

has a mouth-watering selection of 50 kinds of candy in addition to fresh produce.

Just past Grantsville on Route 669 is Yoders Country Market, which, in addition to fresh baked goods, offers all kinds of meats: smoked, fresh, processed and canned. Homemade jams, jellies, applesauce, honey and maple syrup are only some of the made-at-home products. There is also a wide selection of candy, nuts and dried fruits. The Amish-Mennonite community of Grantsville is right off Route 40/48.

Directions: From Baltimore take Route 70 west about 90 miles to Hancock, then continue west on Route 40 to Cumberland, where you take Route 40/48 west to Exit 22 (Route 219 north). Turn left on Alternate Route 40 for Grantsville.

Cranesville Sub-Arctic Swamp

Ice Age Bog

Maryland has two swamps to explore: Battle Creek Cypress Swamp Sanctuary (see selection) and the Nature Conservancy's

Cranesville Sub-Arctic Swamp. This may sound like a shallow boast, but each offers an unusual natural environment for nature lovers to explore.

The **Cranesville Sub-Arctic Swamp**, a 500-acre National Historic Landmark, straddles the boundary between Western Maryland and West Virginia. In fact, the boardwalk lies in West Virginia. The area was once called the Great Pine Swamp because of the abundant giant pine trees, but now it's named for the West Virginia community on its northern edge.

This sub-arctic swamp was formed during the Ice Age, between 7500 and 10,000 B.C. The ice fields halted 100 miles north of this part of Maryland. But the "taiga," or boreal forest, that extended out from the ice formations moved into this area, taking over what was once a deciduous forest. In most regions overrun by the boreal forest, when the ice melted the forest retreated. Now, the boreal forest is found almost exclusively in northern border states and Canada.

But there are exceptions, and one of the exceptions is the Cranesville Sub-Arctic Swamp, where you can still see rare species of flora normally found only in arctic regions. There are complex reasons why this unique area survived. Of major importance is the 2,500-foot altitude, which keeps the climate cool and the growing season short. The location of the swamp also contributes to its survival. The swamp sits in a bowl-shaped valley that is a natural frost pocket.

All of this means the interested visitor has the opportunity to see a very different terrain at Cranesville. Most who venture out on the wooden boardwalk, however, will not be fortunate enough to spot the swamp's most elusive and rarest inhabitant—the northern water shrew. This pennyweight, mouse-like mammal is light enough to run across the top of the watery bog. Yet it will attack animals far larger than itself in its constant quest for food. It does not go after two-footed quarry.

The bog mat you'll see is composed of spongy moss and peat. Wild cranberries, reindeer moss, blueberries, black chokeberries, St. John's wort and mountain laurel compose the low groundcover. Trees include red spruce, hemlock, red maple, eastern larch and mountain ash. This is not a "wow" sight, but rather an unusual and different environment that provides a new world for nature lovers to enjoy.

Directions: From Baltimore, take I-70 west about 90 miles to Hancock, then continue west on Route 40 another 65 miles to Cumberland; take Route 40/48 west to Keysers Ridge, Exit 14. Head south on Route 219 to Oakland; at second light, Green Street, turn right; continue through next light, which becomes Liberty Street, and then becomes Herrington Manor Road. Follow approximately six miles to Cranesville Road; turn left and proceed four miles and just past "Bell Ringer Originals in Wood" sign, turn left onto a dirt road at a sign marked "Cranesville Swamp Nature Preserve;" proceed ½ mile and bear right onto another dirt road; in less than ½ mile, look for electric utility poles and a large marker on the right that indicates the footpath to the boardwalk.

Deep Creek Lake

A Superior Lake

Garrett County, which calls itself Maryland's Best Kept Secret, is rapidly being discovered through its Deep Creek Lake. The word is out—and spreading—that the lake is an absolute vacation delight!

The man-made 3,900-acre lake has 65 miles of shoreline, most of it privately held. One of the few public areas is the 800-foot beach in **Deep Creek Lake State Park**. An ideal spot for a hot summer day, the beach has a wooded picnic area behind it where non-swimmers can relax in the shade and watch the fun.

Many families camp at this state park. Its five nature trails are especially appealing in the spring when the wildflowers bloom and in the fall when the leaves turn. When snow comes to Western Maryland, Meadow Mountain Trail is used by snowmobilers. If you want to rent a snowmobile call Jody Sherman, (301)387-5677. He's located off Route 219 in the McHenry area.

The Deep Creek Lake area is Maryland's largest ski area. At Wisp the elevation is 3,080 and there are vertical drops of 610 feet. Wisp has both downhill and cross-country skiing. Cross-country skiers also use the trails at Deep Creek Lake State Park.

Because 96 percent of the lake's shoreline is privately owned, the best way to explore is by boat. The park has a boat ramp for those with their own boats. If you want to rent a sailboat, powerboat, rowboat or canoe, there are a number of marinas in the area: Bill's Marine Service, (301)387-5536; Crystal Waters Boat Rentals, (301)387-5515; Echo Marina, Inc., (301)387-5910; Mountaineer Marina, (301)387-5170; and Deep Creek Outfitters, (301)387-6977. Several places rent water-skiing equipment. It's a good idea to call ahead and reserve a boat because these marinas do a big business during summer.

Another popular recreation around Deep Creek Lake is horseback riding. Both Double G Ranch, (301)387-5481, and Western Trails Riding Stables, (301)387-6155 or 387-6890, offer a variety of experiences, from ½-hour rides to overnight horse trail rides. They also offer hayrides, camping and winter sleigh rides.

The lake is very popular with fishermen. Garrett County keeps track of the big fish that don't get away. From May through

Deep Creek Lake, a 3,900-acre magnet, draws so many swimmers, sportsmen and skiers to its area that it is endangering Garrett County's claim to being Maryland's Best Kept Secret.

September the county awards weekly and seasonal prizes for the biggest fish caught. Fish must be registered at Johnny's Bait House on Route 219 near McHenry. Prizes were given in one recent year for a 1-pound, 11-inch bluegill; 5-pound, 14-ounce, 25-inch brown trout; 3-pound, 10-ounce, 25½-inch chain pickerel; 1-pound, 12-ounce, 15¼-inch crappie; 6-pound, 10-ounce, 23-inch largemouth bass; 16-pound, 10-ounce, 40-inch northern pike; 3-pound, 8-ounce, 20¼-inch smallmouth bass; 9-pound, 9-ounce, 31-inch walleye and 1-pound, 6-ounce, 15-inch yellow perch. Not even cold weather stops the eager anglers; ice fishing attracts many during January and February. Bring your axe, fishing gear and plenty of warm clothes.

Directions: From Baltimore take I-70 west 90 miles to Hancock, then continue west on Route 40 to Cumberland, where you take Route 40/48 west to Keysers Ridge (Exit 14) and then head south on Route 219. Turn left on Glendale Road for Deep Creek Lake State Park.

Garrett County Historical Museum and Oakland

Oakland Cluster

As you travel around Western Maryland, you'll hear stories about Meshach Browning. You'll learn all about this legendary pioneer hunter at the **Garrett County Historical Museum** in Oakland. He lived along Sang Run, named for the area's wild ginseng plants, the roots of which are worth about $100 a pound. A model of Browning's Sang Run cabin is displayed at the museum. He is credited with killing hundreds of deer, black bear, wildcats and lesser game. Though he lacked formal education, Browning wrote *Forty-Four Years in the Life of a Hunter*, still a hunter's classic 100 years later.

The museum, housed in a 1935 Episcopal Parish House, portrays the lifestyle of both well-known and everyday citizens of the county. It's full of fading photographs of residents and their houses and hotels. Two rooms are re-created: a bedroom of the 1890s/1900s is filled with heavy Victorian mahogany furniture, and a kitchen has period pieces from the 1800s to 1890s. There are clothes, too, including a very uncomfortable-looking wool bathing suit and a rather gaudy orange feather fan.

After your stop at the museum, open June, July and August, Monday through Friday, from 10:00 A.M. to 4:00 P.M., you may want to drive around Mountain Lake Park, just east of Oakland off Route 135. This was where wealthy vacationers built summer homes. It was a Chautauqua-type resort from 1882 to 1942. Many of the fine old Victorian homes have been restored.

In the early years vacationers often arrived at the Baltimore & Ohio Railroad station. John W. Garrett, in whose honor the county was named and who contributed the acreage for Garrett State Forest, was president of the B&O line. The handsome Queen Anne station, now unoccupied, is one of the oldest in the country and an often-mentioned candidate for conversion to a tourist attraction.

Off Old Deer Park Road, now known as Memorial Drive, you'll find the Cornish Manor, an excellent place for a midday break. The house was built in 1868 and serves excellent country meals.

Broadford Recreation Area is just outside Oakland. It's one of the four public swimming beaches in the county. Broadford has a 138-acre lake with 600 feet of sandy beach. There are a bathhouse, snack shop and picnic grounds, as well as paddleboats and rowboats to rent. The lake is popular with both swimmers and fishermen. The beach is open 9:00 A.M. to 8:00 P.M., and the park 9:00 A.M. to dusk. A nominal admission is charged per car.

Directions: From Baltimore take I-70 west 90 miles to Hancock, then continue west on Route 40 to Cumberland, then take Route 40/48 west 33 miles to Exit 14, Keysers Ridge. Take Route 219 south past Deep Creek Lake; turn left on Sand Flat Road and right on Route 135. Near Mountain Lake Park, turn right on Pittsburg Avenue and follow museum signs.

Savage River State Forest

Wilderness and Whitewater

Garrett County has nearly 75,000 acres of wild timberland within three state forests: Potomac State Forest along Backbone Mountain near the headwaters of the Potomac River, Garrett State Forest (see Swallow Falls selection) and **Savage River State Forest**.

Savage River is largest, with roughly 53,000 acres. Elevations within its boundaries range from 1,488 to 3,075 feet, and the two rivers that originate here, the Savage and the Casselman, flow in opposite directions to the Atlantic Ocean and Gulf of Mexico, respectively. In 1951 the Savage River Dam was finished, creating a reservoir of water for Western Maryland communities. Also, when water is released downstream a narrow and difficult 5½-mile whitewater course is created. This challenging course hosts world-class paddling competitions, such as the 1972 U.S. Olympic Trials and the 1989 Whitewater World Championship Races.

Within the Savage River State Forest are two state parks: **New Germany** and **Big Run**. In New Germany the Swauger's Mill Dam contributes to the park's recreational options by creating a 13-acre lake. Visitors can rent rowboats, fish the well-stocked waters

24

and swim. Picnic tables, fireplaces and a pavilion are located near the lake.

New Germany is one of five state parks that have rental cabins (the others are Herrington Manor, Elk Neck, Martinak and Janes Island; see selections). There are also campgrounds. Backpack, or walk-in type, camping is permitted along the 17-mile Big Savage Hiking Trail, recommended for experienced hikers only.

The best way to enjoy the wildlife and wildflowers of this forested park is by taking one of New Germany's nine trails, which are charted and ranked by degree of difficulty on an available park trail map. In winter cross-country skiers enjoy many of these same trails and the park's recreation hall is converted to a warming hut. Limited snowmobile trails have been created on Meadow Mountain near New Germany State Park. A permit is required to use them.

There are also trails and unimproved camp grounds in Big Run State Park. Primitive camping is available in the State Forest.

Directions: From Baltimore take I-70 west for 90 miles to Hancock, then continue west on Route 40 to Cumberland, where you take Route 40/48 west to Exit 24 (Lower New Germany Road) for the park. Maps and permits are available at the New Germany State Park Visitor Center.

Swallow Falls and Herrington Manor State Parks

The Big Muddy

In western Maryland in 1918, Emmanuel Metheny, an Allegheny Mountain man, stopped to help a Packard mired in the mud. Metheny used his old Model T to pull the Packard free. He refused payment for his help but did tell the Packard's passengers they should get a car suitable for the roads; he went on to claim that the Ford Model T was the best car made. This unsolicited testimonial had an unexpected reward. One of the passengers in the Packard was Henry Ford, who later sent his loyal customer a new Ford automobile.

Ford, along with his companions, Thomas Edison and Harvey Firestone, had come to camp on the bank of the Muddy Creek, overlooking Swallow Falls. These titans of American industry returned for another camping visit in 1921, joined by naturalist John Burroughs.

The campsite these influential men chose was in the first state-owned forest in the country. Nearly 2,000 acres of forest land was given to Maryland in 1906 by John and Robert Garrett for the protection of wildlife and the advancement of forestry. The original grant was expanded to 9,248 acres and became the Gar-

Swallow Falls State Park has four falls. It was near this one in 1918 that Henry Ford, Thomas Edison and Harvey Firestone got stuck in a Packard car and were pulled out by a Model T.

rett State Forest. Within this tract is both **Swallow Falls State Park** and **Herrington Manor State Park**.

There are actually four different falls within Swallow Falls State Park: Muddy Creek Falls, Swallow Falls (Maryland's largest), the Lower Falls and Tolliver Falls. Canyon Trail, leading from Muddy Creek to Swallow Falls, is one of the state's most scenic hiking trails. Shaded by high cliffs, it winds along the Youghiogheny River. In the spring wildflowers bloom along the river banks, and even on sweltering summer days it seems cool here. In autumn the foliage brings new color to the trail, while in winter the frozen falls create an icy wonderland.

There are ten miles of trails in the park. One of the more popular is the Swinging Bridge Trail, which provides an excellent point for viewing the 64-foot Muddy Creek Falls. Muddy Creek gets its name from the brackish water found in the Cranesville Swamp where it originated (see selection). The creek meets the Youghiogheny just below Muddy Creek Falls.

You can hike, fish, picnic, camp and cross-country ski in Swallow Falls Park. At nearby Herrington Manor State Park you can swim at one of Garrett County's four public beaches. (The other beaches, described in other selections, are at Deep Creek Lake State Park, New Germany State Park and the Broadford Recreation Area.)

At Herrington Manor beach, on a 53-acre lake, paddleboats and rowboats can be rented. The lake is stocked periodically for fishing. The ten miles of hiking trails can be explored on foot during good weather and on skis after a snowfall. Twenty cabins are available within the park.

Directions: From Baltimore take I-70 west 90 miles to Hancock, follow Route 40 west to Cumberland, then Route 40/48 west to Exit 14 at Keysers Ridge. Go south on Route 219 then turn right on Mayhew Inn Road, then left on Sang Run Road. Make a right on Swallow Falls Road, which takes you to Swallow Falls State Park. For Herrington Manor State Park continue on Swallow Falls Road; it becomes Herrington Manor Road.

Whitewater Rafting

Wild Water

For many visitors Western Maryland's primary appeal is its scenic beauty. The Allegheny Mountains offer waterfalls, tumbling streams, mountaintop lakes and virgin forests. One marvelous way to experience this natural world is by taking a whitewater rafting trip along the Upper Youghiogheny River. The "Yock" flows north into Pennsylvania. You can also cross the West Virginia border and experience the thrills of the Cheat River.

The only problem with the Upper Yock's 11 miles of rapids is that none are for beginners; there are no Class I rapids, the easiest level of navigability. It has Class V rapids, considered extraordinarily difficult, with a series of long and violent sections. There are also some Class VI rapids; sometimes described as "deadly," these are strictly for the pros.

From Western Maryland you can branch out into nearby states for less hazardous whitewater rafting. The Youghiogheny River rafting trips that begin in Ohiopyle, Pennsylvania, accept paddlers aged 12 and over for normal water, and 14 and older for high water. Here the trip is eight miles with a drop of 40 feet during the first mile. The trip boasts eight major rapids separated by small rapids and even a few calm pools.

About 20 miles beyond Maryland's westernmost boundary is Albright, West Virginia, where the Cheat River trips begin. This eleven-mile rafting adventure runs through the Cheat River Canyon and includes 20 rapids with names like Big Nasty, Even Nastier and Devil's Trip. Sounds fun, doesn't it?

Don't come, the experts caution, unless you're prepared. You will get wet, so bring a bathing suit and sneakers on hot days. On cool, cloudy days in summer, or in spring or fall, wear a water-resistant jacket or even wool clothes to retain the body's warmth. Be sure to bring a change of clothes. Trips run rain or shine. The only time rafting trips are canceled is when the river is dangerously high. Most rafts hold four to eight passengers.

There are a number of companies running these exciting whitewater trips. Write or call:

White Water Adventures, P.O. Box 31, Ohiopyle, PA 15470, (800)WVA-RAFT

Cheat River Outfitters, Main Street & River Road, Box 196, Albright, WV 26519, (304)329-2024

Mountain Stream & Trail Outfitters, Box 106, Ohiopyle, PA 15470, (800)245-4090

Wilderness Voyageurs, Inc., Box 97, Ohiopyle, PA 15470, (412)329-4552

Precision Rafting Expeditions, Box 185, Friendville, MD 21531, (301)746-5290

River & Trail Outfitters, Route 2, Valley Road, Box 246, Knoxille, MD 21758, (301)834-8051

Upper Yough Whitewater Expeditions, Inc., River Road, P.O. Box 158, Friendsville, MD 21531, (301)746-5808

U.S.A. Whitewater, Inc., P.O. Box 277, Rowlesburg, WV 26425, (800)624-8060

The Whitewater Classic, Box 99, Sunday Roar, Hico, WV 25854, (304)658-5817 or Star Route 1, Box 124, Oakland, MD 21550, (301)387-4644

ALLEGANY COUNTY

C&O Canal National Historical Park (Upper)

Barge Right In

The railroad and the C&O Canal once vied for travelers and trade. Now they are merely reminders of the early years of westward expansion. It is a rueful footnote to this rivalry that the **C&O Canal National Historical Park** Visitor Center is located in Cumberland's Western Maryland Station Center on Canal Street.

This impressive and commanding station reflected the railroad's success. It was built in 1913, at the height of the railroad era. Inside the station, both railroad and canal memorabilia are on display. Old photographs recall these alternate means of transportation. The C&O Canal National Historical Visitor Center is open Tuesday through Saturday from 10:00 A.M. to 5:00 P.M. and on Sunday from 1:00 to 5:00 P.M.

A path leads from the station to the C&O Canal terminus. From this point it was 184.5 miles along the canal to Georgetown in the District of Columbia. On July 4, 1828, President John Quincy Adams turned the first shovel of earth to begin construction of the canal. On that same day Declaration of Independence signer Charles Carroll laid the first stone in Baltimore for the B&O Railroad. It was to be a race to the west!

The canal did not reach Cumberland until 1850. That was eight years after the B&O Railroad got there. By the time the canal was fully operational it was practically obsolete. The last three locks of the canal, numbers 73, 74 and 75, were finished in 1840. Stop at North Branch and see these locks, as well as a canal boat replica. The boat has a re-created captain's cabin, hay house and on-board mule stable. The canal boats almost always had two teams, so that one team rested while the other worked. Canal traffic was seasonal from the very beginning, because the barges couldn't maneuver once there was heavy freezing. Tours are given of the canal boat on weekends from 1:00 to 5:00 P.M. June through August.

One last canal site you might enjoy is the Paw Paw Tunnel, 30 miles below Cumberland. This was one of the most astonishing engineering achievements of the entire canal project. It was also completed late, 12 years behind schedule. The tunnel, through 3,118 feet of solid rock, was built to eliminate a six-mile set of bends in the Potomac River.

Today you can walk through the tunnel. Wear comfortable shoes and be sure to bring a flashlight. Imagine the tunnel in operation, 1850 to 1924. Talk about a traffic jam! Only one boat could negotiate the tunnel at a time, so there was often a one-mile backup at both ends of the tunnel.

It takes approximately 20 minutes to walk through the tunnel, and as you get near the middle the light dwindles and the sense of being beneath an enormous rocky mountain grows. It's easy to empathize with the workers who hacked and blasted their way through this rock. Violence between the immigrant work crews, cholera epidemics and frequent accidents added to the ordeal.

If time permits after you explore the tunnel, you may want to hike along the Tunnel Hill Trail that leads up and over the ridge above. This is a strenuous walk that takes about an hour.

Directions: From Baltimore take I-70 west 90 miles to Hancock, then go south on Route 522 to Berkeley Springs, West Virginia. Turn right on Route 9 and continue for 28 miles to Paw Paw. Head over the Potomac River bridge back into Maryland and follow signs for the Paw Paw Tunnel on your right. For Cumberland and the C&O Canal Historical Park Visitor Center take Route 40/48 west from Hancock to Cumberland, Exit 43B. Turn left at stop sign, then left again at the next stop sign onto Mechanic Street. Continue through traffic light and turn left to Western Maryland Station Center parking lot for the Visitor Center. For North Branch locks take Route 51 south from Cumberland. The locks are on the left just a short distance outside the city limits.

History House

Up the Stairs, Back in Time

Cumberland's tree-shaded Washington Street has a wealth of historic homes from the last half of the 19th century. Architectural styles range from Federal through Georgian Revival, but the clear favorite is Victorian. Most of the families who built in this section of Cumberland made their money between 1860 and 1920, when both the railroad and the C&O Canal were vying for the westward traffic that passed through Cumberland.

In 1867 the president of the C&O Canal, Josiah Gordon, built his home at 218 Washington Street. The most striking exterior feature of his Second Empire design is the Mansard roof. The house has 18 rooms, plus servants' quarters. Today it is the headquarters of the Allegany County Historical Society, which has overseen the remarkably thorough restoration and decoration of **History House**.

When you enter the house, notice the entranceway ceiling light; this was one of Cumberland's first gas lamps. The first room you'll see is the library, with its substantial collection of books from bygone years, including Gordon's law books. He served as a judge during the last years of his life.

The Victorian parlor where the Gordons entertained has an 1839 square grand piano plus a charming "courting couch." In the music room there is another square grand and a reed parlor organ. The Edison Standard Phonograph and music box reflect popular tastes of the period. The large windows in the dining room make it bright and cheerful, and the draperies that fall in puddles on the floor certainly fit the "age of excess."

The kitchen is located in the basement. The adjoining pantry is the oldest original room in the house; the crude horsehair plaster and the first gas jets can still be seen. The kitchen is filled with dated utensils like a pig scraper and sausage stuffer, while old pots and cauldrons hang in the large, open stone fireplace.

There are several floors above the main level. On the second floor you'll find the 19th-century bedrooms and boudoir, as well as a 1918 bathroom with its commodious footed tub. The bedrooms are filled with heavy Victorian pieces.

There are a number of display rooms on this floor: the Medical Room, Schoolroom and Costume Room. Dental-phobes might feel squeamish when they see the foot-operated tooth drill in the Medical Room. The metal hot water bottle doesn't look pleasant either. There's an early x-ray machine and other old-fashioned instruments. The dunce cap in the Schoolroom was never a popular piece of headwear, but the fashions in the Costume Room are far more upbeat. There is a wedding dress from the late 1870s to early 1880s, afternoon dresses and fashion accessories.

Another upper floor has still more to explore. The highlight here is the Children's Bedroom filled with toys, dolls, a dollhouse and books. The Military Room has a model of Fort Cumberland, a frontier outpost built by the British during the French & Indian War (see Ft. Cumberland Tunnels selection). The military exhibits include artifacts from the Civil War and both world wars. There is also a Genealogy Research Room on the third floor for those tracing their family roots and the sparsely furnished servants quarters.

History House is open May through October Tuesday through Saturday from 11:00 A.M. to 4:00 P.M. and Sunday 1:30 to 4:00 P.M. Admission is charged.

Directions: From Baltimore take I-70 90 miles west to Hancock, then follow Route 40/48 west to Cumberland. Take Exit 43A and stay right through traffic light for ½ block to Washington Street, then turn right.

La Vale Toll Gate House

Pay as You Go

Have you ever become hopelessly confused trying to navigate a road with multiple names? Such confusion is as old as one of the country's earliest links between the Eastern Seaboard and the West: the National Road or Cumberland Road.

This link, now U.S. 40, was called the National Road because it was the first and only road built and maintained by the federal government. George Washington had wanted to build a road as well as a canal linking East and West ever since he had surveyed as a young man in western Maryland.

When Congress began debate on the road's construction, the legislators called it the Cumberland Road in honor of the city. The contract for the first stretch from Cumberland to Eckhart was granted on May 8, 1811, but work was not completed until 1818. At a cost of $21.25 each 24¾ cubic feet of road, the building proceeded slowly and expensively. By 1830 it was decided that the states could assume the costs of any additional building as well as maintenance.

Ohio and then Maryland took over their portions of the National Road and built toll houses to collect money to pay for them. The **La Vale Toll Gate** was the first toll house built along the Maryland section of the National Road and is now the only surviving toll gate house in the state.

The toll house has a two-story, seven-sided main section flanked by two one-story sections. The main part looks like a stunted lighthouse. From the windows in the upstairs bedroom the gatekeeper could see clearly in both directions. He was paid in the first year of operation $200, or 12 percent of the gross receipts. The Report of the Superintendent of the National Road for the following year, 1837, noted that 20,000 travelers had used this section of the National Road and recommended raising the gatekeeper's salary to $300.

The toll rates posted on the gate house windows reveal that a horseback rider was charged four cents, and a four-wheel carriage with two horses, 12 cents. It would also cost 12 cents if you were driving a score of cattle, but only six cents for a score of sheep or hogs. There was no toll for vehicles with wheels eight or more inches wide, nor for mail carriers, soldiers or those going to church or a funeral.

When the railroad reached Cumberland in 1842, traffic along the National Road diminished. In 1878 the toll gate house became the property of Allegany County, which collected tolls until around 1900. Later it was sold to a private owner for a residence. The Maryland Historical Trust assumed ownership in 1969 and began its restoration. The La Vale Century Club now maintains the restored and furnished toll gate house. From June through August, it can be toured on Sunday, Wednesday and Friday from 1:00 to 4:00 P.M. In May, September and October it is open on Sundays only. A nominal donation is requested.

Just five minutes from the Toll Gate House you'll find one of Maryland's best dining bargains at Fred Warner's German Restaurant. It's worth the approximately three-hour drive from central Baltimore to dine on Fred's Wiener Schnitzel (the most tender, delicate veal) served with wafer-thin potato pancakes. Housed in an old stone building that is decorated with needlework, coats of arms, beer mugs, painted plates and hanging grapes, the restaurant offers inexpensive lunch platters, including homemade breads and your pick of a well-stocked salad bar. Fred Warner's has special festivals four times a year during the first part of May, August, October and December.

Fred Warner's is open year round Tuesday through Sunday for lunch and dinner, except during July when it is closed on Sundays and Mondays. Call (301)729-2361.

Directions: From Baltimore go west 90 miles on I-70 to Hancock. Continue west on Route 40 to Cumberland, where you pick up Route 40/48 west. Stay on Route 40/48 to La Vale, Exit 39, which is Route 40 Alternate. The Toll Gate House is on the left just after you exit. To get to Fred's German Restaurant go east on Route 40 Alternate for a short distance and just before the first traffic light bear right on Route 53. Turn left on Route 220, which takes you to Cresaptown and Fred Warner's (on your right).

George Washington's Headquarters and Fort Cumberland Tunnels

Time Tunnel

In a one-room cabin at Fort Cumberland, George Washington studied military strategy and planned his first campaign. Having surveyed in the Cumberland Valley for Lord Fairfax in 1748, Washington, five years later at the age of 21, was given a commission by Virginia Governor Dinwiddie to carry a warning to the French on the Ohio River not to remain in British-claimed territory. He carried out this fruitless mission but on two occasions nearly at the cost of his life. He was ambushed and fired upon by hostile Indians, and he fell into the icy Allegheny River.

A year later, in 1754, when the French still had not heeded the warning, Fort Mount Pleasant was built on the bank of Wills Creek. It was from here that Lt. Colonel Washington led a small force north to a spot just over the Pennsylvania state line (Fort

George Washington, at the age of 21, planned his first military campaign in this one-room cabin at Fort Cumberland in Allegany County. Ron Lytle

Necessity National Battlefield Park) and fought his first battle. Washington built a small temporary fort "of necessity" but had to surrender when he was attacked by a far superior force.

In 1755 a large fort was built on the Maryland hill overlooking Wills Creek. Fort Cumberland, as it was called, was the biggest fort in the colony at that time, measuring 400 feet long and 160 feet wide. The dimensions of the fort are marked out on the streets of Cumberland, also the original location of Washington's headquarters.

General Braddock rode a chariot into Fort Cumberland in May 1755. George Washington, as his aide-de-camp, marched with him on the ill-fated attack on Fort Duquesne. The British lost the battle and their general, but the colonies gained their greatest hero (Washington's heroism would contribute to his appointment as commander of the American revolutionary forces). Though he had had three horses shot from under him and his uniform was riddled with bullet holes, Washington helped two other officers carry the mortally wounded General Braddock from the battlefield. Then he returned to battle, riding all night to lead the men and wagons to safety.

As president, Washington came again to Fort Cumberland in 1794 to review the troops marching north to suppress the Whiskey Rebellion in Pennsylvania. Despite its historic significance, the fort fell into disrepair. When the land was sold to private developers, the one-room cabin that had been **George Washington's Headquarters** fortunately was saved and eventually moved to the banks of Wills Creek (now Riverside Park), where it has been restored. When you peer through the windows of the cabin, you see a mannequin dressed like the youthful British officer Washington was. A taped message provides background on Washington's involvement in the French and Indian War and on Fort Cumberland.

If you plan ahead you can arrange through the pastoral offices of Emmanuel Episcopal Church (301)777-3364 to explore the **Tunnels of Fort Cumberland**. The church is built on the site of the fort and some of the network of trenches that crisscrossed and surrounded Fort Cumberland are still visible amid the foundations of the church.

These stone-lined trenches are the only surviving earthworks from the French and Indian War. One section is identified as a possible powder magazine. Walking along these winding tunnels, you can get quite a thrill realizing that Washington may well have found his way along the very same route.

On your way to the tunnels, be sure to stop for a look at this Gothic church. Two of the windows were done by Tiffany himself, a third by his studio. The windows reveal such depth of color they seem to glow with an internal fire. The *Adoration of the Shepherd* by Bongereau over the altar is not to be missed. The church is at 16 Washington Street in Cumberland's historic district (see History House selection).

Directions: From Baltimore take I-70 west to Hancock about 90 miles. From Hancock continue west on Route 40 to Cumberland. Take Exit 43B, left onto Mechanic Street. At Baltimore Avenue, turn left. Baltimore Avenue runs into Washington Street. Continue straight up Washington Street.

WASHINGTON COUNTY

Albert Powell Trout Hatchery

Hatching 500,000 Fish Stories

If you have never seen a fish hatchery but are curious about how one operates, visit the **Albert Powell Trout Hatchery** just off I-70 east of Hagerstown. Although there is no visitor center or display area, you can stop at the hatchery office to ask questions and stroll a central walkway between a series of raceways brimming with fingerlings.

Before young trout are released into the outdoor raceways they are incubated and hatched indoors. This Washington County facility receives close to 500,000 trout eggs each year from Washington State commercial hatcheries. From hatching trays the newborns are transferred to troughs where they are held for approximately three months.

The young fingerling trout are transferred to the outside raceways when space becomes available during the spring stocking season. Approximately 150,000 year-old trout 11 to 12 inches long are stocked in Maryland waters by this hatchery annually; another 20,000 are kept to grow an additional year. At the end of the second year they are roughly 16 inches long. Some of these larger trout are included in every truckload of fish that leaves the hatchery each spring. Powell Hatchery also supplies fingerlings to the Bear Creek Rearing Station in Garrett County. This facility rears approximately 60,000 fingerling trout to adult size. Powell Hatchery supplies adult trout from Washington County eastward, while the Bear Creek Rearing Station stocks its trout in Garrett and Allegany Counties.

You can visit the Albert Powell Trout Hatchery from 9:00 A.M. to 4:00 P.M. There is no charge.

If you are in the area on Sunday afternoon you can head south on Route 66 to Beaver Creek Road and visit the **Beaver Creek Country School.** This turn-of-the-century one-room school is filled with interesting curios. The old wooden desks are lined up in front of the teacher's desk. Slate tablets and pencils, an old chalkboard, wallcharts and books complete the picture. There are even mannequins dressed in period outfits representing both teacher and students.

Across the hall there is a museum room, which is arranged in sections. The first represents an old-time millinery shop, the second a cobbler's shop, another is a section of a Victorian parlor, and there is also a display area for kitchen utensils.

The Beaver Creek Country School is open Sunday afternoons June 1 through October 1 from 2:00 to 5:00 P.M. A nominal admission is charged.

Directions: From Baltimore take I-70 about 60 miles to Exit 35 (Route 66). You'll see the fish hatchery on your left as soon as you get on Route 66 north. From the fish hatchery go south on Route 66 to Beaver Creek Road, where you make a right. Proceed up Beaver Creek Road and take a right on Beaver Creek Church Road for the Country School.

Antietam National Battlefield

Where Have All the Young Men Gone. . .

The fields and hillsides around Antietam Creek are empty now; the air is clean and all is quiet. But the modern exhibits help today's visitors imagine a landscape of fallen soldiers, the air choked with smoke and the sound of constant gunfire.

Private letters shown at the **Antietam National Battlefield** Visitor Center give a poignant perspective to what is called the bloodiest day of the Civil War, September 17, 1862. Confederate Lieutenant Pendleton commented, "Such a storm of balls I never conceived it possible for men to live through. Shot and shell shrieking and crashing, canister and bullets whistling and hissing most fiend-like through the air until you could almost see them. In that mile's ride I never expected to come back alive." Similar sentiments were expressed by Lieutenant Graham with the 9th Regiment, New York Volunteers. He wrote, "I was lying on my back, supported on my elbows, watching the shells explode overhead and speculating as to how long I could hold up my finger before it would be shot off, for the air seemed full of bullets. When the order to get up was given I turned over quickly to look at Col. Kimball, who had given the order, thinking he had become suddenly insane."

In addition to this verbal picture there is a visual reminder of the battle, a large painting done by Captain James Hope from a sketch he made on the battlefield amid the chaos of the conflict.

An audio-visual program helps put the events at Antietam in perspective. A 26-minute film, *Antietam Visit*, shown on the hour, focuses on President Lincoln's visit with Commander-of-the-Army George B. McClellan after the battle. Lincoln reviewed the troops, visited the numerous wounded and urged McClellan to pursue the Confederates into the South. Special interpretive programs are given by park rangers and volunteers on a scheduled basis.

After this introduction you're ready to tour the battlefield. There were three phases to this one-day battle that left more than 23,000 casualties. Your tour begins with the morning action, which took place from 6:00 to 9:00 A.M. Much of the early fighting took place in the northern part of the field around a cornfield and the Dunker Church. The church you'll see was reconstructed in 1961–62. The original was destroyed not in battle but during a storm in May 1921. Additional information is available at the Visitor Center explaining the history of the Dunker, or Anabaptist, Movement.

A much contested area during the morning hours was the cornfield. Union General Joseph Hooker reported, "In the time that

Antietam, the one-day battle that left more than 23,000 casualties, is known as the bloodiest day of the Civil War. Along "Bloody Lane" (above) 4,000 men fell in four hours.

I am writing every stalk of corn in the northern and greater part of the field was cut as closely as could have been done with a knife and the slain lay in rows precisely as they had stood in their ranks a few moments before. It was never my fortune to witness a more bloody, dismal battlefield."

Bad as the morning action was, it solved nothing; neither side conclusively won their ground. There was worse to come. For nearly four hours during the midday, 9:30 A.M. to 1:00 P.M., the opposing forces fought along a sunken country lane. There were 4,000 casualties and the road was known thereafter as Bloody Lane. The tower you'll see overlooking this section was built in 1896 and used by visitors and military organizations as a vantage point from which to study the battle strategy.

The third and final afternoon phase, 1:00 to 5:30 P.M., centered around the Lower Bridge, now called Burnside Bridge. Four Union divisions under General Burnside had been attempting to cross the bridge since 10:30 A.M. Holding them off were 450 Georgia riflemen. This impasse had a key impact on the day's outcome since it prevented Burnside's forces from reinforcing other battle sectors. Burnside and his men finally crossed the bridge around 1:00 P.M., but then spent two hours reforming their line before driving the Georgia troops towards Sharpsburg. This delay, too, proved disastrous. It gave A.P. Hill time to arrive from Harpers Ferry with his Confederate division and drive Burnside back. Hill's action helped the Confederate army escape.

At the conclusion of your battlefield tour, take the footpath to the Hawkins Zouave Monument. It marks the spot where the battle ended at 5:30 P.M. You can look out over the entire battlefield and reflect on the tragic loss of so many young men from both North and South.

Of the 12,410 Federal casualties, 4,776 are buried at Antietam National Cemetery. The more than 10,700 Confederate dead are buried elsewhere. Despite such heavy losses, this was not a decisive victory for either side. Lee's failure to successfully carry the fighting into the North caused Great Britain to delay recognition of the Confederate government. Five days after the Battle of Antietam, Lincoln issued the Emancipation Proclamation. He had hoped to do it at a moment of Union strength, not on the heels of a federal debacle. The proclamation freed all the slaves in the rebellious states, providing a dual northern purpose for the war: the preservation of the Union and the abolition of slavery.

Civil War enthusiasts will want to take advantage of the unique opportunity to stay overnight on the battlefield in the historic Piper House, the headquarters of Confederate General James Longstreet. After the battle the farm house served briefly as a field hospital.

There are four bedrooms, each with its own bath, in the 19th-century log and frame Piper farm house. Period antiques fill the rooms and a sense of history fills the house. Rooms at this battlefield bed and breakfast should be reserved at least a month in advance and prices range from $45 to $65. Call (301)797-1862 or (301)432-5466.

Another bed and breakfast, The Inn at Antietam, overlooks Antietam National Cemetery. This attractively furnished turn-of-the-century Victorian house has rooms from $35.50 for singles to $45 to $75 for doubles. The southern breakfast is more reflective of gracious hospitality than continental caution; it's a repast to be remembered. Call (301)432-6601 for reservations.

Antietam National Battlefield Visitor Center is open daily except Thanksgiving, Christmas and New Year's Day. Hours are 8:30 A.M. to 5:00 P.M. September through May and 8:00 A.M. to 6:00 P.M. June through August. A nominal admission fee is charged. Cassette tapes can be rented ($3) with details of all the major spots of interest along the battlefield tour, which takes approximately 1½ hours.

Directions: From Baltimore take I-70 west past Frederick to exit for Alt. Route 40. Take Alt. 40 west to Boonsboro where it intersects with Route 34. Take Route 34 south to Sharpsburg. The Visitor Center is north of Sharpsburg on Route 65.

Boonsborough Museum of History & Crystal Grottoes Caverns

Caverns and Curios

Just a few miles apart, the Boonsborough Museum of History and Crystal Grottoes Caverns offer treasures both natural and unnatural, that is, man-made. Although speaking of the unnatural, the museum does have a display of oddities associated with the magic of Wizard Zittle, a faith healer who lived near Boonsboro in 1845. Superstition and witchcraft are among the many topics investigated at this remarkably thorough museum. Many of the Civil War artifacts were found on nearby Antietam, South Mountain and Harpers Ferry battlefields. You'll rarely find such a comprehensive collection of carved "mini balls," the name given to lead bullets that soldiers shaped into poker chips, checkers, mustache combs, chessmen, tops, bottle stoppers, initials and decorative shapes.

Mementos of Confederate Officer Henry Kyd Douglas fill another case. This young soldier grew up at nearby Blackford Plantation, which now serves as the C&O Canal National Historical Park Headquarters. Look for the letter Douglas wrote to his father on Union stationery with the federal emblem crossed out. Henry is the author of the now famous *I Rode with Stonewall*. A copy of the original text, which was first called *The Stonewall Papers*, is displayed. So is the diary Douglas kept during the war and an original order signed by Stonewall Jackson.

Weapons appear to be everywhere, from prehistoric Indian arrowheads to hand-made "shanks" confiscated from a local prison. Not all the weapons were used on this side of the Atlantic. There is a matador's sword, a Japanese sword from World War II and a set of African witch doctor's knives.

One of the most horrifying items on display is the hand-wrought slave punishment collar, lined with long, iron spikes. One wonders how a person could possibly endure wearing it and yet some slaves, we are told, were made to wear these collars night and day.

A more poignant memento is a piece of wooden fence from the Antietam battlefield. Young Sergeant Wright rushed the fence and was shot in both legs. He received the Congressional Medal of Honor for his valor and later returned to the battlefield to claim a piece of the fence. To this piece of fence, he affixed a small plaque that reads, "I volunteered to help pull this down. September 17, 1862."

The museum also has a fully stocked 19th-century general store that runs the gamut from handwrought items of 1795 to mass-produced products of 1875. The glassware display is quite extensive. Though you are given a printed guide, the owner-director Doug Bast, who has been called a historical packrat, is on hand to tell about the many unusual items he has single-handedly amassed. The museum is open May through September on Sunday from 1:00 to 5:00 P.M. and other times by appointment. Call (301)432-6969 or (301)432-5151. A nominal admission is charged.

Heading out of Boonsboro on Route 34 you'll quickly spot the **Crystal Grottoes Caverns,** Maryland's only commercial underground caverns. The caves were discovered in 1920 when the state was building Route 34. The road crew was quarrying limestone when the drill bit fell into the as yet undiscovered cave. They dynamited the drill holes, crawled into the opening and saw for the first time what came to be known as Crystal Grottoes. The caverns opened to the public on April 2, 1922, and have stayed in their natural state.

No colored lights or fancy signs mar the natural beauty of the limestone formations. There are some large chambers, and many of the formations sparkle with their crystalline covering. It takes about 45 minutes to explore them all.

The caverns are open daily from 9:00 A.M. to 6:00 P.M. with the last tour starting at 5:30 P.M. There is an admission charge, roughly comparable to an evening movie admission.

Directions: From Baltimore take I-70 west past Frederick to exit for Alt. Route 40. Take Alt. 40 west to Boonsboro. The museum is at 113 North Main Street. Go south on Route 34 to the caverns just out of town on the left.

Fort Frederick

Frontier Defense

Once there was a chain of forts protecting Maryland's western frontier; of these only **Fort Frederick** has survived. The frontier settlers wanted to stay out of the conflict between the English on the coast and the French who were firmly entrenched in Canada—neither nation was of much concern to the people struggling to carve homes out of the wilderness. But the French prompted their Indian allies to attack the homes along the Maryland frontier. In 1756, following General Braddock's defeat by the French at Fort Duquesne, the Governor of Maryland insisted that the Maryland Assembly appropriate money to build a fort.

Governor Horatio Sharpe took a personal interest in the North (now Fairview) Mountain fort. After supervising much of the work, he named it Fort Frederick in honor of Maryland's Lord Proprietor, Frederick Calvert, Sixth Lord Baltimore. The flag you'll see flying over the fort shows the Union Jack, indicating the colony's allegiance to England, plus the black and gold colors of the Calvert family.

Fort Frederick was a more formidable fort than was traditionally built along the frontier. It was both larger and more enduring; unlike other forts in the chain, its stockade walls were stone instead of wood or earth. Thus it has withstood the ravages of time.

There is another reason why the fort still stands: It was never attacked. Perhaps the imposing walls deterred assault, even though the fort was important as a supply base for the English during the French and Indian War. In the American Revolution it was reactivated as a prison camp for British and Hessian prisoners and remained unmolested. A small skirmish was fought at Fort Frederick on Christmas Day, 1861, with Union troops holding the fort against Confederate raiders.

To fill in the historical details about Fort Frederick, stop first at the Visitor Center and watch the 30-minute movie; it will make the self-guided walking tour more meaningful.

The tour map (available at the Visitor Center) will direct you up the path to the fort. On your right you'll see the garrison garden. Eating salted meat (with occasional fresh game), dry beans and bread could get monotonous, so the troops garrisoned here planted vegetables outside the stone walls to supplement their diet. Food was so scarce during the American Revolution that fort commandant Colonel Rawlings permitted local farmers to hire his British and German prisoners, who were fed in return for their labor.

Just outside the fort walls you'll see a cannon resembling the four that guarded the diamond-shaped corner bastions. A cannon this size was capable of firing six-pound iron balls. As you pass through the gateway you'll see two barracks within the 1½-acre fort compound. Guides dressed in uniforms of the French and Indian War period are on hand to answer questions about the fort and about army life from 1756 to 1763. The barracks' rooms have been furnished to represent enlisted men and noncommissioned officers' quarters of the late 1750s. You're invited to step into the public room and get a feel of 18th-century barrack life. Don't try to bounce on the beds though; they're made of uncovered wooden planks. Two men shared a bunk; this was considered quite commodious compared to sleeping arrangements for transient troops—they had to make do with blankets on the hard floor.

Across the parade ground is the west barracks. These two barracks were planned to hold about 4,000 enlisted men, but the fort was rarely garrisoned up to strength and the rooms were used for other purposes. In the west barracks you'll see a storage room, laundry and dining area. The second floor has been converted into a museum depicting the history of the fort.

The location of the governor's house, which served as fort headquarters, is now indicated by stone foundations at one end of the parade ground. Also marked are the officers' quarters and a storehouse. There was not sufficient documentation to accurately rebuild these structures. Much of the restoration of Fort Frederick was done in the 1930s during the Depression by the Civilian Conservation Corps. They excavated the ruins, repaired the dilapidated stone walls and restored the stone foundations of the barracks.

The barracks and Visitor Center are open from 8:30 A.M. to 5:00 P.M. from Memorial Day to Labor Day. There is no charge except for special events. Each May the reactivated Maryland Forces present "Fort Frederick Rendezvous" depicting life during the French and Indian War, frontier skills and ranger tactics. In late June "Military Field Day" is held here with roughly 350 uniformed men representing all three conflicts in which Fort Frederick played a role. In late July and again in late August "French and Indian Days" are celebrated with marching and drillling. In late September there are competitive matches during the "Governor's Invitational Firelock Match." The schedule ends with a ghost walk on Halloween.

You can picnic at Fort Frederick, and Captain Wort's Sutler Shop sells snacks, soft drinks and crafts. Two nature trails provide more diversion if you have a day to spend at Fort Frederick. And there is a primitive family campground on the bank of the Potomac River. You can fish in the Potomac and in the 92-acre Big Pool Lake.

Directions: From Baltimore take I-70 west about 80 miles to Exit 12. Take Route 56 south toward Big Pool. Fort Frederick will be on your right.

Gathland State Park

A Monument "Quite Odd"

Gathland State Park, just outside Burkittsville, encompasses the ruins of Gapland, the South Mountain home of George Alfred Townsend, the youngest reporter to cover the Civil War. It is also the site of Townsend's commemorative arch honoring all correspondents of the war. Townsend went on to become a noted journalist and author during the Reconstruction Period. He used

Gath as one of his pen names. The first three letters were his initials; the added *h* was inspired by the biblical passage, "Tell it not in Gath, publish it not in the streets of Askalon" (II Samuel 1:20).

Townsend eventually used Askalon for the name of the third of nine major buildings he erected on this 100-acre tract. Planning, designing and building were a diversion for Townsend, a change of pace from his hectic writing schedule.

A walking tour of Gathland State Park (to which there is a self-guiding tour map) starts at Gapland Hall. This was once a substantial fieldstone summer and weekend home. A stone tablet embedded when the house was built in 1885, but long since lost, explained the derivation of the name: "I sought for a man that would stand in the gap before me in the land" (Ezekial 22:30). The main wing of the house has been restored but lacks the original ornamentation, grillwork and porch.

The path continues down to Gapland Lodge, now serving as a park museum. It is open on weekends May through September from 10:00 A.M. to 6:00 P.M. This, too, was built in 1885 and served as a servants' quarters, kitchen and summer dining room.

The next stop is eye arresting. The War Correspondent's Arch is the most unusual structure Townsend designed. Ruthanne Hindes, a journalist, described it this way in her biography of Townsend: "In appearance the monument is quite odd. It is fifty feet high and forty feet broad. Above a Moorish arch sixteen feet high built of Hummelstown purple stone are super-imposed three Roman arches. These are flanked on one side with a square crenellated tower, producing a bizarre and picturesque effect." The arches are said to represent Description, Depiction and Photography. The arch cost $5,000 to build and donations were made to the building fund by Thomas Edison, Joseph Pulitzer and many others.

Stop four on your walking tour is the previously mentioned Askalon, the third of Townsend's original buildings. He built a large wooden frame house, using it first as a stable, then as servants' quarters. Continuing on, you come to the barn ruins. The next stop, Mt. Gath, is a private residence and can only be noted, not visited. Mt. Gath was a guest house added by Townsend in 1892.

Moving up the trail, you'll come to the ruins of the library where Townsend had his living quarters. Finally, you'll see the mausoleum where Townsend hoped to be buried. He was actually buried in Philadelphia. Over the empty tomb the inscription, signed Gath, reads: "Good Night."

If this short hike is not enough, you can pick up the Appalachian Trail, which passes through the park. A six-mile hike will take you to the Weverton Cliffs. You can also pick up an auto tour map of the South Mountain Battlefield, which covers 12 miles and takes about 30 to 45 minutes.

Directions: From Baltimore take I-70 west past Frederick to Exit 49, Alternate Route 40. Take Alternate Route 40 west to Middletown, then follow Route 17 south to Burkittsville. From Burkittsville go west one mile on Gapland Road to the top of South Mountain for Gathland State Park.

Hager House and Washington County Museum of Fine Arts

A Window on Maryland Frontier Life

Everyone loves a romantic story, and tourists are no exception. Legend has it that Jonathan Hager as a young man in Westphalia, Germany, fell in love with Elizabeth Kershner. When she emigrated to America, the legend goes, he stowed away on the *Harle*, a Dutch ship, and followed her. Records show that he did indeed sail on the *Harle*, arriving in Philadelphia on September 1, 1736.

Hager was 22 years old when he arrived. For the next three years he explored the wildernesses of Virginia, Maryland and Pennsylvania. On June 5, 1739, he obtained a warrant for 200 acres he called Hager's Fancy. The land he bought already had "3 acres of corn field fenced in and two sorry [poorly built] houses."

Hager built a two-and-a-half-story stone house on the foundations of one of the earlier dwellings. His stone house rested on two springs, giving him a protected water supply in the event of Indian attack. Its 22-inch walls could serve as a frontier fort if necessary. (You'll notice the windows on the lower floor are wider on the inside than on the outside, making it easier to defend the house.)

Elizabeth Kershner, whom he followed to America, as the story goes, was a neighbor on this western Maryland frontier. They were married a year after he settled in present day Hagerstown. When Hager formed the town, he named it Elizabeth Town, but everyone else called it Hager's Town.

Because it was a frontier home, this place is quite different from the coastal colonial plantations. You can still see the pig bristle in the plaster. The house is original but the furnishings are not; they do, however, represent life on the frontier in the 18th century. You'll notice Hager's front room also served as a trading post. A variety of hides on the table indicate what kind of game was found in the region in the 1740s: rabbit, deer, beaver, bear and even buffalo.

Take note of the tightly woven basket that rests in the Hager parlor. It was said that if a woman could make a split oak basket

Hager House was built in 1739 by the founder of Hagerstown. Its 22-inch walls could serve as a fort and the two springs, on which it rested, gave Hager a protected water supply.

so tight it could carry water she was a good marriage partner. It would be helpful if she also made candles. It took 39 candles to equal the light cast by one 40-watt bulb.

From the front room you'll move to the kitchen, or gathering room, the center of family life. It has far more dishes and utensils than would have been found in a frontier home but they represent the simple pottery and pewter you would have seen. Pewter dishes contained lead, which was responsible for some of the ill health and early deaths of this period. You'll learn that when a couple decided to wed they would, like married couples, eat off the same plate, thus announcing their intentions. The old stone fireplace is surrounded by cooking pots and dried herbs.

At **Hager House** you get to explore both upstairs and downstairs. In the master bedroom upstairs there is a four-poster canopy bed. It was customary during the 18th century to use the bedroom as a social center, so you'll also see table and chairs as well as a 1725 clavichord. Hager was a lay minister and may well have conducted services in this bedroom. If you're interested, you may also see the attic, which may have been used as extra sleeping quarters or for storage.

Next you'll see the basement where the two springs still flow. The large fireplace was used for cooking during the summer and by Hager for minor forging jobs.

In six years his family had outgrown their place and he sold it at three times its initial per-acre cost to Jacob Rohrer, in whose family the property remained until the 20th century. Hager purchased a 1,780-tract two miles away. He called his second home Hager's Delight, but nothing remains of this house. On November 6, 1775, Hager was accidentally killed when a log hit him in the chest while he was supervising the building of the German Reformed Church on land he had donated to the town. Hager has been called the Father of Washington County. The Hager House is open Thursday through Saturday 10:00 A.M. to 4:00 P.M. and Sunday 2:00 to 5:00 P.M. It is closed Mondays. Admission is charged.

While in the City Park area, take time to explore the nearby **Washington County Museum of Fine Arts,** which is open at no charge Thursday through Saturday 10:00 A.M. to 5:00 P.M. and Sunday 1:00 to 6:00 P.M. The museum's major emphasis is on American art. You'll see portraits by Thomas Sully and the Peales; landscapes by George Inness and Albert Bierstadt; still-lifes by Severin Roesen and John LaFarge. Maryland artists are also well represented: John Beale Bordley, Hugh Bolton Jones and Grace Hartigan. The Old Masters are included in the museum's permanent collection. Much of the gallery space is used for special exhibitions.

The Washington County Museum of Fine Arts was a gift to the county from William Henry Singer, Jr. in honor of his wife Anna Brugh Singer. With the museum also went the art the Singers had collected on their European trips. William Singer was, himself, an American Post-Impressionist, and some of his paintings now hang in the Singer Gallery within the museum.

Directions: From Baltimore take I-70 west to Exit 32 (Route 40) into Hagerstown. Route 40 becomes Franklin Street. Turn left at Prospect Street for City Park, where you will find both the Hager House and the Washington County Museum of Fine Arts.

Maryland Heights and Kennedy Farm

Staging a Raid on Harpers Ferry

The historic town of Harpers Ferry is in West Virginia. But a sizable portion of Harpers Ferry National Historical Park is in Maryland, as is the **Kennedy Farm,** which served as the staging area for the historic 1859 raid by John Brown and his band of abolitionists.

Behind St. Peter's Catholic Church in the town of Harpers Ferry you'll find the stone steps that lead up to Jefferson Rock and the famous view therefrom, which Thomas Jefferson described as "worth a voyage across the Atlantic." (At that time Jefferson had not yet crossed the Atlantic.) Across the Potomac River on **Maryland Heights** there is another overlook that provides a vantage point for viewing the town nestled on the mountain side. Two trails traverse Maryland Heights: Overlook Trail and Stone Fort Trail. The latter leads to the remains of a Civil War fortification. On the West Virginia side of the river the Loudoun Heights Trail connects with the Appalachian Trail.

To trace the events that put Harpers Ferry on the map, start at the Kennedy Farm, known locally as the John Brown Farm. Here Brown and his followers planned their raid on the Harpers Ferry arsenal. The community was curious about the newcomers, particularly because it was known that they included blacks. John Brown kept all his band inside, however, and refused to admit any visitors into the Widow Kennedy's farm house. A month after the raid, *Frank Leslie's Illustrated Newspapers* printed a sketch of the farm. Newly restored, it looks much today as it did in that sketch.

In the steps of Brown and his committed band, you make your way from the farm to the Harpers Ferry arsenal. As you travel, think back to October 16, 1859, when the raiders attacked the Federal arsenal hoping to obtain arms for the slaves they anticipated would flock to their banner. They gained neither recruits nor arms. Indeed, helping to defeat them were two soldiers who went on to lead Southern troops—Lt. Col. Robert E. Lee and Lt. J.E.B. Stuart. Ten of the raiders were killed when the Federal troops stormed the armory fire engine house (now called John Brown's Fort). Four raiders escaped, but Brown and another four conspirators were captured. As the ringleader, Brown was tried and convicted. He was hanged on December 2, 1859, less than two months after his unsuccessful raid—swift justice even in those days!

At the Harpers Ferry Visitors Center you can watch a seven-minute film encapsulating these dramatic events. A longer 30-minute film is shown at the John Brown Museum just down the street. Throughout the day the National Park Service offers special tours that are well worth catching. Authentically clad mid-19th-century "residents" introduce you to the community and the gun factory that employed many of the townsfolk. The armory was defended by the North and seized by the South. You'll miss a lot of local color if you explore on your own, but there is a helpful guide for those who just want to amble around town.

Most of Harpers Ferry sites can be enjoyed without charge. If you bring a picnic to enjoy along the river, you can have a very inexpensive but pleasant family outing. For those who feel no outing is complete without shopping, the town does offer a number of quaint shops and boutiques.

The Kennedy Farm is open weekends May through October from 9:00 A.M. to 1:00 P.M. For additional information call (301)791-3130. The Harpers Ferry National Historical Park Visitors Center and exhibits are open daily 8:00 A.M. to 5:00 P.M. During the summer the special tours are given from 10:00 A.M. to 4:00 P.M. On Friday and Saturday evenings a special presentation of the historical drama *Hearts and Minds* is given on the town green at 8:30 P.M. It highlights the influence that Harpers Ferry has had on our lives and our history.

Directions: From Baltimore take I-70 west to Frederick. At Frederick take Route 340 west toward Harpers Ferry. Before crossing the Potomac River into Virginia, take the Harpers Ferry Road north to Samples Manor and then go north on Chestnut Grove Road to Kennedy Farm. For Harpers Ferry, continue west on Route 340 and follow signs.

Miller House

From Hanging Staircase to Patent Medicines

What you'll see today on a tour of the **Miller House** in Hagerstown is a typical townhouse of the 1820s and an eclectic collection of clocks, dolls, carriages, pottery and country-store commodities. The house's graceful hanging staircase is one of its most outstanding architectural features. The tour starts in the front drawing room, which was the formal room for receiving visitors in the mid-1800s. Both formal and informal evenings were enjoyed here; the family played games, read aloud and sang. You'll see a "tea caddy," customarily locked to protect the expensive green and black tea from servant pilfering. The gilded valances over the window represent the 1850s, but the other furnishings are from 1818 to 1825.

A curious architectural feature, a gib door, actually a window that doubled as a door, can be seen in the back drawing room. The hallway off this room leads to the older wing of the house, built in the flounder style, so called because it was flat and narrow with windows on only one side.

The back wing of the house was built in Hagerstown in 1818 by a local potter, Peter Bell. He had originally bought half of Lot 91 in Jonathan Hager's plan of Elizabeth Town in 1802 and erected a log cabin on it. His second building on the other half of the lot was used as a pottery by his son, Peter Bell, Jr. and grandson, John Bell. Examples of their work can be seen today in one of the dependencies of the main house.

The main section of the house was built for William Price, who, though he served as a Maryland legislator and on the U.S. District Court, is known today for having been the grandfather of Emily Post, the etiquette expert. The house passed to the Neill family in 1844. They owned it until 1911, when it was purchased by the Miller family. Dr. Victor D. Miller, Jr. built a one-bay addition in 1915. It was the Miller descendants who gave their family home to the Washington County Historical Society, which has its headquarters here now.

The house has an early 19th-century kitchen with utensils and a large fireplace for cooking. In the basement you'll find a turn-of-the-century country post office complete with a mannequin postmistress. There is also a country store with fully stocked shelves. The patent medicines include Dr. Fahrney's Teething Syrup, concocted from alcohol, morphine and chloroform. Equally potent was Dr. Tenney's Pleasant Syrup, a compound of alcohol and belladonna believed to get rid of round worms. The store has an extensive collection of kitchen utensils, other household tools and farm equipment.

Back upstairs are the music room, the Civil War room and the canal exhibit. The old clock collection and the doll display are quite impressive. You'll discover that the tall clocks, or tall case clocks like the ten in the Miller exhibit, began to be called grandfather clocks in 1898 after a popular song, "My Grandfather's Clock." At the end of the tour you visit the dependencies and see the pottery and carriage collections.

The Miller House gives visitors a look at life within a townhouse in Hagerstown between 1820 and 1850. Its graceful hanging staircase is an architectural gem.

The Miller House is open Wednesday through Friday 1:00 to 4:00 P.M. and Saturday and Sunday 2:00 to 5:00 P.M. It is closed January, February and March. Admission is charged.

Directions: From Baltimore take I-70 west to Hagerstown. At Exit 32 take Route 40 west into the city to Prospect Street. Turn left, then left again onto Washington Street. The Miller House is on your right.

Washington Monument State Park

You Too Can Salute Washington from Tent, Mountain Top or Stagecoach Inn

The first county named for George Washington also boasts the first monument built in his honor. The townfolk of Boonsboro in Washington County didn't want to raise money for the monument; they wanted to build it with their own hands as a labor of love. On July 4, 1827, at 7:00 A.M. most of the 500 residents of Boonsboro met at the public square and marched behind the Stars and Stripes to the summit of South Mountain to build their monument.

The mountain had an abundant supply of "blue rocks" to use for the stone tower. No mortar was used to bond the huge stones. They were carefully cut and laid to form a dry circular wall. By the end of the day the townsfolk had completed 15 feet of the monument, half of the plan. After that hard work the Declaration of Independence was read, and three veterans of the American Revolution climbed the newly built steps and fired a three-round salute.

They agreed to complete the monument at the end of "the busy season." And, true to their word, once the crops were harvested, they gathered again and added the last 15 feet. Their speedy work gained for Boonsboro the distinction of erecting the first monument dedicated to George Washington. The citizens of Baltimore had raised $178,000 by lottery and started their monument in Washington's honor 12 years earlier, but theirs was still not finished by 1827.

It has been said, "As monuments go, none was ever built with purer or more reverent patriotism." Had it been built with mortar as well, it might have withstood the weather and vandalism that reduced it to rubble within 55 years. In 1882 the Odd Fellows Lodge of Boonsboro rebuilt the monument and added a canopy over the top and a road up the mountainside. A crack appeared within a decade, and the monument crumbled in ruins once again.

The tower you see today was rebuilt between 1934 and 1936 by the Civilian Conservation Corps. The original cornerstone was

Washington County, the first county named for the first president, also has the first monument to him. It was built in 1827 by nearly all 500 residents of Boonsboro.

reset, and a facsimile of the dedication tablet was added: "Erected in Memory of Washington July 4, 1827 by the citizens of Boonsboro."

If the weather is clear it's worth the climb up the 34 steps to take in the three-state panorama. You will be rewarded by an appealing vista of the Potomac River winding through the rolling countryside. **Washington Monument State Park** now encompasses 108 acres and is open year-round. There is a circular hiking trail and the Appalachian Trail passes through the park. The Cumberland Valley is a flyway for migratory birds, and each year ornithologists gather here for a count of passing hawks and eagles. The park has 13 acres set aside for family tenting.

Be sure to stop at the Visitor Center open daily sunrise to sunset except for the months of November through April. The center has a taped account of the building of the monument plus a geological explanation of how South Mountain was formed. There are Civil War arms and artifacts. South Mountain was the site of a skirmish fought on September 14, 1862, before the armies met at Antietam. The Battle of South Mountain was a delaying action. General James Longstreet, commanding the major section of Lee's Army of Northern Virginia, held the passes leading over South Mountain, thus preventing General McClellan's troops from crossing. Although the Southerners under Longstreet were vastly outnumbered, they managed to stall McClellan a full day. It wasn't until September 17 that the two armies met along Antietam Creek (see selection).

General D.H. Hill, who covered Longstreet's march to Hagerstown, made his headquarters in a house now known as Old South Mountain Inn Restaurant. You can dine at this historic inn among ghosts that date back to around 1750. When the National Road was built outside the inn's door, the stagecoach brought many a distinguished traveler, including Henry Clay and Daniel Webster, who stayed often. In 1876 the inn became the summer residence of Madeleine Vinto Dahlgren, widow of Admiral Dahlgren. She called it her Sky Farm. The inn is open Tuesday through Friday 5:00 to 9:00 P.M.; Saturday, noon to 10:00 P.M. and Sunday, noon to 8:00 P.M. Sunday brunch is served 10:30 A.M. to 2:00 P.M. For reservations call (301)371-5400.

Directions: From Baltimore take I-70 west past Frederick to Exit 49, Alt. Route 40. Take Alt. Route 40 west five miles beyond Middletown to the top of South Mountain (Turners Gap). At Turners Gap, Old South Mountain Inn is on your left and the entrance to Washington State Park is on your right.

Ziem Vineyard

Wine Time

Ziem Vineyard is a genuine "mom and pop" operation. Bob Ziem, a chemist by training, wanted to develop a vineyard and winery as a retirement business. He and his wife Ruth moved from bustling Bethesda to a 55-acre farm in Washington County in the early 1970s. Little did they realize how busy the weekends would be before Bob retired from the Navy Department in 1986.

The Ziems have proved that a successful business can develop from a hobby. Bob Ziem is a self-taught vintner, no doubt aided by his chemistry background. After the first vines were planted in 1972, the erstwhile hobbyists gradually added the equipment needed to produce the first Ziem wine five years later. Now the Ziems grow 16 grape varieties on seven acres and bottle 2,000 to 3,000 gallons of wine a year.

Ziem wines are 100 percent varietals, which means the grapes are not blended. The wine is settled, racked and aged in barrels. The red wine is aged in 55-gallon oak barrels. Because red wines are not filtered there is apt to be sediment at the bottom of the bottle. This sediment is found in the finest red wines of the world and does not adversely influence the taste of the wine. Ziem white wines are aged for a shorter period in plastic barrels.

Nearly all of the work at the Ziem Vineyard is done by the owners. When Bob Ziem was only a weekend vintner, Ruth kept trying to figure out "if she was too smart to drive a tractor or not smart enough." Bob's retirement solved the problem—he drives the tractor.

The Ziems welcome visitors from 1:00 P.M. to dusk on Thursdays and Fridays. They'll show you around and give you a chance to purchase their Maryland wines. On Saturday from 11:00 A.M. to dusk and Sunday from 1:00 to 6:00 P.M. the Ziems offer a variety of their wines for tasting. On pleasant afternoons you can enjoy the outdoor tasting area alongside a picturesque stream; on inclement days there is an indoor tasting room. Ziem Vineyard is open at other times by appointment. If you are driving a long distance, it is advisable to call ahead, (301)223-8352, even on those days with scheduled hours. Ziem Vineyard is closed Monday through Wednesday and on major holidays.

Directions: From Baltimore take I-70 west to the intersection with I-81 at Hagerstown. Head south on I-81 to the last Maryland exit, for Antietam Battlefield. You'll exit on Route 68 and 63 combined, but take Route 63 when it turns to the right for Downsville. Ziem Vineyard is three miles from this point just outside Downsville on Route 63.

FREDERICK COUNTY

Barbara Fritchie House and The Home of Roger Brooke Taney

Dramatic Duo

Some students of history may dispute the facts, but if the details are questionable the sentiment and character are true—Barbara Fritchie was a stalwart Union supporter during the Civil War who proudly flew the Stars and Stripes from her upstairs window in Frederick. The story passed down by Frederick townsfolk is that a youngster was sent to warn 96-year-old "Auntie" Barbara that Confederates were going to be marching through town. Fritchie, who kept a small silk U.S. flag in her Bible, misunderstood the message. Thinking it was Federal troops coming, she went out with her small flag and waved it to the passing soldiers. The resulting confrontation was immortalized by abolitionist poet John Greenleaf Whittier in part as follows:

> Up rose old Barbara Fritchie then,
> Bowed with her four score years and ten,
> Bravest of all in Frederick-town,
> She took up the flag the men hauled down;
> In her attic-window the staff she set,
> To show that one heart was loyal yet.
> Up the street came the rebel tread,
> Stonewall Jackson riding ahead.
> Under his slouched hat left and right
> He glanced; the old flag met his sight.
> "Halt"—the dust-brown ranks stood fast,
> "Fire"—out blazed the rifle-blast.
> It shivered the window, pane and sash;
> It rent the banner with seam and gash.
> Quick, as it fell, from the broken staff
> Dame Barbara snatched the silken scarf;
> She leaned far out on the window-sill,
> And shook it forth with a royal will.
> "Shoot, if you must, this old gray head,
> But spare your country's flag," she said.
> A shade of sadness, a blush of shame,
> Over the face of the leader came;
> The nobler nature within him stirred

To life at that woman's deeds and word;
"Who touches a hair of yon gray head
Dies like a dog! March on!" he said.

Thus, Barbara Fritchie's name became enshrined among the heroes and heroines of American history. Doubt may exist about the details of this Civil War confrontation, but this feisty lady did indeed make her mark on Frederick. She was 40 when she married 26-year-old John Fritchie, son of suspected Tory spy Caspar Fritchie, and the match kept local tongues busy with gossip. The story of her life is reviewed in the orientation slide program you'll see before you begin your tour of the **Barbara Fritchie House.**

Rooms both upstairs and down have furnishings that belonged to Barbara and John Fritchie. Many historic heirlooms have been lost due to the repeated flooding of Carroll Creek. In the room where Barbara once entertained local townspeople and family, you'll see the desk where Federal General Jesse Reno penned a letter to his wife on his way through Frederick. He died two days later at the Battle of Antietam. Upstairs there is the poet's corner dedicated to Whittier's tribute and the bedroom where Barbara died 13 years after her younger husband. Outside there is a triangular garden with 18th-century herbs and flowers.

The Barbara Fritchie House at 154 West Patrick Street is open daily Monday through Saturday from 10:00 A.M. to 4:00 P.M. and Sunday 1:00 to 4:00 P.M. Closed on Tuesdays.

Just up the road, at 121 South Bentz Street, is the house of Chief Justice Roger Brooke Taney, who delivered the Supreme Court opinion in the famous 1857 Dred Scott case. Among other things, the decision held that black slaves were inferior beings; it became an ember that helped ignite the Civil War.

Years earlier, Taney had set up a law practice in Frederick with Francis Scott Key. Key eventually moved to Baltimore, but Taney, who had married his partner's sister Anne, remained. The house on South Bentz Street was his country home.

Taney visited his rural home on weekends. Today it is furnished with Taney heirlooms. The drawing room, dining room and bedroom are furnished, and outside you can explore the kitchen and slave quarters. Upstairs there is a small collection of memorabilia associated with both Taney and Key. **The Home of Roger Brook Taney** does not have regular hours, so you must arrange your visit in advance by calling Frederick Tourism, (301)663-8687.

Close to both the Fritchie and Taney houses is Manayunk Tavern, at 207 W. Patrick Street. The name of this popular restaurant comes from a Lenape Indian word meaning "drinking place," and though the bar affords patrons liquid refreshment, it is the menu that keeps customers coming back for lunch and dinner. Entrees change weekly, if not sooner, and make good use of fresh produce and flavorful seasonings.

Directions: From Baltimore take I-70 west to Frederick; use the South Market Street exit. Go north on Market to Patrick Street. Turn left for the Barbara Fritchie House. To park, go past the house and turn left after the creek bridge. You can then take a short walk up to the Taney House on South Bentz.

Brunswick Museum

All Aboard!

The railroad boomtown of Brunswick had its heyday in the late 1800s. Its significance is recognized by the inclusion of 320 acres at the town's center on the National Register of Historic Places. Most of the buildings in this district have survived intact, as has the spirit of the town. It is still essentially a rail community; according to residents, it's the only one of its kind in Maryland.

Russell Baker described the town as it was in the 1920s in his book *Growing Up*: "On the outer edge of my universe lay Brunswick. I first walked in that vision of paradise hand-in-hand with my father, and those visits opened my eyes to the vastness and wonders of life's possibilities. Two miles north of Lovettsville, across the Potomac on the Maryland shore, Brunswick was as distant and romantic a place as I ever expected to see. To live there in that great smoking conurbation, rumbling with the constant thunder of locomotives, filled with the moaning of train whistles coming down the Potomac Valley, was beyond my most fevered hopes. Brunswick was a huge railway center on the B&O Main Line, which linked the Atlantic coast to Chicago and midwestern steel centers. Approaching it was almost unbearably thrilling. You crossed an endless, rickety cantilevered bridge after pausing on the Virginia bank to pay a one-dollar toll. This was a powerful sum of money, but Brunswick was not for the pinchpennies of the earth."

The railroad arrived in Brunswick in 1850, eight years before the C&O Canal. To fully appreciate that accomplishment, visit the model railroad layout on the top floor of the **Brunswick Museum.** This is the kind of place where you're apt to see children tugging at their fathers to get them to "come on." The HO layout is a genuine spellbinder with about 700 pieces of rolling stock—freight cars, locomotives, passenger cars and cabooses— huffing and puffing along a ⅓-mile track. The track represents the actual Chessie line from Union Station in Washington to Brunswick Yard, which is depicted in the layout as it was during the 1950s, when it was seven miles long. This is one of the most extensive model railroads you're ever likely to see. Enormous effort has been expended to depict such stops along the line as Silver Spring, Rockville, Gaithersburg, Dickerson and Point of Rocks. The two main track lines cross rivers, negotiate tunnels and chug through towns.

On the museum's two lower floors you'll discover more about railroading and about the town of Brunswick. The Victorian era is recaptured both at home and at work. Period furniture fills a turn-of-the-century parlor, kitchen and nursery. Display cases are filled with popular fashions of the 1890s. Household utensils and photographs help complete the picture of home life in an earlier age. Exhibits of the working world feature old farm tools and an extensive collection of railroad and canal tools. The museum itself is located in the 1904 brick Red Man's Lodge, the meeting place of a fraternal organization interested in Indian lore.

To get the feel of the town take time to walk or drive the streets of downtown Brunswick. You'll see Victorian houses and shops as well as the "company town" railroad houses that have changed very little over the years.

The Brunswick Museum, 40 W. Potomac Street, is open mid-April to mid-December on Saturdays from 10:00 A.M. to 4:00 P.M. and Sundays 1:00 to 4:00 P.M. Admission is charged.

Directions: From Baltimore take Route 70 west. At Frederick head southwest on Route 340. Then turn left on Route 17 for Brunswick and take a left on Potomac Street for the museum.

Byrd Winery and Berrywine Plantations

Time for Wine

Daytrippers like variety in their destinations. A brief stop at a local winery offers a change of pace. There are two vineyards in Frederick County that can be combined with a visit to the region's historic and natural attractions.

You can drop in on the Byrds. They—like many families in Virginia, Pennsylvania, New York, California, Oregon and other grape-growing states—own and operate a vineyard and winery. They'll show you a short slide program to introduce you to their winery. You'll see the steps Sharon and Brett had to follow to graft the grapes, prepare the fields, harvest their crop and produce their wine. They obviously didn't miss a step. In their first four years of operation they won 16 medals—the total is now up to 39! The Byrds began planting in 1972 and produced their first wine in 1976—the first year for wine production in western Maryland.

Brett Byrd has said, "People used to think I was stupid, now they think I am a genius." His Cabernet Sauvignon won three gold and a silver medal in national competitions for the last four consecutive years with four consecutive vintages. With this track record more and more wine critics are noticing Byrd Winery. Other wines they produce include Chardonnay, Sauvignon Blanc, Johannisberg Reisling, Gewürtztraminer, William Byrd Cabernet Sauvignon, William Byrd Chardonnay and Byrd Cellars Red, White, Blush and Manor Rosé. You can enjoy tasting some of these estate-bottled wines after you tour the winery.

Byrd Winery is open for tours, tasting and wine purchases February through May on Saturday and Sunday from 1:00 to 5:00 P.M. EST and from 1:00 to 6:00 P.M. DST There is no charge for tours. Closed January and major holidays.

Frederick County has a second family-run winery, the Linganore Wine Cellars at Berrywine Plantations. You'll know you're getting close when you see rows upon rows of what looks like short telephone poles. Berrywine is an Aellen family concern. As Anthony Aellen, the young manager, describes it, "a hobby that got out of hand." Anthony explains that his grandfather used to make about 35 gallons of wine each year in his basement. He gave his wine-making equipment to Jack and Lucille Aellen, who, with their six children, were living on a 250-acre dairy farm in Maryland's Linganore Valley. Within five years they had begun converting the dairy farm to a winery, planting the first grapes in 1972 and making wine by 1976. By 1983 the federal government designated the Linganore Valley as Maryland's first grape-growing area.

The Aellens enjoy experimenting; they produce roughly 30 varieties of wine each year. These include May Wine, Medieval Mead, and wine made from peaches, plums, elderberries, raspberries and a host of other fruits. After you tour the wine-making operation in the old barns you can enjoy a tasting. When the fruit is in season you're encouraged to try first the fruit and then the wine for comparison. Berrywine Plantations hosts monthly festivals from June through October, except September (see Calendar of Events). Berrywine is open year-round from 10:00 A.M. to 6:00 P.M. and Sundays noon to 6:00 P.M. Closed major holidays.

Directions: For Byrd Winery take I-70 from Baltimore, continue ten miles past Frederick to Exit 42 (Myersville). From the exit ramp take Main Street through town to Church Hill Road (about one mile outside town). Turn right on Church Hill Road and continue for another mile to Byrd Vineyards on the left. You will notice the grape vines growing on the hillside. For Berrywine Plantations take I-70 west from Baltimore about 30 miles to the exit for New Market. Take Route 75 north for 4.5 miles, then turn right on Glisans Mill Road. If you cross a concrete bridge, you'll know you missed the turnoff. Stay on Glisans Mill Road for 3.7 miles to the winery on the right.

Catoctin Mountains

Where Whiskey Flowed and Water Falls

On quiet days in the mountains during the summer of '29 you'd occasionally hear the thump from the moonshiner's wooden keg, but on July 29, 1929, it was still. No noise betrayed its location.

Two men drove along Big Hunting Creek until they came to a narrow, rough road up the mountainside draw. They parked, and toting an empty whiskey jug, started up the draw. Before they'd gone very far, they were halted by a rifle-toting still blockader (so called after the blockade runners of earlier seafaring days). They were told to "git" and git they did—but only long enough to assemble the rest of the posse. The raid on the **Blue Blazes Whiskey Still** was underway.

Stories are still told in Frederick County about the shoot-out that ensued. You can hear about this dramatic confrontation from the volunteers who operate the Blue Blazes Whiskey Still. The present still is not nearly so large as the operation raided back in '29. The original was no fly-by-night setup. It was one of the biggest stills ever destroyed in Maryland, having produced over 25,000 gallons. Such big stills were called steamer stills and held roughly 40 barrels of moonshine. The smaller apparatus operated at **Catoctin Mountain Park** since 1970 was originally a Smokey Mountain still seized by Treasury agents, or revenuers. But it wore out, so the usable parts were used to build another old-time model.

A self-guided nature trail leads from the National Park Service Visitor Center to the Blue Blazes Still. This is just one of the 16 trails that offer more than 30 miles of hiking within the Catoctin Mountain Park and **Cunningham Falls State Park,** directly across Route 77. You can also take a 14-mile scenic drive along the Catoctin Ridge; it begins at the Visitor Center on Route 77 where you can obtain a map of both parks.

The most scenic spot in these two parks is Cunningham Falls. Even armchair travelers can negotiate the easy five-minute walk from the Route 77 parking turn-off to the falls. Two other trails lead to the falls from the William Houck Area: the Lower Cunningham Falls Trail of moderate difficulty and the strenuous Cliff Trail.

The cascading Cunningham Falls drops 78 feet and offers many photographic possibilities, so be sure to bring a camera. If you have a zoom lens or binoculars you'll be able to enjoy a closeup look at the woodland birds. On hot summer days the falls might whet your urge for a swim. In that case, head over to the 40-acre Hunting Creek Lake, where there are two sandy public beaches and a bathhouse for changing. On summer weekends it's advisable to arrive by 10:00 A.M. if you want to find a parking spot. Those more interested in fishing than dipping can throw a line in the well-stocked lake or in one of the park's many streams. A license is required for anyone over 16. Canoes are rented during the summer and fall.

Other park options include camping, picnicking, cross-country skiing, horseback riding on designated trails, snowshoeing and sailing.

At the southern end of the Cunningham Falls State Park off Route 15, on Route 806, you'll see the remains of the Old Catoctin Furnace, one of three furnaces operated here from 1776 to 1903. The Mountain Tract, as the surrounding land was called, was issued to Benedict Calvert and Thomas Johnson for the purpose of erecting an iron works. In the last triumphant stages of the Revolution this furnace supplied ten-inch shells for the Continental Army. The stack you see today is from the Isabella Furnace built in 1867. Signs explain just how this furnace operated.

Directions: From Baltimore take I-70 west to Frederick. Head north on Route 15 for 13 miles to Catoctin Furnace. Then take Route 77 west, which leads to both the Catoctin Mountain Park Visitors Center and the parking turn-off for the easy walk to Cunningham Falls.

Frederick Historic District

Old but Not Square

Florence, Italy, has its lucky bronze boar. In Frederick, Maryland, there is an iron dog some would say is lucky, too. This faithful pet in front of Dr. John Tyler's house was stolen in 1862 by Confederate troops as they marched through Frederick. They intended to melt it down for bullets, but the dog was found undamaged after the battle at Sharpsburg (see Antietam selection).

As is true for all historic cities, it is much better to take an escorted walking tour than to head out on your own with a self-guided brochure. The background stories and anecdotes the guides relate add a depth you're unlikely to uncover alone. Brochures can be obtained and tours arranged at the Visitors Center, 19 East Church Street (call (301)663-8687). Approximately ten of the 20 recommended tour sites are along Church Street, where the early German and English settlers established their churches. These include the Evangelical Lutheran Church (1738–1855), Trinity Chapel (1763–1807), All Saints Episcopal Church (1855) and the Evangelical Reformed Church (1848). Natives still regale visitors with the story about Stonewall Jackson attending the Presbyterian church in Frederick. It seems Jackson slept through

About half of the tour sites in historic Frederick are found on Church Street. All Saints Episcopal is but one of four churches built by German and English settlers.

the impassioned sermon the Reverend Zacharis preached about the necessity of preserving the Union. When leaving the church the Confederate General, who was giving his all to severing the very ties Zacharis was trying to bind, complimented the confused minister on his wonderful sermon.

In addition to these historic old churches, the town also boasts a number of figures from the pages of history who lived here. Many of their homes have survived. Civil War heroine Barbara Fritchie flew her flag from her Frederick townhouse. A few doors away is the home of John Hanson, first President of the United States under the Articles of Confederation. The home of *American Creed* author William Tyler Page is around the corner from Dr. John Tyler's on Church Street. Just beyond the perimeters of the inner city walking area is the home of Supreme Court Justice Roger B. Taney (see selection).

Frederick has two new shopping areas you may want to explore, plus Patrick Street's Antiques Row. Between Church Street and Second Street on East Street you'll find Shab Row. This former "shabby area" is a series of restored log cabins and Federal-style townhouses that have been converted to craft boutiques and antique shops. In the next block, at the corner of Patrick, Church and East Streets, is Everedy Square, a renovated pots and pans factory, with unusual specialty shops and a restaurant.

There are several charming spots where you can enjoy a midday break for lunch or an early dinner. On Market Street you can find saloon-like atmosphere and good food at Bushwaller's. The restaurant is housed in a building erected in 1840 for a group of French refugees from the slave uprising in Haiti. Although the saloon has the look of a long-time Frederick landmark, it actually opened in 1981. To enhance the old-timey feeling, the walls are lined with old photos, drawings and memorabilia.

Also on Market Street you'll find a quite different but equally appealing eatery, the Province at 131 North Market. Colorful quilts hang on the walls and the rear dining room overlooks the restaurant's much-used herb garden.

If you want to take the good taste of Frederick home with you, stop at McCutcheon's Apple Products on South Wisner Street. They sell an absolutely delicious country-style apple butter, as well as their popular pear butter. Jellies, preserves and cider are also made and sold at this family-owned and operated business.

Directions: From the Baltimore Beltway (I-695) take I-70 west to Frederick. At Frederick, use the Patrick Street/Historic District exit and follow the signs to the Visitors Center.

Grotto of Lourdes and National Shrine of St. Elizabeth Ann Seton

Contemplative Combination

Two shrines in Emmitsburg provide inspiration for the devout of all denominations. The *Grotto of Lourdes* was the first Catholic Shrine established in the 13 original states. Father Dubois came to western Maryland and in 1805 founded St. Mary's Catholic Church. He discovered a cave with a natural spring on a mountainside near his church. Dubois placed a cross in front of the cave. Subsequently other priests added paths and a fountain. In 1875 Patrick Duffy, a seminarian at Mount St. Mary's College, decided this would be an ideal place for a replica of the famous French shrine known as Lourdes.

A kneeling statue of St. Bernadette of Lourdes reminds visitors of the French saint, but she is not the only saint remembered here. There is a replica of Our Lady of Lourdes as she appeared to St. Bernadette. The path to the shrine is flanked with azaleas and rhododendron. It is particularly scenic in spring when the blossoms provide a contrast to the mountain greenery. At the base of the path there is a 120-foot companile with 14 bells. A gilded bronze statue of Mary, Mother of God, crowns the bell tower.

Near the parking lot you'll see a replica of the log cabin that Mother Seton and her followers used for six weeks when they first arrived in Emmitsburg in 1809. This cabin is an invitation for you to continue investigating the years Mother Seton spent in Emmitsburg. Your next stop should be the **National Shrine of St. Elizabeth Ann Seton,** approximately two miles away on Route 15 north.

The life and work of St. Elizabeth Ann Seton, who is credited with having founded the parochial school system in the United States, are presented at the Visitor Center of the National Shrine. A 12-minute slide presentation provides background, which lends greater significance to the pictorial story, exhibits and personal memorabilia on display. If you want to study each panel of the displays, you should plan to spend an hour or more here. Daughters of Charity are available to answer any questions you may have.

If you have time for a leisurely visit, you can follow "The Seton Way," a self-guided walking tour. The first stop is the 200-year-old Stone House, where Mother Seton established her religious community after moving out of the log cabin. When speaking of the Stone House, Pope John XXIII said, "In a house that was very small, but with ample space for charity, she sowed a seed in America which by Divine Grace grew into a large tree."

This imposing campanile stands near Emmitsburg at the entrance to the replica of the Grotto of Lourdes, the first Catholic Shrine established in the 13 original states.

The spartan furnishings in the house reveal the simple life-style of Mother Seton and her followers. It is fascinating to learn that she arrived in Emmitsburg by covered wagon. Hers was virtually a frontier existence for a time.

Life improved when she and her 16 residents moved into the "White House" in February 1810. Here she finally had ample room to teach her ever-expanding enrollment drawn from all races and religions. The first floor of the White House consisted of a chapel and classroom. The second floor provided sleeping quarters for the children and students while the third floor was occupied by the sisters. The classroom has authentic furnishings from Mother Seton's tenure. There is a grandfather clock made by an Emmitsburg craftsman and on the walls are samplers stitched by the school's sisters and boarders.

The chapel on the first floor retains its original altar. You can see where Mother Seton knelt to receive communion. Adjoining the chapel is the room where she died on January 4, 1821. There is a replica of her bed, which was on wheels so it could be moved to permit her to participate in the daily Mass.

The last stop on the walking tour is the cemetery. Mother Seton was originally buried beside an oak tree next to her sister-in-law, Harriet Seton. In 1846 a mortuary chapel was completed for her remains at the request of her son, William Seton. At the time of her beatification by Pope John XXIII in 1962 her remains were exhumed and placed in a small bronze casket. In 1968 they were transferred to a resting place beneath the altar of St. Elizabeth Ann in the Shrine Chapel at St. Joseph's Provincial House of the Daughters of Charity. At her canonization on September 14, 1975, Pope Paul VI said, "Elizabeth Ann Seton is a Saint. She is the first daughter of the United States of America to be glorified with this incomparable attribute."

The Seton Shrine is open daily 10:00 A.M. until 5:00 P.M. except on Christmas, the last two weeks in January, and on Mondays from November to April. The Eucharistic Liturgy is celebrated Saturday and Sunday at 9:00 A.M. and on Wednesday through Sunday at 1:30 P.M. The masses are followed by the blessing with a relic of Saint Elizabeth Ann Seton.

Directions: From Baltimore take I-795 and Route 140 west to Emmitsburg. Make a left at the town square onto Seton Avenue and go ½ mile to the Seton Shrine.

Lilypons Water Gardens

Fish 'n' Fry

Lilypons can make two claims to fame; it is the largest propagator of ornamental aquatic plants in the country (perhaps in the world) and it is the smallest town in Maryland. Both distinctions were an outgrowth in a very real sense of the ripple effect.

G. Leicester Thomas, Frederick County farmer and business-man, began growing waterlilies and raising goldfish on his 275-acre farm in a pond near the road. The beauty of the flowers and darting fish caught the attention of passing motorists. Before long Leicester Thomas was selling enough plants and fish to warrant expanding his hobby into a business. Thus **Lilypons Water Gardens** and Three Springs Fisheries were born.

Having founded a business that from its earliest days in 1917 sold a great deal of its merchandise by mail (now it is about 60% mail order), Thomas needed a post office. He was an enthusiastic fan of Lily Pons, then at the height of her Metropolitan Opera career. Thomas wrote the diva that if she had no objections he would like to name his business and post office in her honor. She readily assented and even attended the post office dedication on June 22, 1936. For years she regularly mailed her Christmas cards from the Lilypons Post Office.

Though the setting remains much as it was, the business has become a major industry with offices on the second floor of the old farm house. There are now 500 ponds at Lilypons and a second facility in Brookshire, Texas.

The farm is open 51 weeks a year (closed Christmas week), but the best time to visit is during June, July and August when the lilies and lotus flower. Contrary to expectation the fish are not gold in early summer but rather gray-black. The fish fry are allowed to grow to two inches, then harvested and sold.

Scavenger birds find the fish delectable. A keen-eyed osprey, attracted by the fish's bright colors, can consume as much as $300 worth of goldfish or Koi (Imperial Japanese carp) in a day. While the birds may be a threat to profits, they are a delight to visitors. Herons, egrets, bitterns, osprey and kingfishers and also such waterfowl as wooducks, mallards and migratory geese might be spotted.

Only 45 miles from Baltimore and 35 miles from Washington, Lilypons Water Gardens is open Monday through Saturday from 10:00 A.M. to 5:00 P.M. and Sunday noon to 5:00 P.M. March through October. From November through February hours are 10:00 A.M. to 3:00 P.M. Monday through Friday.

Directions: From Baltimore take I-70 west about 40 miles to Exit 54. Take Route 85 (Buckeystown Pike) south eight miles to Lilypons Road and turn left.

New Market

To Market, To Market, To Buy. . .

"Everything old is new again" could well be the motto of **New Market,** the Antiques Capital of Maryland. This tiny town, virtually one long street, boasts more than 35 antique shops for visitors to explore.

Now on the National Register of Historic Places, New Market has been serving travelers since it was founded in 1793. Its location on the National Pike between Baltimore and Frederick made it an ideal spot to overnight. There were six to eight inns to accommodate the traffic, most with barns and pens for the livestock.

Today there are two charming bed and breakfast inns on Main Street. Jane and Ed Rossig's Strawberry Inn, (301)865-3318, is the oldest in Frederick County. Practically next door is the National Pike Inn, (301)865-5055, run by Tom and Terry Rimel. As befits this antique haven, the rooms in both country inns are furnished with period pieces.

In order to maintain the ambience of New Market, the only stores permitted by the town council are antique shops, aside from a country store and service-related businesses that cater to the community. The old-time, small-town flavor is remarkably intact and the diverse architectural styles make a stroll down Main Street worthwhile even for those with only a minimal interest in antiques.

Antique enthusiasts should plan to spend at least half a day here, with time for a meal at Mealey's Inn. The name is derived from Dick and Nellie Mealey, who, with a partner, bought the Utz Hotel, as it was then called, in 1919. The inn's oldest section is a colonial log house built the same year the town was founded. It probably served as both house and shop. Additions and changes saw Mealey's evolve into a Colonial brick, then a late Federal brick design. The main dining room was once the Pump Room, and the old pump that once furnished water for the Utz Hotel guests now rests in front of the fireplace. Today Mealey's is owned by the Jefferies, and it is more popular than ever. Reservations are a must on weekends. Call (301)865-5488.

New Market is worth visiting on any pleasant weekend, but in late September during the weekend-long New Market Days it is even more fun. The streets are lined with craftspeople demonstrating and selling their wares, and there is a festive atmosphere in the shops.

All of the shops and restaurants are open on weekends. Mondays all shops and Mealey's are closed. Mealey's opens on Tuesdays, and from Wednesday through Friday about 15 other shops are open also. When you arrive in town stop in front of the Post Office and pick up a guide to Historic New Market at the Visitors Information Bulletin Board.

Directions: From Baltimore take I-70 west. Use Exit 62 (Route 75) and proceed north for one block for the left turn onto Route 144 and Main Street in New Market.

Rose Hill Manor and Schifferstadt

Carriages and Crafts, Farm and Flowers

Rose Hill Manor is a historical house museum planned with children in mind. The downstairs rooms contain strictly hands-on exhibits that give youngsters a chance to be actively involved with the 18th century.

This rural Georgian manor house was built in 1790 by John Grahame and his wife Anne Johnson Grahame. The house was built on land given the couple by the bride's father Thomas Johnson, first elected governor of Maryland. One of the most significant contributions of Thomas Johnson's long and distinguished political career was his nomination of George Washington as Commander-in-Chief of the Continental Army. After Governor Johnson retired, he spent the last nine years of his life living at Rose Hill with his daughter and son-in-law.

Rose Hill Manor guides recall the days when Thomas Johnson lived with the Grahames. The costumed docents invite visitors into the touch-and-see parlor, allowing time for younger guests to enjoy the 18th-century toys. The textile room gives visitors a chance to try their hand at quiltmaking or at throwing the loom shuttle to advance the work in progress. A sizeable number of the 300 items included in the Rose Hill Children's Museum are to be found in the kitchen. You can don an old-fashioned apron and mop hat, and turn the hand of a kraut cutter or roll the dough for the beaten biscuits.

The hands-on approach is not followed in the roped off upstairs rooms. The bedrooms and governor's study are furnished with valuable period pieces.

The manor house is but one part of this 43-acre park. There are five additional areas to explore. On weekends when Rose Hill hosts special events, both a blacksmith and tinsmith demonstrate their old-world skills in the fully stocked work areas. Speaking of old world, a log cabin has been moved onto the park grounds. The rustic home, furnished with handmade furniture and utensils, will take you back to the day of the settlers who made Frederick County their home in the early 18th century.

As you make your way from one area of the park to the next, take time to smell the flowers. The 18th-century garden is filled

Rose Hill Manor, in a 43-acre park, invites youngsters to touch and try as many as 300 different household tools including such items as a loom, rolling pin and kraut cutter.

with aromatic herbs—mint, lavender, oregano and basil. A vegetable patch, like the one that once served the manor's needs, is in full growth by mid-summer. Flowers were grown to grace the table. In a large empty field the park personnel have recently planted a wildflower patch, which they plan to expand over the next few years.

Two museums—the Farm Museum and the Carriage Museum—provide exhibits of the nitty-gritty tools of trade for farmers and the conveyances of an earlier era. There are hundreds of farm implements in the bank barn and dairy barn. Exhibits depict the evolution from wooden plows to steam tractors. The Carriage Museum has more than 20 restored vehicles ranging from the buggy with the fringe on top to a Russian sleigh.

Walk-in tours of Rose Hill Manor are available Monday through Saturday from 10:00 A.M. to 4:00 P.M. and Sunday 1:00 to 4:00

P.M. April through October, and weekends March, November and December. The house is closed January and February. Throughout the year colonial craft demonstrations are scheduled, highlighting such 18th- and 19th-century skills as soapmaking, candle dipping, quilting, carpentry, broommaking, spinning and waving. Check the Calendar of Events for specific happenings.

Just blocks away from Rose Hill along Carroll Creek is **Schifferstadt,** another 18th-century house, but one that is far more modest. Schifferstadt was completed in 1756, making it the oldest house still standing in Frederick. There are those who consider Schifferstadt to be the finest example of German colonial architecture in the country. The house was built by Joseph Brunner and his son, Elias. They named it after their family's birthplace near Mannheim, Germany. The Brunner family name is first mentioned in the Frederick area rent rolls in 1744, after they emigrated to Maryland from Philadelphia. In 1746 the family purchased 303 acres of "Tasker's Chance" for ten English pounds, or roughly $40. It was on this land they built Schifferstadt.

The walls of the sandstone house are 2½ feet thick. The stones at the front are uniformly laid, but on the back and sides they are haphazard. The native oak beams are all hand-hewn. You can still see the wooden pegs that pin the braces together. The house tour gives you a chance to see the underside of the wooden roof beams in the attic, where you'll also get an unusual perspective of the huge vaulted chimney. This architectural tour covers the cellar as well as the attic. The cellar is also vaulted and extends beneath the northern half of the house, which was the original portion. The wing was added during the 1820s. The house is not furnished, but you will see the original five-plate jamb stove that is dated 1756. It was cast in Mannheim, Germany, and bears the German inscription, "Where your treasure is, there is your heart." The brick-wing addition has a seven-foot squirreltail, brick bake oven.

The wing also houses the Schifferstadt Gallery, with many one-of-a-kind handmade items. At the artist-run Artisan's Cooperative you'll find pottery, wheat weavings, woodcarvings, stained glass, herbal wreaths, fine porcelain, stencil art, woven goods, baskets, paintings, jewelry, leather goods and much more. Schifferstadt is open daily 10:00 A.M. to 4:00 P.M. from April through December.

Directions: From Baltimore take I-70 west to U.S. 15 north in Frederick. For Rose Hill take Motter Avenue Exit off U.S. 15. For Schifferstadt take Rosemont Avenue Exit.

Sugar Loaf Mountain

How Sweet It Is!

On a clear day, though you can't see forever, you can see a great deal of the picturesque Maryland countryside from 1,283-foot **Sugar Loaf Mountain**. It stands alone, a landmark for those traveling across the surrounding terrain. Reportedly first charted in 1707, the mountain was named by early settlers who felt it resembled a loaf of sugar bread.

From Sugar Loaf's summit you'll see Virginia's Bull Run to the south, the Catoctin and Blue Ridge mountains to the west, and Frederick Valley to the north. Mention of Sugar Loaf appears in many historic journals. General Braddock passed by in 1775 on his way to the disastrous Battle of Fort Duquesne. During the Civil War the mountain was used as a Union lookout post. From here a sentry spotted General Robert E. Lee leading his men across the Potomac River just before the Battle of Antietam. Afterward, wounded soldiers from both North and South were treated at log cabins still standing at the base of Sugar Loaf Mountain.

Gordon Strong discovered the charms of Sugar Loaf during a 1902 vacation. He was so impressed he purchased acreage, gradually acquiring the entire mountain. In 1912 Strong built a Georgian colonial mansion, Stronghold, high on Sugar Loaf's slopes. One of the illustrous guests here was President Franklin Delano Roosevelt. Roosevelt was as taken with Sugar Loaf as Strong had been, and wanted to acquire the mountainside estate as a presidential retreat. In spurning Roosevelt's overtures, Strong suggested the President turn his attention to the 10,000 acres already owned by the government outside Thurmont. At Roosevelt's direction, Shangri-La, a mountain hideaway, was built on the federal land. During the Eisenhower administration it was renamed Camp David after the President's son.

Although few visitors since Roosevelt have considered buying Sugar Loaf, many have been captivated by its scenic beauty. In fact, it is now protected as a National Natural Landmark. There are trails along Sugar Loaf's slopes, and if you have a mount you can enjoy the riding trail.

If mountain climbing, even on little mountains, is too strenuous for you, there is a winding road that leads within a quarter of a mile of the top. The road has numerous overlooks where you can stop and enjoy the view. Sugar Loaf can be visited from 7:00 A.M. to sunset daily. A snack bar is open on summer weekends and holidays, and there are picnic tables and rest rooms.

Directions: From Baltimore take I-70 west about 30 miles to exit for New Market and Route 75. Go south on Route 75 to

Hyattstown and turn right onto Route 109. Pass under I-270 and go another 3.3 miles to Comus. Turn right on Route 95 and go 2.5 miles to Sugar Loaf Mountain.

CARROLL COUNTY

Carroll County Farm Museum

Down on the Farm

In 1985 Hollywood turned its spotlight on rural America with three movies—*Places in the Heart, Country* and *The River*. But this kind of attention is nothing new; for years the **Carroll County Farm Museum** in Westminster has been depicting the life of independent farmers of the 19th century.

This is not a museum in the traditional sense. Although there are a few display cases filled with carefully labeled articles, this is primarily a re-creation of the way of life of a land-owning farm family in the 19th century. On such farms the farmer planted enough to feed his family and his livestock. He acquired mechanized equipment very gradually, relying primarily on horse power. His wife preserved and canned the excess crop, and the seeds were saved for the next year. Market days were major events for the entire family.

The house at the Carroll County Farm Museum was built in 1852 to serve as the County Almshouse. The farm was worked from the late 1850s until 1965 when it became this museum. Six rooms of the house are now furnished, in fact many would say over-furnished, in the Victorian style of the late 19th century. The layered look is definitely in—tables are covered with not one but three decorative cloths. Ornate picture frames are draped with swags of lace to draw the eye from one picture to the next.

As you tour the house it becomes evident that although the days were long and the life hard, farming did enable a family to acquire a few of the finer things. While you're exploring, see how many objects you can name. The kitchen offers a treasure trove to be identified. Few can pin a name on the whipped cream churner, though most can identify the apple corer.

The guides, dressed in period costumes, will direct you to other utensils and tools still in use in the craft barns, where blacksmiths, weavers, spinners, quilters, tinsmiths and potters demonstrate their skills and wares. After watching these craftsmen, you can check out the farm support buildings, which include a spring house, smokehouse, the barns and animal pens. The farm is just part of a 140-acre park. There are nature trails

The Carroll County Farm Museum re-creates the way of life on a family farm in the 19th century. In one barn, blacksmiths, tinsmiths, weavers and others demonstrate skills.

to hike if you have the time and a place to picnic under the trees surrounding the pond.

The Carroll County Farm Museum is open weekends noon to 5:00 P.M. May through October and every day except Monday from 10:00 A.M. to 4:00 P.M. during July and August. A gift shop is open Tuesday through Friday from 10:00 A.M. to 5:00 P.M. Throughout the year the farm sponsors a series of fairs and festivals (see Calendar of Events).

Directions: From Baltimore take Route 140 northwest to the Westminster area. One mile south of Westminster turn left off Route 140 onto Center Street. Go 1½ miles and the Carroll County Farm Museum is on the right off Center Street.

Greenway Gardens, Piney Run Park and Cascade Lake

Three Faces of Nature

A trio of natural treats awaits you in Carroll County. If you like to watch things grow, then **Greenway Gardens & Arboretum** offers a twofold allure. Owners Dottie and Zeeger de Wilde have ambitious plans for their 27-acre garden complex. Over the next decade they will be adding new garden focal spots, new trees on their rolling hills and new plants.

Already some of the de Wildes' dreams are realized. They've developed a small Desert House with a wide variety of succulents, including several huge seven-year-old century plants. These fast growers are already five feet high and five feet wide with yard- long leaves.

The outdoor plants are most colorful in the spring and fall. Zeeger de Wilde is a native of the Netherlands so it's not surprising that in the spring roughly 40,000 tulips, plus a profusion of daffodils and hyacinths, blossom here. In autumn the golds, bronzes and rusts of the chrysanthemums blend with the sunset hues of the surrounding foliage. It's also worth remembering that the best times for viewing roses are when they peak in late spring and mid-fall before the first hard frost.

At any time of year nature lovers can enjoy the arboretum with its collection of trees from near and far. Horticulturists can browse through garden books in Greenway's library, and craft enthusiasts can check the schedule of nature craft workshops. Bird watchers appreciate the numerous nesting areas at Greenway.

Greenway Gardens & Arboretum is open daily, except Christmas Day, from 9:00 A.M. to 5:00 P.M. (4:00 P.M. January through March) and noon to 5:00 P.M. on Sundays. Thursday evening they stay open until 9:00 P.M. Admission is charged.

Less than 15 minutes away is **Piney Run Park.** The park's 300-acre lake provides a picturesque setting for picnickers and boaters, and multiple options for fishermen. The lake is stocked with rainbow trout. Other fish include large- and smallmouth bass, crappie, bluegill, channel catfish and freshwater rockfish, although the last must be returned to the water. You can either fish from the shore or rent a canoe or rowboat and try your luck farther out. From November through March fishing is allowed from the shore only.

For fun on the lake you can rent paddleboats or enjoy a pontoon ride, available hourly on weekends June through August from 1:00 to 5:00 P.M. A nature center introduces you to the region's flora and fauna, and five miles of nature trails crisscross the park.

During the winter the trails are used by cross-country skiers. And when the lake freezes, ice skating is permitted.

Piney Run Park's main season is April through October weekdays 9:00 A.M. to sunset and weekends 6:00 A.M. to sunset. From November through March park personnel are available at the nature center. Visitors can park outside the gate and still take advantage of the hiking, fishing, skating and skiing.

Not too far away in Hampstead is seven-acre **Cascade Lake,** where visitors are encouraged to swim by park personnel and the setting as well. Cascade looks like a Norman Rockwell depiction of the old swimming hole. There's a floating diving platform, a big sliding board and boats to rent. Swimmers can bring inner tubes, rafts and other floatables. This family-oriented public park has a reasonable admission, shaded picnic areas, a playground and a game room with video games and pool tables. Cascade Lake is open from Memorial Day to Labor Day. One note of caution: On hot summer weekends the parking lot is generally filled to overflowing by 1:00 P.M. For information call (301)374-9111 or (301)239-2310.

Directions: From Baltimore take I-70 west, exit on Route 32 north, then turn left on Route 26 for Piney Run Park. For Greenway Gardens continue on Route 26 past the Piney Run Park entrance and turn right on Route 97. Head north on Route 97 to Nicodemus Road and turn right. Greenway Gardens is at 328 E. Nicodemus Road. When traveling from Baltimore to Cascade Lake take Route 140 northwest to Route 30. Go north on Route 30 to Hampstead. Turn left on Route 482 and make a right on Snydersburg Road. Cascade Lake is at 3000 Snydersburg Road. To reach Cascade Lake from Greenway Gardens return to Route 97 and go north to Westminster. Turn left onto Route 140 and then right onto Route 27. Take Route 27 northeast about two miles, then bear right on Route 482. When approaching from this direction turn left on Snydersburg Road.

Hard Lodging, Strawbridge Shrine and Uniontown

A Piece of the Rock

Hard Lodging, the name Solomon Shepherd gave his home in the 1790s, could easily refer to the solid rock foundation on which it rests. Shepherd actually named his estate after a nearby land grant. The townfolk, however, called the house on the rock-top Solomon's Folly.

When you tour this house, which is now on the National Register of Historic Places, one of the first areas you'll be shown is the basement. The floor on this lower level is the irregular rock ledge on which the house stands. The house is a typical English-style house influenced by design touches associated with Delaware, including a brick belt course (a distinctive brick design that separates the first and second floors) and a water table (a strong molding beneath the front windows to throw off rainwater).

The main section, now the dining room and overhead bedrooms, was built in the 1790s. Added later was a service wing, which is currently decorated as an Early American den and living room. The last owner, Mrs. Thelma Littlefield Shriner, had an informal wing with sun porch built on in 1950.

Much of the furniture is from the Empire Period, 1815–1820, although some pieces are older. Some of the furnishings have an interesting history. In the entrance hall the Empire secretary, or desk bookcase, belonged to the Jerome family, who were friends of Mrs. Shriner's grandfather. Jenny Jerome was Winston Churchill's mother.

Mrs. Shriner amassed an eclectic, but interesting, collection of furnishings. The silver service in the dining room also belonged to the Jeromes. Decorative pieces in the dining room include Limoges plates and a Currier and Ives lithograph. One piece that delights visitors is the five-faced cookie jar. Tours are given by the Historical Society of Carroll County. To make arrangements call (301)848-6494 or 848-9531.

There are two additional points of interest north and south of New Windsor that can easily be combined with a stop at Hard Lodging. One is **Strawbridge Shrine**, but don't be misled by the name. What you'll see is a replication of the 1764 meeting house of the first American Methodist congregation and a rustic cabin. The cabin was the home of John Evan, Methodism's first American convert, from 1764 to 1827. Robert Strawbridge came to America from Ireland after being converted to Methodism by John Coughlin, one of John Wesley's preachers. The homestead where Robert Strawbridge lived is privately owned and cannot be toured. There are no set hours at the Shrine; you may explore on your own.

North of New Windsor lies the village of **Uniontown**, whose main street hasn't changed since the turn of the century. There are no chic boutiques or elegant eateries here. A walking-tour brochure gives architectural details of the picturesque private homes lining Uniontown Road. Those who really like to get away from the hustle and bustle should try the Newel Post, a Victorian bed and breakfast in town. Call (301)775-2655 for details.

One last spot you should include on your day's itinerary is the International Gift Shop at the New Windsor Service Center. Handicrafts from around the world are sold under the auspices of the Church of the Brethren World Ministries Commission. The

Gift Shop is open Monday through Saturday from 9:00 A.M. to 5:00 P.M. Closed on holidays.

Directions: From the Baltimore Beltway (I-95) take Route 26 west 20 miles to Route 27 and turn right. Go left at the intersection with Route 407 and then right on Route 31, New Windsor Road, then turn right on Wakefield Valley Road and right on Strawbridge Lane for Strawbridge Shrine. For Hard Lodging return to Route 31 and head north. Turn left on Route 75 for a short distance.

Maryland Midlands Railway Excursions

Fall Colors, Spring Apple Blossoms

It sounds more like an electric buzz saw than the expected choo choo, but you're still riding the rails for real on the **Maryland Midlands Railway.** Although these excursions into scenic Western Maryland are just a side line for this short-line railroad, passengers definitely have fun enough to think they are a specialty. Day-trippers board at the company's headquarters in Union Bridge, easily accessible from I-70 or I-270. The 84-year-old brick railroad station looks like a Hollywood set for Hello Dolly, but when the train heads toward the station with its Mars light turning, it looks like a Spielberg vision of the future from a "close encounter."

Families with young children often choose the shorter 18-mile, 1½-hour Sunday Local railroad excursion that runs from Union Bridge to Rocky Ridge and back. It's an ideal introduction to rail travel. The fare is $6 for adults and $4 for children 12 and under. Most excursion passengers, however, opt for the "run up the mountain" on the Blue Mountain Limited, a four-hour, 50-mile trip (fare, $15 and $8). This was the former Western Maryland Railway's scenic main line to the mountains. The climb to Blue Ridge Summit at the top of the Catoctin Mountains swings past Camp David, the President's retreat. In autumn, when the woodlands are full of color, special trains run in conjunction with the nearby foliage festivals. Billowing clouds of apple blossoms float over the hillsides in the spring. The rolling farmland, rippling streams and narrow passageways cut through the rocky hills make this a dramatic ride in any season. Standing in the open gondola car or on the observation platform, you'll feel the pull of the rails. It's easy to understand how enthusiasts get hooked.

For information on regular excursions and special trips, call (301)775-7718. Excursion trains run weekends from June through early November. Trains are available for boarding 20 minutes before departure.

Directions: From Baltimore take I-70 west to Route 75 at New Market. Take Route 75 north for 14 miles to Union Bridge. The train station is on the left on North Main Street (Route 75).

Montbray Wine Cellars

The Clone Zone

Montbray Wine Cellars has a unique brand of protection: an old German "fire letter." Now on display in the barn above the aging cellar, this traditional German prayer letter seeking God's protection against fires was discovered by Dr. Hamilton Mowbray in 1964 in a tack box hidden in a hewn beam. It was accompanied by a second letter dated May 31, 1899, that described how it was found by the writer when he was building a new barn. The original fire letter, written in the mid-to-late 18th century, included three verses of St. John.

If the fire letter brings back the past, Montbray's "clone vineyard" certainly heralds the future. Dr. Mowbray and plant physiologist William Klul were the first to successfully clone a grapevine from a single cell. Their success led Mowbray to plant the world's first clone vineyard of vines propagated from a single cell of the French hybrid Seyve-Villard.

The differences cloning makes appear to be all positive. It makes new plants less expensive and much easier to transport. A million plants can potentially be shipped in a little jar. According to Dr. Mowbray, clone vineyards produce a far more vigorous vine with more bunches of bigger, tastier grapes.

The winery was started in 1964 when Dr. Mowbray and his wife Phyllis acquired the 100-acre Silver Run Valley farm. The name comes from the family name de Montbray, from the town in Normandy. Montbray produces five wines: a Chardonnay, Johannisberg Riesling, Cabernet Sauvignon, Montbray Garnet and the award-winning Seyve-Villard. A *Washingtonian Magazine* panel voted Montbray Chardonnay and Montbray Cabernet Sauvignon best out of eight wines of each kind from wineries in Virginia and Maryland. The Seyve-Villard was recently named by the wine writer for the *Baltimore Sun* as the best white wine from the mid-Atlantic states.

Visitors are welcome at Montbray Wine Cellars Monday through Saturday from 10:00 A.M. to 6:00 P.M. and Sunday from 1:00 to 6:00 P.M. (if a weekend visit is planned, you are requested to call ahead, (301)346-7898). You can get a look at the operation, perhaps chat with Dr. Mowbray, and taste their wines.

Directions: From Baltimore take Route 140 (Reisterstown Road) to Westminster. From Westminster take Route 97 north for seven miles to Silver Run Valley Road and turn right. Montbray

Wine Cellars is two miles ahead on the left. There is a second smaller operation, White Marsh Cellars, not too far away in Hampstead.

Union Mills Homestead and Gristmill

Shriver Family Saga

The Shriver family, founders of **Union Mills**, are savers. This becomes apparent as you tour the family homestead. In addition to the furnishings and memorabilia accumulated by six generations of Shrivers who have lived here, there are also diaries, accounts and records. Only the Adamses of Massachusetts have more detailed family records.

The Shriver brothers, Andrew and David, came to Maryland in 1797. They each built a two-room log house separated by a "dog walk." The cost for building both houses was $86; the exact figure is listed in the accounts kept from the very beginning. On their 100 acres the brothers next built a sawmill, followed by the gristmill you'll see on your visit. Records show that 100,000 bricks were fired for the gristmill but only 70,000 were used. A tannery and shops for a blacksmith, cooper and carpenter were added later.

Once the family businesses were functioning smoothly, David Shriver moved to the Shellman House (see selection) in Westminster, and then to Cumberland, on the National Road that he surveyed. Andrew stayed at Union Mills, where both his family and his home expanded over the years. Andrew fathered 11 children, and the house was eventually enlarged to 23 rooms. The various additions are easily seen from outside.

Andrew Shriver campaigned for Thomas Jefferson. The grateful president rewarded Andrew with the postmastership of the Union Mills community. Andrew's original eight-slot postmaster's desk still sits in his office, one of the house's four original rooms.

The Civil War divided the country; it also divided the Shriver family. The second Andrew, son of Andrew Shriver, inherited the homestead and tannery. His brother William had a nearby house, called The Mills, and the gristmill. Andrew Kaiser was a Protestant, a Republican, and though he owned slaves he was a Northern supporter. Two of his sons served in the Union army. William, a convert to Catholicism and a Democrat, did not own slaves but he supported the South. Four of his sons fought for the Confederacy.

The tensions within the family reached their peak just before the Battle of Gettysburg when troops from both armies were fed at the homestead. On June 29, 1863, J.E.B. Stuart's 2,400 rebels camped in the farm's apple orchard (plans are underway to replant this orchard). At about 2:00 A.M. they were all fed pancakes prepared in the kitchen's huge fireplace by "Black" Ruth Dohr. Not long after the Confederates had departed, Union General Barnes arrived. He was given a bedroom at the homestead and he and his officers were entertained in the parlor by the Shriver daughters. They sang and danced. Accounts of the evening mention that one song heard that night was "When the Cruel War Is Over."

When the war was over the Shrivers returned to the business of business. The family tannery won an award at the 1876 Centennial in Philadelphia. The certificate, which still hangs at the homestead, commends their "oak sole leather from Texas hides." The house itself served as an inn for travelers along the coach road from Baltimore to Pittsburgh. Washington Irving stayed here, talking late into the night in front of the fire. James Audubon also enjoyed the hospitality of Union Mills Homestead while he was researching and writing about Baltimore orioles. Audubon watched an oriole build a nest in the willow tree outside his window.

Unlike other historic homes, Union Mills Homestead has no period rooms. Here you'll find an amiable lived-in mix of furnishings. As one of Andrew Shriver's descendants remarked, "No one seems ever to have thrown anything away!"

Across from the house is the restored water-powered gristmill. The mill operated from 1798 to 1942 and was one of the first mills to use the revolutionary designs of Oliver Evans. Evans's *The Young Millwright and Miller's Guide*, published in 1795, included the greatest innovations in milling since before the time of Christ. The first mill to incorporate these ideas was at Ellicott Mills (see selection). Both George Washington and Thomas Jefferson employed the new design. The Union Mills gristmill is one of the most accurate restorations of an Evans design in the country.

You can buy flour milled at Union Mills, as well as other items, at the gift shop in the restored Miller's House. Also restored is the Old Bark Shed, where on selected weekends blacksmithing, carpentry and woodworking are demonstrated.

Union Mills Homestead and Gristmill are open June until September, Tuesday through Friday from 10:00 A.M. to 5:00 P.M. and Saturday and Sunday from noon to 5:00 P.M. They are open weekends only in May, September and October. Admission is charged.

Directions: From Baltimore take Route 140 west to Westminster. Then head north on Route 97. Union Mills is on the right on Route 97 seven miles north of Westminster.

Westminster

A Strange Doll, Civil War Legend and Country Inn

The dolls displayed in most museums, though not bandbox perfect, still retain their age-old shape and allure. At the Carroll County Historical Society's doll exhibit, however, there is a doll with none of that. This bedraggled object was once the property of a young boy who made a practice of burying the doll, exhuming it, and then restaging its funeral. Youngsters touring the museum react along sex lines to this story: the boys love it and the girls are appalled.

Though this one doll looks the worse for wear, other toys in Miss Carroll's Children's Shop represent the heights of bygone elegance. A display case filled with international dolls, miniature houses, a children's tea set, a 1920 grocery store from F.A.O. Schwartz and other old playthings fill this popular exhibit on the second floor of the Kimmey House on Main Street in **Westminster**.

Westminster, the county seat and second oldest town in Carroll County, offers a pleasant way to absorb a good deal of Maryland's past without much effort. A short walk along Court Street takes you past a mix of architectural styles: Gothic, Second Empire, Italian Villa, even a sophisticated version of a Pennsylvania farmhouse. Two of the houses on the Court House Square Walking Tour are open to the public, the Kimmey House (with the children's shop described above) at 210 E. Main Street and the Shellman House at 206 E. Main.

The five-bay, 2½-story Shellman House was built in 1807 by Jacob Sherman as a wedding gift to his daughter, Eve. In the 1860s it was deeded to the Shellman family. A restoration to its 1830s appearance has not eliminated a slightly more recent luxury. In 1870 a sink was installed on the second floor so wash basins and slop jars could be emptied without the bother of a trip downstairs. The Shellman House basement has a collection of old tools and kitchen utensils.

One of the town's fascinating legends concerns Mary Shellman. During the Civil War, Confederate General J.E.B. Stuart passed through Westminster as he headed from the Baltimore area to a rendezvous with Robert E. Lee's Army of Northern Virginia. In Westminster Stuart met Mary Shellman and was so charmed he briefly delayed his passage. Thus Stuart was not available as advance reconnaissance for Lee when he crossed into Pennsylvania. The significance of Stuart's absence can be debated, but it is true that the subsequent accidental meeting of

Miss Carroll's Children's Shop, on the second floor of the Kimmey House in Westminster, displays all kinds of toys, mostly elegant, from the past.

Lee and Hooker's armies became the highly significant Battle of Gettysburg.

The Historical Society of Carroll County opens the Kimmey House and the Shellman House 9:00 A.M. to 4:00 P.M. Tuesday through Friday year-round. From June through September the houses are also open on Saturday from 10:00 A.M. to 4:00 P.M. and Sunday noon to 4:00 P.M. Closed on major holidays. A nominal admission is charged.

A third house, the home of the town's founder, William Winchester, enables visitors to spend the night or a quiet weekend. This farmhouse, built in the 1760s, is now a charming bed and breakfast called the Winchester Country Inn. It has five guest bedrooms filled with period furniture.

The two main rooms, the hall and parlor, are served by a central fireplace. The cheery blaze warms early morning diners who feast on fresh fruit, local eggs, country meats and home-baked breads and rolls. On pleasant evenings guests relax on the front porch with complimentary wine or tea. During the week you can often obtain a room without a reservation, but weekends are busy. To plan a stay call (301)876-7373.

Directions: From Baltimore take Route 140 west to Westminster. Turn left onto Center Street following the signs to Carroll County Farm Museum. The Inn is on Center Street diagonally across from the Farm Museum (see selection).

HOWARD COUNTY

Ellicott City

Main Street—Main Attraction

Unlike Humpty Dumpty, **Ellicott City** was put back together again—and again. In 1868 the town was flooded, causing the death of 50 inhabitants and $1 million in damages. Then in 1972, the town was flooded in the wake of Hurricane Agnes. The community was next devastated by a fire on the night of November 14, 1984, which destroyed a number of Main Street shops. If all that is the bad news, the good news is that Ellicott City is better than ever!

Bustling specialty boutiques, artists' galleries, antique shops and old country stores line Main Street. The more than 50 shops include a Magic Emporium, where talented salesfolk earn their livelihoods tricking the customers; the Stillridge Herb Shop, where aromatic fragrances waft out the door; and the Chateau Wine Supplies, where wine buffs can find all of the Maryland-produced vintages. On one side of Main Street the shops back up to a sparkling stream, and the shopping arcade even has a porch overlooking the gurgling water. On the other side of Main Street the shops, many of which were constructed in the early 1800s, are built right into the granite hills. At the Forget-Me-Not Factory's upstairs galleries, the handmade pottery and sculpture sits on the rocky outcroppings. You can even see seepage from underground streams moistening the rocky wall.

Pick up a walking tour guide, available at almost all the shops in town, and enjoy the historical background of the stores you explore in this old mill town. Ellicott City, originally called Ellicott's Lower Mills, was established in 1772 by three brothers from Bucks County, Pennsylvania. Joseph, John and Andrew Ellicott purchased 700 acres of wheat land, plus the water rights so that they could power a gristmill. The Ellicott brothers built roads from their town to the markets in Baltimore and a wharf in the harbor at Baltimore from which they shipped their products. Ellicott Mills became firmly linked with Baltimore in 1830 when the city became the first railroad terminus in the United States.

The first historic run of Peter Cooper's engine, later called the Tom Thumb, took place on August 28, 1830. The daring riders who made the inaugural trip jotted down notes to prove that the human mind could function while traveling at the dizzying speed of 14 miles an hour. Before Cooper built his engine, trains were pulled by horses. This led to the expression "iron horse" It was die-hard supporters of the old ways against proponents of the new-fangled engines that led to the legendary race between the Tom Thumb and a horse.

The Ellicott City **B&O Railroad Station Museum,** located in the 1830 granite stone station, is filled with railroad memorabilia and has an HO scale model railroad layout covering the first 13 miles of track between Baltimore and Ellicott City. The route comes alive when museum lights dim and track lights glow. There is also an 18-minute audio-visual presentation on the early days of the B&O Railroad.

You'll see reconstruction of the Freight Agent's Quarters, where he lived and worked. The agent's $400 annual salary did not go far, even in the 1830s. The museum is open January through March on Saturday from 11:00 A.M. to 4:00 P.M. and Sunday from noon to 5:00 P.M. From April through December hours are 11:00 A.M. to 4:00 P.M., Wednesday through Saturday and Sunday noon to 5:00 P.M. It is closed on major holidays. Admission is charged.

Ellicott City recalls the small towns of yesterday and is filled with old-fashioned finds. Those who favor the lace and jewelry of earlier eras will love the specialty shops. It is not a town to

On Tongue Row in Ellicott City, the original stone buildings, built in the 1840s by Mrs. Ann Tongue as living quarters for millhands and their families, are now specialty shops.

hurry through; take your time and browse. If you arrive early, you can have breakfast at Breakfast (3723 Old Columbia Pike), where the sign outside quotes Nathaniel Hawthorne: "Life within doors has few pleasanter prospects than a neatly arranged and well provisioned breakfast table." Later in the day high tea is served from 2:00 to 5:00 P.M. For lunch you can enjoy the rustic charm of Cacao Lane, where if you're lucky you can sit by a window on Main Street. The Dauville Restaurant offers a French country ambience, while at the Phoenix Emporium the atmosphere is that of a turn-of-the-century café. If you just want to snack, try the fresh baked goods at Leidigs Bakery, the dessert treats at Scoop du Jour, or the deli items at Baxter's. Ellicott City has something for everyone.

Directions: From Baltimore take Route 144 (Frederick Road) west to Ellicott City.

Savage Mill

Maryland's Warp and Woof

Listed on the National Register of Historic Places, **Savage Mill** combines history, shopping and peaceful woodland trails. You'll weave your way through studios and specialty shops and past reminders of Savage Mill's significant contributions to Maryland's economic history.

Restored Savage Mill opened in the spring of 1986 and ambitious plans are already on the drawing board for restoration of additional mill buildings. The mill dates back to 1810, when the Williams brothers—George, Amos and Cumberland—began building a dam and millrace to harness the power generated by the 52-foot Little Patuxent River falls. Named for John Savage, who purchased the property in 1822, this was one of many Maryland mills that prospered due to the proximity of the port of Baltimore. Raw cotton imported at Baltimore was turned into cloth at the mills and then shipped to other states.

Savage Mill specialized in manufacturing cotton duck, a heavy material often used for sails and tents. By 1936 the mill encompassed 16 buildings and had some of the largest looms in America. These looms were sometimes used to make canvas sheets for Hollywood backdrops. The sheets measured 208 inches in width and weighed 17 pounds per yard.

Historical displays have been placed between boutiques and art galleries. Photographs and exhibits tell the story of the workers at the old Savage Mill. You'll see a picture of the mill workers' houses. These were homes to families that earned all of four dollars a month for working six-day weeks of 10–12 hour days. Other photographs show the 1919 company store, the class of

1924 at Savage High School, and the mill superintendent's house. During World War II the mill had 400 workers turning out 400,000 pounds of cloth each month.

Most of the retail shops are in the New Weave Room. The Old Weave Room has artist studios and antique shops. The adjacent Spinning Building has additional antiques and collectibles and a tower that gives a bird's eye view of the complex. As you climb the winding old stairs, notice the metal nubs along the handrail; they were added to discourage the youngest mill workers, some of whom were barely eight, from sliding down the banister. Also off the Spinning Building is the Paymaster's Office. Amid its Victorian splendor mill business was transacted.

Many of the artists who work at Savage, as well as many visitors, find the historic Bollman Truss Bridge a tempting subject for photographs and paintings. This is the sole surviving bridge of its type in the world. Its picturesque suspended iron framework is dramatically framed by the verdant landscape.

Warfield's Restaurant now provides a midday respite, offering soups, salads, sandwiches and luncheon specials. A sundeck overlooking the millrace affords the option of al fresco dining. There are plans for another restaurant to be added overlooking Little Patuxent River.

Savage Mill is open Monday through Saturday from 10:00 A.M. to 5:30 P.M. and Sunday from noon to 5:30 P.M.

Directions: From Baltimore take I-95 south to Route 32. Take Route 32 east to Route 1. Go south on Route 1 to Gorman Road and turn right. Signs will direct you to the parking lot of Savage Mill.

Stillridge Herb Farm

You'll Relish These Herbs

In 1972 Mary Lou Riddle planted four herbs—orange mint, lavender, lemon balm and oregano—in her farmhouse garden. All but the orange mint died. Rather than become discouraged and give up, Mary Lou kept trying. And how. Today she runs thriving **Stillridge Herb Farm** and its several retail outlets (see Savage Mill and Ellicott City selections).

Visitors are welcome to drop by and see the patterned gardens or "yard patches" of herbs that Riddle now nurtures with astonishing success. You can also visit the greenhouse and the herb house or stillrooms, where the harvested herbs are hung to dry. It's here the wreaths, herbal arrangements, tussie mussies (17th-century nosegays) and other items are made for the Stillridge Herb Shops. The Stillridge Herb Wreath has been featured in several issues of *House and Garden* magazine. This intricate wreath uses 30 different fragrant herbs, herbal flowers and cinnamon sticks. A complete herb shop is located at the farm.

The best way to explore the world of herbs is to reserve a seat at one of Mary Lou Riddle's herbal luncheons. A typical menu includes Mai Wine Bowl, Burnet Spread on Crackers, Tomato Herb-Butter Soup with Marjoram, Herb Bread, Salad with Herb Dressing, Rosemary Chicken Casserole, Peas with Tarragon Butter and Rose Geranium Ice Cream. If you like these seasoned specialties, then pick up a copy of Riddle's cookbook, *Through My Kitchen Window*. Few luncheon guests depart without purchasing some herbs, and Mary Lou is happy to advise gardeners on the intricacies of growing and using them.

Herb lectures given at Stillridge teach the basics about growing herbs, the legendary properties of these aromatic plants and their multiple uses. These lectures also include herbal refreshments. To obtain information or make reservations, call (301)465-8348. Stillridge Herb Farm is open Monday through Saturday from 9:00 A.M. to 4:00 P.M.

Directions: From the Baltimore Beltway (I-695) take Exit 16 onto I-70 west. At the first exit (Route 29), head north and then turn left at the blinking light onto Route 99 (Old Frederick Road). Proceed approximately three miles and you'll see the sign for Stillridge Herb Farm on your right.

BALTIMORE COUNTY

Ballestone Manor and Heritage Society Museum

Manor on the Green

There is one spot on the Rocky Point State golf course where golfers are not allowed: the carefully fenced grounds of **Ballestone Manor**. This historic 18th-century plantation house is built on land given to George Washington's maternal great-great-grandfather, William Ball. In 1659 Cecilius Calvert, the second Lord Baltimore, granted Ball 450 acres on Back River Neck.

Ball, a Virginian, considered this Maryland acreage an investment and never built on it or visited it. It was the Stansbury family who built a 2½-story, three-bay Flemish-bond brick house in the post-Revolutionary period, around 1780. These were years of economic growth for Baltimore and the surrounding countryside because of the prosperous mercantile trade.

In 1819 the estate was purchased by the Leakin family, who expanded the house with a 1½-story brick addition, plus a two-

Ballestone Manor, 100 years in the building, graces land given to George Washington's maternal great-great-grandfather William Ball, by the second Lord Baltimore in 1659.

story frame structure that is no longer standing. The final expansion was done by Edward Miller between 1850 and 1880. He raised the roof to a full two stories and added a columned portico with a Victorian millwork railing.

The house, built over a hundred-year period, fell victim to time, the elements and vandalism. It was saved and restored by the Heritage Society of Essex and Middle River and furnished by the Maryland Historical Society. Docents, attired in period clothes, conduct tours of Ballestone Manor on Sundays from 2:00 to 5:00 P.M. in June, July and August.

The dining parlor is filled with Federal pieces, and across from the entranceway is a parlor representing the later Victorian era. Upstairs there is an 1840 Empire bedroom as well as a children's bedroom. After you tour the main house, do stop in the out-kitchen. Although the kitchen is a modern addition, it does suggest an 18th-century dependency.

You'll find more regional history at the museum operated by the Heritage Society in the old firehouse in Essex. The walls are now lined with display cases, and furniture and costumed mannequins fill the rooms. There are literally thousands of artifacts that tell the story of the Essex and Middle River area. One room has fire-related regalia, while another has a collection of memorabilia from the nearby Martin Marietta airplane plant. There's also an old drugstore and a 1920 vintage school room. An avenue of shops includes a toy store, music shop, general store, post office and the Essex Candle Company, which operated from 1932 to 1950. The **Heritage Society Museum** is at 516 Eastern Boulevard in Essex. It is open on weekends from 1:00 to 4:00 P.M. Donations are welcome.

Directions: From Baltimore take U.S. 40 less than a mile north of I-695, then turn right on Rossville Boulevard to Stemmers Run Road. On Stemmers Run Road proceed to the intersection with Eastern Boulevard in Essex. Turn right for the Heritage Society Museum. For Ballestone Manor proceed straight ahead on Eastern Boulevard. Turn right onto Back River Neck Road and proceed for a short distance to Ballestone Manor.

Boordy Vineyards

Lift Your Spirits

"Maryland's climate is eminently suited to the culture of the grapevine, but with one notable exception, little advantage is taken of it. The exception is the admirably run **Boordy Vineyard** in Riderwood, near Baltimore, where J. & P. Wagner . . . experiment widely with different types of grapes. . . . They also make wines, if only to demonstrate how good eastern American wines from hybrids can be, if properly handled. The result, so far as quality goes, is laudable, and their contribution to American winemaking is enormous."

Since Alexis Lechine wrote the above in the *New Encyclopedia of Wines and Spirits* in 1977, more Maryland vintners are taking advantage of the climate he praises. But Boordy continues to have a special place in the history of winemaking in Maryland and indeed across the country.

Philip Wagner had tried to cultivate California varieties on his Riderwood farm during the 1920s and 1930s, but the Maryland climate proved inhospitable for them. Wagner, a reporter for the *Baltimore Sun*, was sent with fellow correspondent and wine buff H.L. Mencken to France during World War II. Wagner did more than cover the conflict. He used the opportunity to persuade French farmers to part with cuttings of their hybrid grapes.

When Wagner returned to Riderwood, he established experimental plantings of these hybrids. When they proved ideal for the Maryland climate, he established not only a winery, but he also sold his newly discovered French hybrids to vintners across the country. Wagner once said, "There isn't a state in the union now, with the possible exception of North Dakota, that doesn't have them."

Wagner's Boordy Vineyards produced wine that was acclaimed from coast to coast. By 1965, demand exceeded output. Looking around for new fields, Wagner prevailed upon his friends, the Defords, to plant grapes at their Long Green Farm in Hydes. In 1980, when he decided to retire, Wagner sold Boordy Vineyards to the Defords, who had to evict 150 cattle from their dairy barn to convert it into a winery. The grapes came in early that year, and changes were still being made on the barn when the first truckloads of harvested grapes arrived.

The Defords continued Wagner's practice of obtaining grapes from a number of farms, and they now get staggered harvests from different regions in Maryland and Virginia. Combining these grapes with those grown at Hydes, they produce about 18,000 gallons annually. They make five whites: Maryland Premium White, Vidal Blanc, Chardonnay, Seyval Blanc and Seyval Blanc Sur Lie Reserve. Additionally, they produce three rosé wines: Maryland Premium Rosé, Vin Gris and Boordy Blush. Finally, there are three reds: the always available Maryland Premium Red, the irregularly available Petit Cabernet and the seasonal Nouveau.

Wines can take five to six years from the time the vines are planted to the time the finished wine is ready to drink. Some fine wines take considerably longer. The exception to this slow maturing is Boordy's Nouveau, similar to the French Beajolais Nouveau. This fruity wine is ready to drink just three weeks after the harvest. For the last several years Boordy Nouveau has been awarded top prize at the International Eastern Wine Competition. Other Boordy award winners are its 1982 Seyval Blanc and 1983 Vidal Blanc. Also, Boordy wines have been chosen for state and national ceremonial occasions and served to such visitors as Pope John Paul and the Duke and Duchess of Kent.

Visitors are welcome at Boordy for tours and tastings Monday through Saturday from 10:00 A.M. to 5:00 P.M. and Sunday 1:00 to 5:00 P.M. There is also a series of Harvest Parties between mid-November and Christmas to enjoy the latest Nouveau. Everyone is welcome. Call (301)592-5015 for details.

Directions: From the Baltimore Beltway (I-695) take Exit 29, Cromwell Bridge Road, and go northeast for 2.9 miles. Turn left on Glen Arm Road and proceed 3.2 miles to the intersection with Long Green Road. Turn left and continue 2 miles to Boordy Vineyards entrance on the left.

Cloisters Children's Museum

Where the Fanciful Flowers

A museum for children designed to stir their imagination and encourage them to put it into play could have no more exciting a setting than the medieval castle that houses the **Cloisters Children's Museum**. This too frequently overlooked museum in Baltimore County is perfect for a mid-winter family excursion. Although three nature trails can be explored in warmer weather, most of the museum's charms can be enjoyed within its stone walls.

You may wonder what a turreted castle, complete with cloister, windmill and chapel, is doing in Maryland. The answer is as improbable as the castle: It was a birthday present! In 1930 Sumner Parker built this Tudor-Revival folly, modeled on castles of medieval France and England, for his wife, Grace Dudrea Parker. Mrs. Parker willed it to the City of Baltimore and in November 1977 it opened as an activity-oriented museum.

The 27-room castle is listed on the National Register of Historic Places. Parents will enjoy the rich furnishings, which the Parkers acquired on travels through Europe and the United States. The eclectic collection includes decorative pieces from the 14th to the 20th centuries. Stone for the castle walls was quarried on the 53-acre estate, and the trees felled for the huge beams once grew on the grounds.

In the regal-looking gallery the walls are lined with paintings and throne-like chairs flank the doorway. The small suit of armor once belonged to a young prince. Just off the gallery is a small chapel with stained-glass windows that cast multicolored patterns on the stone floors when the sun shines through them.

A doll house in the entranceway is a preview of the children's exhibits on the upper floors. While the first floor is hands-off, the second floor is definitely hands-on. There's an architectural exhibit that invites youngsters to tinker with giant building blocks and pipes. A playroom is filled with hard-to-resist enticements: a small castle, a large wooden doll house, a pint-size helicopter and a children's grocery store. Children are encouraged to experiment with sound in the music room. They can discover how long or short a sound lasts, the different sounds produced by a variety of materials, and how sound changes pitch. The dress-up room is one of the most popular in the museum. Kids can don wedding dresses, evening gowns, police and firemen's uniforms, a doctor's white coat or an Indian headdress. They're encouraged to act out their own plays or put on a performance with the puppets in the lilliputian theater. Finally, a print shop provides a variety of methods for youngsters to make their mark.

The Cloisters Children's Museum is open Wednesday through Friday from 10:00 A.M. to 4:30 P.M. and on weekends from noon to 4:00 P.M. Admission is charged.

Just before reaching the museum, you'll see a sign for the **Irvine Natural Science Center**. This is an extremely small two-room collection of nature specimens. A limited number of nature books are offered for sale. The museum is located on the grounds of St. Timothy's School. There is also a trail through the woodlands and meadows of this 234-acre campus.

For those who want to take a midday lunch break or enjoy an early dinner, the Valley Inn is on Falls Road almost directly across from the Children's Museum. This establishment operated as an inn as early as 1832, and the land on which it was built once belonged to Charles Carroll, the barrister.

Directions: The Cloisters is located on Falls Road, just outside Baltimore Beltway (I-695) Exit 23. From the exit, follow signs for Falls Road. At the light turn left onto Falls Road South. Look for the Cloisters sign one-half mile down the road.

Fire Museum of Maryland and Valley View Farms

Pumping Iron

Over 60 fire-fighting vehicles dating from 1822, and an impressive array of support equipment, fill the 23,000 square feet of display and storage space at the **Fire Museum of Maryland**, one of the country's largest fire museums.

Although there are rows and rows of equipment, visiting the Fire Museum is certainly not dull. Clanging bells, fire sirens, ongoing fire calls, and the chance to operate an old pump engine combine to create a sensory barrage.

Fire-fighting procedure is explained at the firehouse watch desk. A desk similar to this could be found in firehouses across the country through the 1940s and 1950s. Volunteers demonstrate the alarm telegraph, and at the back of the museum you see a replica of the central alarm office. Both at the watch desk and in the alarm office there are alarm boxes that may be actuated by visitors. But volunteers are careful to explain how vital it is to turn in alarms only when there is an emergency. (Check the schedule at the museum's movie theater; you might be able to catch a short film on fire safety and fire fighting.) In addition to learning how and when to use a fire alarm, young visitors are sometimes permitted to ring one of the fire bells. Some of the larger bells produce an ear-piercing ring.

Also explained are the different types of fire alarms. You'll learn who and what determines whether a fire is a single-alarm fire. Then you'll see how that message is conveyed to the men at the firehouse. Fire companies had ceremonial, as well as functional, equipment. One glossy parade piece on display is the 1875 L. Butler & Sons hose carriage. Nearby is an 1853 James Smith pumper that still works. You can try your hand at pumping water with this vintage model. It may seem easy, but those on the line had to keep pumping until the fire was out. Another pumper, a 1931 USA Pumper made at Ft. Holabird, Maryland, is on display just outside the museum entrance. Unlike the equipment inside, this picturesque old piece is available for children to climb on. It also provides a great photo opportunity.

As you wander down the rows of equipment, you can see the evolution from hand pump to steam pumping engines, and from hand-drawn wagons to horse-drawn vehicles. The 1916 fire engine that Walter Christie revolutionized by installing a tractor engine marked another step forward. It was one of the first gas engine fire-fighting pieces.

Most of the pieces are big and most are painted bright red. Even companies that painted their trucks what one volunteer terms "slime lime" are now re-painting them red. There are small display cases filled with fire hats and helmets, old speaking trumpets, and kerosene and whale oil lanterns.

The Fire Museum of Maryland was founded by Stephen G. Heaver in 1971. His substantial collection is the heart of the museum, although additional pieces have been added or loaned. Staffed by volunteers, this is a non-profit operation supported by admission fees. Hours are Sunday 1:00 to 5:00 P.M. from May through November.

Just seven miles north on York Road in Cockeysville you can visit **Valley View Farms** Country Store, the "Nation's largest, most complete and most unique Christmas shop." Under a twinkling canopy of lights, 100 decorated Christmas trees offer more than 5,000 decorations, the makings of which are displayed around the trees. In many cases you can buy the ornaments ready-made.

A second area, the International Christmas Shoppe, has decorations and hand-made specialty items from more than 50 countries. There are exquisitely carved nativity crèches from more than 15 countries. All but a special few can be purchased. There's an antique German music box that is not for sale, but there are an amazing array of others available from $10 to $10,000. Many of the hand-carved German figurines are also musical toys. Another Christmas favorite, the Nutcracker, is available in myriad forms. Angels come in spun glass, brass, wood, ceramic, straw, pewter, paper-mâché, crystal, porcelain and wax. These are only a few of the thousands of items gathered from around the world.

Valley View Farms has a Do-It-Yourself House Decorating Department, a Delicatessen and a Produce Department (open until Thanksgiving) with farm-fresh products. Valley View Christmas Shoppe is open daily September 15 through December 24 from 7:00 A.M. to 9:00 P.M.

Directions: From Baltimore Beltway (I-695) Exit 26 go north on York Road, Route 45, for one block. The Fire Museum of Maryland is on the right behind the Heaver Plaza Office Building. For Valley View Farms continue north on York Road.

Gunpowder Falls State Park

Maryland's Largest

Did you know Baltimore County has 173 miles of Chesapeake Bay shoreline? The idea that there are a number of scenic beaches (including a Miami Beach) north of Baltimore surprises even some long-time Marylanders. Both Miami and Rocky Point Beach are part of the county's Department of Recreation and Parks. But the largest park in the county, and indeed in Maryland, is **Gunpowder Falls State Park**. Within its 15,000 acres you can swim, fish, boat, tube, white-water canoe, hike, ride, camp and picnic.

Big and Little Gunpowder Rivers meet in Baltimore County for the last eight miles of their journey to the Chesapeake Bay. There's a wonderful, but probably apocryphal, legend about how the rivers were named. When European settlers gave gunpowder to the Indians, so the story goes, the Indians planted the black powder along the riverbanks in hopes it would grow.

You can find reminders of America's colonial past within Gunpowder Falls State Park. A popular colonial fording spot can be seen where the Old Post Road passes Long Calm Ford. The only double-dormed mill in the United States, Jerusalem Mill, is on Jericho Road. David Lee built the mill in 1772. He also built a two-story building in which he produced guns for the Revolutionary army. A little farther south, downriver on Jericho Road, you'll see a covered bridge over the Little Gunpowder River.

There are several separate sections of the park. Two of the most popular are the Bay-fronting Hammerman/Dundee area and the more northern Hereford area, where you'll find the park's white-water rapids. Near the town of Sweet Air there are 1,155 acres of hiking and horseback trails. There are also trails in the Central area along the Big and Little Gunpowder Rivers. The Northern Central Railroad Trail is the most historic section; it offers 7.2 miles of improved gravel surface from Ashland north to Monkton (an unimproved 14-mile extension of this trail reaches north to the Pennsylvania line) and is popular with hikers, bikers, horse-back riders and joggers. From this trail fishermen have access to the Lock Raven watershed and the Gunpowder River south of Phoenix Road.

Since the days when Indians fished the waters, sportsmen have flocked to this area. The blue crab, a Chesapeake Bay delicacy, can be found from late summer through early fall. At the mouth of the Gunpowder River, licensed fishermen can fish for striped bass, perch and pickerel. To the north, along the river in the Hereford area, possible catches include bass, carp and catfish.

Gunpowder Falls State Park is open year-round during daylight hours. Only the Hammerman area has an entrance fee.

Directions: From I-695 take I-95 north and proceed to the first exit, White Marsh Boulevard. Take White Marsh Boulevard to Route 40 north. Continue on Route 40 to Ebenezer Road and continue eight miles to the Hammerman area of the park. For the Hereford Area take Exit 33 (Route 1) north off I-695.

Hampton National Historic Site

Ridgelys Right on the Money

The Ridgely family always seemed to be at the right place at the right time. The first Marylander, Robert Ridgely, was deputy secretary of the young colony in St. Mary's County in 1671. Charles the Planter settled on the rich farmland of Anne Arundel County while Charles the Merchant moved into Baltimore County when land was easily and cheaply obtained. It was, however, Captain Charles the Builder who really made the family fortune by capitalizing on the iron ore deposits discovered on the family holdings in Baltimore County. The Ridgely's Northampton Ironworks supplied cannons and shot to the Continental Army.

Captain Charles took the vast fortune he acquired during the Revolutionary War and built the largest and one of the most ornate Georgian mansions of his day. In fact, the National Park Service's Historic Structures Report of 1980 says **Hampton Mansion** "is one of 71 outstanding examples of Georgian architecture still in existence in the United States. Its opulence has survived to the present virtually intact." The eye-catching design pulls your eye up the white columns at the front door, past the second floor balcony to the octagonal white dome crowning the cream color mansion. Charles Ridgely, indulgent but not extravagant, gave architect-builder Jehu Howell permission to add the dome provided the cost did not exceed 180 pounds.

There were those who questioned Captain Charles' judgment when he began what was likened to "the castle of some feudal baron" on land still home to wolves. His nearest neighbors lived in crude cabins. Folks called the house Ridgely's Folly. Captain Charles died before all the work was complete. His heir and nephew Charles Ridgely Carnan, who would reverse his middle and last names according to the dictates of the will, acquired Hampton Mansion from his uncle's widow. Young Charles then became a representative in the Maryland General Assembly (1790–95), a Senator in the Assembly (1796–1800) and Governor of Maryland (1815–18).

It was Charles Carnan Ridgely who began the landscaping that would become as renowned as the house itself. The 1859 edition of A.J. Downing's *A Treatise on the Theory and Practice of Landscape Gardening* states, "It has been truly said of Hampton that it expresses more grandeur than any other place in America." The garden has pairs of parterres on three terraces, or falls. The Hampton parterres were laid out in a formal geometric style. Four parterres on the first two terraces have been restored to approximate their appearance prior to 1830. The first terrace features spring bulbs and seasonal flowers while the second level has two rose parterres. Peonies have been planted on the third level.

If the first owner built it and the second owner landscaped it, the third owner's wife spent a lifetime decorating Hampton. Eliza Ridgely, whose portrait hangs in the Great Hall, traveled throughout the world acquiring art treasures and furnishings for her grand Maryland home. When the Marquis de Lafayette visited Eliza and her husband, he was impressed with her beauty and her elegant home. He also commented on the size of the hall, saying, "You could drive a team of horses through it." Many of Eliza's acquisitions as well as other Ridgely family pieces still grace the rooms. Present plans are for each room to reflect a decorative period popular during the lifetimes of the six generations of Ridgelys to live at Hampton. Currently one of the most striking rooms is the dining room painted a brilliant Prussian blue, the first commercial chemical color. Prussian blue is also used in the Hammond-Harwood House in Annapolis (see selection). The blue is picked up in the curtains, where it is combined with gold and trimmed with gold and orange tassels. Quite a striking window treatment!

After your house tour, purchase a garden and grounds guide to direct you to all the sites on the estate. The walking tour map has six main stops with keys for both trees and points of interest. Hampton is the center of what was once a vast agricultural plantation and industrial complex. There are 22 historic structures on the 60-acre site. The grounds are open daily from 9:00 A.M. to 5:00 P.M. except Christmas and New Year's Day. The house is open Monday through Saturday from 11:00 A.M. to 5:00 P.M. and

Sunday from 1:00 to 5:00 P.M. with the last tours at 4:30 P.M. Hampton is operated by the National Park Service and there is no charge. A Tea Room at the mansion is open for lunch.

Directions: From the Baltimore Beltway (I-695) take Exit 27 north, Dulaney Valley Road. From Dulaney Valley Road make an immediate right onto Hampton Lane. Hampton N.H.S. is ¼ mile down Hampton Lane on the right.

Sagamore Farms and Foster Farms

Maryland's Horse Country

There are approximately 500 thoroughbred horsebreeding farms in Maryland, and Baltimore County has 137 of them, more than twice that of any other county. The oldest and best know of these is **Sagamore Farms**.

This picture-postcard farm, with its rolling green hills and pristine white fences, was a gift from Margaret Emerson Vanderbilt to her son Alfred on his 21st birthday. From the time he acquired Sagamore in 1934, Alfred strove to make it one of the best training and breeding farms in the country.

His success is evident in the number of successful racehorses bred and trained at Sagamore Farms. Vanderbilt's best-known thoroughbred is Native Dancer. He was sired by one of Sagamore Farms' first great racehorses, Discovery, whose offspring won 1,712 races for a total purse of $5,625,643. But Native Dancer was the champion of champions. He won 21 of his 22 starts. Like his famous sire, Native Dancer went on to produce 44 winners, including Restles Native, who is still standing stud at Sagamore.

Sagamore Farms is a breeding and training farm. The breeding area has a stallion barn, two mare and foal barns, a barn for barren mares, a yearling barn and a breeding shed. After the foals are weaned, they are taken from the stalls they've shared with their mothers and moved to the yearling barn. They remain in the yearling barn until late fall. They then move to the racing barn.

In the racing section of the farm the young horses are schooled and conditioned to build their stamina. They are exercised on the race track, first running 1¼ miles a day, and working up to 1½ miles at a gallop. Some Sagamore horses race directly from the farm, others are trained and sold. Sagamore also rehabilitates injured horses.

It is the training area that visitors see: the outdoor track, the exercise pens and the quarter-mile indoor track. In the morning you are more likely to see the horses being trained, while in the afternoon they are apt to be in their stalls or out on the track.

Sagamore Farms, now owned by Jim Ward, has approximately 200 horses. It is a busy, working farm and visitors will have to be content with just a glimpse of this fascinating horse-breeding haven.

Just a few miles down the road is a quite different farm. **Foster Farms** is one of the few Maryland farms still growing mushrooms. From early November through July up to six houses are filled with this unusual crop. The Fosters started raising mushrooms in 1934 and once had them growing in 31 houses. But the market has declined and so only a few houses are still in use.

You can visit the farm daily from 8:00 A.M. to 5:00 P.M., and they'll be happy to take you into the mushroom houses and explain how they grow these eatable fungi, so prized by gourmets.

Directions: From Baltimore Beltway (I-695) Exit 22 go north on Greenspring Avenue (Route 519) approximately eight miles to Tufton Avenue (Greenspring becomes Worthington Avenue just before you reach Tufton Avenue). Turn right on Tufton Avenue, then left on Belmont Road. Sagamore Farms is on the right at 3501 Belmont Road. For Foster Farms, continue one-half mile further on Worthington Avenue and turn left on Bonita Avenue; the entrance to the farm will be on your left.

HARFORD COUNTY

Havre de Grace

Amazing Grace

Though the British burned Havre de Grace on May 3, 1813, damaging 60% of its structures, the town has 800 buildings with "historic attributes," and more than 60 identified with date plaques. You can hit the high spots on a self-guided tour beginning at the **Concord Point Lighthouse** and ending at the Lockhouse.

The most picturesque spot in town, the Concord Point Lighthouse is open on Sundays from 1:00 to 5:00 P.M. May through October. Here you can pick up a brochure on the self-guided tours. The brochure is also available at the Chamber of Commerce at the Mini-Mall on Washington Street Monday through Friday, 1:00 to 5:00 P.M. If you arrive on Sunday, don't miss the chance to climb the lighthouse. You'll have an impressive view of the Susquehanna River flowing into the Chesapeake Bay. The lighthouse was authorized in 1826 and built of Port Deposit granite. Work was completed on May 21, 1829. One family, the O'Neills, served as lightkeepers until 1920—during its entire history of manual operation. The first of the lightkeepers, John O'Neill,

A self-guided tour of historic Havre de Grace takes you past many of the 800 buildings that survived the British burning of the town in 1813. The canal lockhouse dates from 1840.

who singlehandedly manned the town's hill battery, had been captured and imprisoned by the British in 1813. He was sentenced to be hanged, but was saved by the intervention of his daughter, Matilda. To arrange a lighthouse tour on a day other than Sunday, call (301)939-1340 or (301)939-2016.

From the lighthouse it's only a block down Market Street to the new **Havre de Grace Decoy Museum**. A total renovation has provided a new home for the decoy carvings of Madison Mitchell, Paul Gibson, Charles Bryant and others. It too is open only on Sundays, 1:00 to 5:00 P.M., at no charge.

Next, the tour takes you by Tydings Park just past the 1920 Bayou Hotel. The park provides a lookout over the Susquehanna Flats, first viewed by Captain John Smith in 1608 on his voyage up the Chesapeake Bay.

Havre de Grace's long history is divided into six periods. The period from 1780 to 1830 is sketchily recorded because the fire laid waste to so much of the town. Only the Rodgers House at 226 N. Washington Street is conclusively dated as an 18th-century building. George Washington made note of stops at the Rodgers House in 1785 and 1795.

The period from 1830 to 1850, which brought the Susquehanna & Tidewater Canal and the concurrent railroad corridor, was probably the most interesting in the city's history. The growth slowed in the middle period, 1850–80, with the end of the canal era and the Civil War.

Then came the Victorian period, 1880–1910, with its gingerbread houses. Bay windows, towers, gables, turrets, stained glass, irregular windows and heavily carved porch trim are much in evidence on the tour. The city's late period, 1910–40, was marked by bungalows and weekend homes built by an influx of sportsmen. The contemporary period, 1940 to the present, accounts for a small number of new houses in the historic district.

All but four houses on the self-guiding tour can be seen as you drive up Union Street. Fourteen houses dating from 1801 to 1896 line this historic street. You'll also see some community churches and the Havre de Grace City Hall.

The in-town tour ends at the **1840 Lockhouse**. Once a combined office and living quarters for the locktender, the Lockhouse is now the home of the Susquehanna Museum and is open April through November on Sundays, 1:00 to 5:00 P.M. A short historical audio-visual program on the Susquehanna & Tidewater Canal is shown. You'll learn that the canal was 45 miles long and had 19 locks, one of which you see directly in front of the house. There is also a pivot bridge that permitted wagons and mules to cross the canal to the river wharves. The parlor, kitchen and upstairs bedrooms have been furnished in the style of the canal era.

Directions: From the Baltimore Beltway (I-695) take I-95 north 25 miles to the exit for Route 155, the last exit before crossing the Susquehanna River. Follow Route 155 south into Havre de Grace. Turn left on Erie Street and drive several blocks to Conesteo Street. Turn left on Conesteo and almost immediately you'll see the red brick lockhouse. The Concord Point Lighthouse, where the self-guided tour begins, is at the south end of town. From the Lockhouse Museum go south on Union Avenue to Commerce Street. Turn left and go east to Market Street and the lighthouse.

Ladew Topiary Gardens

I'll Be Seeing Yew

Harvey Ladew was an international jetsetter long before the term was coined: a man of multiple interests—scientific, artistic and athletic—with the money to satisfy each whim. When Ladew purchased his Maryland farm in 1929, he was so eager to host a party he invited guests before the renovation was finished. The rough floor nails tore the hems of the ladies' gowns.

No doubt these ladies forgave him, but there may have been others less forgiving at the dinner party he once gave where guests and horses were served at table with silver dishes! Ladew's farm was purchased for a fox-hunting retreat, and the hunt motif is everywhere—on the china, in photographs and paintings, on clocks and wall hangings.

Ladew achieved notoriety when he rode in two hunts, one in America and one in England—within 72 hours. Often a quarry himself, he never was caught by any of the ladies who vied for his attention. He preferred the unencumbered life of bon vivant and world traveler. On a scientific journey in Bolivia he had a mouse named after him, *Thomasomy Ladewi*. He would rather have had the title, King of the Dudes, that his uncle, E. Berry Wall, gained after making 40 complete costume changes in one day during the 1888 season in Saratoga Springs, New York. Ladew himself came to be known as the best dressed man in America.

He decorated his home with great imagination. A dressing room, frequently used by his siter Elise, has one wall covered by a trompe l'oeil painting of his. He painted a chest with lace-trimmed undergarments spilling out of open drawers, and chairs on either side cluttered with a black tricorn hat, a negligee and a black lace mask. The morning glory flowers Ladew painted around the mantle and windows of the bedroom are much more circumspect. You may visit his studio if you want to see other examples of his painting.

The library is one of the most beautiful rooms in the house. It was added by Ladew after he returned from England with an oval desk too large for any of the existing rooms. Being nothing if not determined, Ladew built an oval library around the desk. Whimsy intrudes even here; he hung a tennis net under a hunt table to hold his empties. He also built an escape door into the bookcase so that he could make a getaway if a party got too dull.

It was while visiting England that Ladew acquired a passion for topiary, the art of sculpturing trees and shrubs. You'll see his favorite figures, a mounted hunter riding behind the hounds after a fox, bounding across the front lawn. The garden boasts a giraffe, camel, goat, reindeer, rabbit, scottie and even a unicorn. The aviary has swimming swans, nesting hens, a rooster and lyrebirds. A striking vista is presented by a corridor of topiary hedges more than a third of a mile long!

With so much emphasis on topiary art, most first-time visitors are pleasantly surprised to discover 15 flowering garden "rooms" also designed by Ladew. Many of these rooms, as he called his garden areas, are color coordinated. The white garden has 35 varieties of flowers all in white. There are also pink, yellow and red gardens. Other motifs include the berry garden, the Victorian garden, the wild garden, the rose garden, the iris garden and the water lily garden. The steps leading to the garden of Eden are carved with a Chinese proverb Ladew evidently took to heart: "If you would be happy for a week, take a wife; if you would be happy for a month, kill your pig; but if you would be happy all your life, plant a garden."

Humor abounds inside and out. You'll leave this Maryland estate wishing you could have attended just *one* of Mr. Ladew's parties.

Ladew Topiary Gardens is open Tuesday through Friday from 10:00 A.M. to 4:00 P.M., Saturday and Sunday noon to 5:00 P.M. The house is open only on Wednesday, Saturday and Sunday. A café serves lunch during garden hours. Admission is charged.

Directions: From the Baltimore Beltway (I-695) take Exit 27 and go north on Route 146 (Dulaney Valley Road). Ladew is just five miles past Jacksonville (or 14 miles from the Beltway) on Route 146.

Susquehanna State Park & Steppingstone Museum

An Earlier Step for Mankind

In woodsy Harford County you'll discover the multiple delights of **Susquehanna State Park—Steppingstone Museum**, the Carter Mansion, the Jersey Toll House and Rock Run Mill—and these are just the historic attractions. There are also nature trails, fishing areas, campgrounds, picnic tables and a boat launching ramp.

Captain John Smith once thought the mighty Susquehanna River, named for the Indians Smith encountered, might be a route to the fabled Northwest Passage, a water route to the Asian continent. He was so enthusiastic about the river he declared, "Heaven and earth seemed never to have agreed better to frame a place for man's commodious and delightful habitation."

Susquehanna State Park capitalizes on its riverfront location. This section of the Susquehanna is popular with fishermen in April when the shad run up the river. At other times pike, perch and bass lure the sportsmen. In addition to the river's recreational and scenic appeal, three of the historic points of interest are located at the juncture of Rock Run and the Susquehanna River.

A stone four-story, water-powered grist mill was built here in 1794 by John Stump. This picturesque riverside mill is open 2:00

to 4:00 P.M. on weekends and holidays from Memorial Day through September. The mill's 12-ton wheel still grinds flour that is sold at the mill.

Just upriver is the Jersey Toll House, once the residence of the canal tollkeeper at Rock Run. Inside you will see a diorama of this part of the Susquehanna River in 1850. Carter Mansion is on a hilltop overlooking the river. This 13-room house, now furnished with antiques, was built in 1804 by John Carter. The stone house has an indoor smokehouse and a wine cellar in the cool basement. The Jersey Toll House and Carter Mansion are open 10:00 A.M. to 6:00 P.M. on weekends Memorial Day through September. There is no fee.

The most interesting attraction in the park is the Steppingstone Museum, a short distance from the Rock Run area, off Quaker Bottom Road. This outdoor living history agricultural museum presents a complete picture of rural life around 1900. The modest stone farmhouse with walled rear terrace is furnished comfortably. The parlor has a heavy Victorian sofa and you can imagine the family gathered around the piano for an evening sing along. There's also another small parlor filled with books, a well-stocked kitchen, and up the narrow, winding staircase, a small bedroom.

In one of the adjacent barns you'll find the J. Edmund Bull Antique Tool Collection. Tools are arranged by their use—layout tools, rough shaping tools, smoothing planes, shaping tools, finishing saws and many others. There is usually a volunteer on hand to demonstrate how they were used.

Volunteers also man the large shed that houses the support industries on which the farmer depended. You'll see a blacksmith practicing his craft, a cooper making barrels or perhaps a woodworker or tinsmith. Another large barn has an Old Country Store filled with hand-crafted items, hard candy, plus a wide array of exhibits. The faded family-size Flexible Flyer conjures up Normal Rockwell images. There's a collection of old carriages, unusual kitchen gadgets and looms. Volunteers frequently demonstrate the looms as well as carding, spinning and weaving. You will find a few craftspeople at Steppingstone Museum, but its festivals feature a full range of craft demonstrations (see Calendar of Events). The Steppingstone Museum is open weekends May through the first Sunday in October. Admission is charged.

Directions: From the Baltimore Beltway (I-695) take I-95 north for 25 miles to the exit for Route 155. Take Route 155 west. After ¼ mile turn right on Earlton Road and follow for ½ mile. Then make a left on Quaker Bottom Road, follow for roughly one mile to Steppingstone Museum entrance on the right. For the Rock Run area stay on Quaker Bottom Road to Rock Run Road and turn right. The Carter Museum will be on your right and the

Jersey Toll House and the Rock Run Mill will be along the Susquehanna River.

U.S. Army Ordnance Museum

Anzio Annie Survives

As you wander up and down the museum's rows of tanks, armored cars, howitzers and associated artillery, you're likely to overhear stories recounted by visiting veterans about the days when their lives depended on these weapons. Such stories are more than matched by the legends and lore associated with field pieces in the **U.S. Army Ordnance Museum** collection at the Aberdeen Proving Ground.

Anzio Annie, a major piece in the collection, is the name the Allies on Anzio gave the German Leopold gun that held them pinned to a sandy beachhead. The Allied High Command was mystified by it; they couldn't imagine how a gun large enough to fire a 550-pound shell could escape their bombing and naval attacks. But the Leopold survived numerous raids. The puzzle was solved when the Allies broke from their beach position. The Germans retreated, leaving Anzio Annie hidden in a mountain tunnel. The gun was mounted on 24 railroad wheels and was only rolled out to be fired. Annie is the only German railroad gun known to survive World War II.

Another massive weapon is the atomic cannon introduced in the early 1950s. This 166,638-pound weapon fired both conventional and atomic munitions at targets up to 18 miles away. Speaking of large weapons, consider the Nazi V-2 rocket on display. It's scary to learn that if Heinrich Himmler, head of the SS, had not arrested two top V-2 engineers they very likely would have perfected a rocket capable of hitting New York City. And the space age might well have started earlier, for the rocket contained the basic elements of later space vehicles.

These are just some of the more than 300 pieces in the outdoor exhibit, which, when combined with the indoor displays, forms the world's most complete weapons collection. The weapons have more than historical value; they are also highly useful for research. They enable engineers to develop and modify existing models, as well as learn how to defend against various weapons.

As you enter the museum you'll see the Civil War–era Gatling gun, which illustrates the research value of this collection. In 1902–1904 experiments were done with the Gatling gun to develop a more rapid firing weapon. At that time the need for speed was not critical so the experiment was discontinued. When aircraft armaments were needed in the 1940s, the Ordnance Museum supplied information from the earlier tests and the Gatling

The U.S. Army Ordnance Museum, the world's most complete weapons collection, houses—outside and indoors—exhibits from the Revolution through the Vietnam war.

gun principle was used to develop the Vulcan, an aircraft weapon.

The museum's exhibits include the history and development of ammunition, the evolution of the combat helmet, examples of every kind of rifle imaginable, as well as case after case of rocket launchers, machine guns, submachine guns, chemical weapons plus examples of uniforms and jeeps used by the Army.

Young boys love this museum, veterans relive the past, and history buffs are fascinated by the explanations of how and where the weapons were used. Even visitors without a built-in interest will be intrigued. There is so much to see you should plan on a leisurely visit.

The U.S. Army Ordnance Museum is open at no charge Tuesday through Sunday from noon to 4:45 P.M. It is closed Monday and on National holidays. The museum does open for Armed Forces Day, Memorial Day, Labor Day, Veterans Day and Independence Day. You will have to stop at the gate house as you enter the U.S. Army Aberdeen Proving Ground. The MP will take down your license and registration numbers and give you a Visitor Pass for your car.

Directions: From the Baltimore Beltway (I-695) take I-95 north 21 miles to the exit for Route 22. Turn right on Route 22, the Aberdeen Thruway, and proceed to the Aberdeen Proving Ground Harford Military Police Gate.

Babe Ruth Birthplace and Baltimore Orioles Museum

A Guaranteed Hit!

If the cry, "Play ball!" stirs your blood, you're sure to enjoy the **Babe Ruth Birthplace and Baltimore Orioles Museum**. The Babe, at least an electronic representative, is back at the Baltimore rowhouse where he was born on February 6, 1895. As you enter you'll see a sign proclaiming, "Baseball Spoken Here," and spoken is the right word. The bionic Babe will greet you and tell you about the museum. You'll hear recorded reminiscences from baseball greats and from avid fans as well as from the writers and photographers who covered the game.

The narrow rowhouse at 216 Emory Street, just 12 feet wide by 60 feet long (the museum encompasses three adjacent houses as well), belonged to Babe Ruth's grandparents. The Babe did not have an easy childhood, and his wild ways didn't help. At eight he was sent to St. Mary's Industrial School for Boys, part reform school for incorrigible boys and part orphanage. The school offered much that George Herman Ruth didn't like, but it did introduce him to the love of his life: Here he learned to play baseball. One of the most poignant items in the museum is the school hymnal, inscribed, "World's worse [sic] singer—world's best pitcher," signed George H. Ruth.

George's finest hour as a pitcher came in the 1918 World Series, four years after he entered the major leagues. He pitched 29⅔ scoreless innings for the Boston Red Sox, a record not beaten until Whitey Ford's streak in 1961.

Ruth went on to set batting records with the New York Yankees. He hit 60 home runs in 1927, a feat no player equalled until 1961 when Roger Maris knocked 61 balls out of American League parks. Only one player, Hank Aaron, ever hit more total home runs than the Babe's 714. Aaron soared beyond with 755. The museum has a 714 Home Run Club Room with a plaque for each of the Babe's home runs. Here also is career information on the only 13 players to hit more than 500 homers.

There is a Maryland Hall of Fame Room that highlights the six local players in the Baseball Hall of Fame. Since this is the official Baltimore Orioles Museum, fans can watch a ten-minute video spanning 30 years of Orioles' action, and see photographs and memorabilia on the hometown team.

Babe Ruth and Jimmie Foxx star at the Baltimore Orioles Museum. At the Babe's birthplace nearby, one hears that the great pitcher/hitter learned to play baseball at a reform school.

Museum hours are 10:00 A.M. to 5:00 P.M. daily, April through October. From November through March hours are 10:00 A.M. to 4:00 P.M. daily. Closed Christmas Eve and Day, Thanksgiving and Easter. Admission is charged.

Directions: Babe Ruth Birthplace is located on Emory Street, two blocks south of Pratt Street and the University of Maryland Hospital.

B&O Railroad Museum, Mount Clare Mansion and City Fire Museum

Train of Thought

The story of the American railroad begins at Mount Clare in Baltimore, when Maryland's Charles Carroll laid the first stone for the Baltimore and Ohio Railroad on July 4, 1828 (coincidentally on the same day President John Quincy Adams turned over the first shovel of soil for the building of the Chesapeake and Ohio Canal just outside Washington, D.C.). Carroll said about his involvement in the B&O Railroad inauguration, "I consider this among the most important acts of my life, second only to the signing of the Declaration of Independence, if second even to that."

At the **Baltimore and Ohio Railroad Museum** you can explore this pivotal transportation revolution. Fifty locomotives and full-size models are housed in the museum's Mount Clare station roundhouse. The station is considered the birthplace of the American railroad and the oldest station in the United States. The first American trains ran from this spot to Ellicott City, and it was here that Peter Cooper built the engine he called his Tea-kettle, nicknamed by others Tom Thumb.

Cooper's Tom Thumb is known as the early locomotive that lost a legendary race with a horse. As sometimes happens with such stories, fiction has clouded fact in this tale. Although a race evidently did take place, just when and where have never been firmly established. It might have been on August 28, 1830, during the engine's inaugural 13-mile run between the Mount Clare station and Ellicott City, except no horse could have matched the engine's time of 26:22 minutes, and the many news accounts of the run do not mention a race. It is far more likely that the race took place in 1831, during the celebration of Charles Carroll's 94th birthday. The fan belt broke during this run, slowing the train enough for a horse to beat it.

The B&O Railroad Museum is known worldwide for the size and scope of its collection. Many of the prize railroad cars are on the roundhouse's 22 spokelike tracks. There are vintage Pangborn engines, Imlay coaches, trains from the Civil War (when the military first used railroads) and later wars. From World War I there are "40 and 8" trains, so called because they carried 40 men and eight horses.

113

America's love affair with trains began on Mount Clare with the start of the Baltimore and Ohio Railroad on July 4, 1828. It is kept aglow by the B & O Museum's world-famed collection.

Trains overflow to the front and back of the museum. These are popular with young visitors who play conductor and engineer on the vintage engines. The museum is open Wednesday through Sunday from 10:00 A.M. to 4:00 P.M. Admission is charged.

The ten acres on which Mount Clare Station was built was virtually given to the B&O Railroad by James MacCubbin Carroll for the bargain price of $1. Carroll's nearby family home, Mount Clare Mansion, is also open for tours. This pre-Revolutionary Georgian estate is the oldest in Baltimore, circa 1756. It was built by Charles Carroll the Barrister, who helped write the Declaration of Rights for Maryland and the Maryland State Constitution. The house is furnished with Carroll family pieces. You can tour the house Tuesday through Saturday from 11:00 A.M. to 4:00 P.M. and Sunday from 1:00 to 4:00 P.M. It is closed on Mondays and holidays.

Baltimore has another small museum that focuses on transportation. The **Baltimore Streetcar Museum** at 1901 Falls Road has an audio-visual program and offers streetcar rides on its one mile track. The museum is open year-round on Sunday from noon to 5:00 P.M. During June, July and August it is also open Thursday 7:00 to 9:00 P.M. and on Saturdays noon to 4:00 P.M. (See also National Capital Trolley Museum.)

Loosely related to the subject of transportation, getting firemen to the fire is part of the story at the **City Fire Museum** near Belair Market (see Markets selection). The museum has a few examples of antique equipment, fire department insignias and badges and photographs of the great Baltimore fire of 1904. It is open at no charge Monday through Friday 9:00 A.M. to 4:00 P.M. A more comprehensive collection of fire engines and equipment can be found at the Fire Museum of Maryland in the Baltimore suburbs.

Directions: The B&O Railroad Museum is located at 901 W. Pratt Street, a few blocks west of Martin Luther King Jr. Boulevard in downtown Baltimore. For the Mount Clare Mansion take Pratt Street from the B&O Museum to Martin Luther King Boulevard, and turn right. Turn right again at Washington Boulevard and follow it to Carroll Park; the mansion is at the top of the hill on the right.

Baltimore Center for Urban Archeology

They Dig History

Everyone loves a mystery, particularly everyone at the **Baltimore Center for Urban Archeology**, or BCUA. Here trained specialists and eager volunteers are historical detectives solving the mysteries of the past; their clues are uncovered artifacts. For example, a spoon with the initials DAR helped solve this mystery: How did an early industrial site, such as the brewery (that's the Great Baltimore Brewery), relate to early residents and local inhabitants? The spoon belonged to Rebecca Peters (those were her grandparents' initials), who lived with her husband and seven children next to the brewery they owned and operated between 1782 and 1812. From items found in the family privy BCUA staffers were able to deduce details of the Peters's life style.

The Center's museum, which opened in September 1986, is the first of its kind in the United States. Baltimore is the second city after Alexandria, Virginia, to establish a center to preserve archeological sites within an urban environment. Descriptive panels in the museum explain procedures used in solving archeological mysteries, including how a dig is conducted and how the uncovered artifacts are sorted and interpreted.

Interested visitors may volunteer to spend several hours, or several days, helping at one of BCUA's digs. But you don't have to leave the museum in order to have a hands-on archeological experience. Inside the museum is a full-scale excavation pit with artifacts embedded in the dirt. Here you can try your hand at digging and then you learn to chart your find. To find out what happens after an artifact is removed from a dig, you observe the volunteers in the working laboratory area. Here too you can help wash, identify and catalog some of the 280,000 artifacts currently in the collection. Only a small portion of these artifacts is displayed; the remainder is in storage in the museum basement.

The BCUA is part of the network of Baltimore City Life Museums. It is sandwiched between the Carroll Museum and the 1840 House, completing the re-creation of a mid-19th century block. It opens onto the H. Chace Davis Jr. Courtyard, and during the summer some of the laboratory work is done there among the ornamental shrubs, trees and flowers from the mid-1800s.

The Baltimore Center for Urban Archeology charges a small fee and is open Tuesday through Saturday 10:00 A.M. to 4:00 P.M. and Sunday, noon to 4:00 P.M. During the summer the museum is open until 5:00 P.M.

Directions: The BCUA is at 802 E. Lombard Street just east of the Inner Harbor in downtown Baltimore.

Baltimore Maritime Museum

Ship to Shore

Two very different ships comprise the **Baltimore Maritime Museum** at the Inner Harbor's Pier 4. The *U.S.S. Torsk* was the head of a submarine wolf pack; the *Chesapeake* was a floating lighthouse.

On August 14, 1945, the *Torsk* sank two Japanese men-of-war. The next day word came that the war had ended. Thus it was the *Torsk* that fired the last torpedoes of World War II. The submarine holds another record: It is the "diving-est" ship in the world, with 11,884 submersions.

After World War II the *Torsk* was converted to a snorkel-equipped GUPPY submarine. It was involved in operations during the 1960 Lebanon crisis and the naval blockade of Cuba in 1962. The *Torsk* was transferred to Maryland in 1972 and now affords visitors a real feel for life aboard a submarine.

Visitors may find even a short stay claustrophobic in the crew's 14- by 30-foot quarters. It's sobering to realize the conditions under which 26 men lived; no movie or book adequately conveys the entombed feeling you'll get as you explore this submarine. You'll leave with a new respect for submariners.

The second ship of the Baltimore Maritime Museum is the lightship *Chesapeake* built in Charleston, South Carolina, in 1930. Lightships were used where traditional lighthouses could not be constructed, near harbors or channel entrances. Seven years before the *Chesapeake* was built, a lightship began guarding the approach to New York Harbor.

The *Chesapeake* is on the National Register of Historic Places, but it's a "place" that doesn't stay put. This is one of the few lightships that is still operational, and it visits other cities as a representative of the city of Baltimore. When the *Chesapeake* is docked at Pier 4, it can be toured on a combination ticket with the *Torsk*.

Tours are given from the end of May to mid-September from 10:00 A.M. to 5:00 P.M. and from mid-September until the end of May Thursday to Monday from 10:00 A.M. to 4:30 P.M. Admission is for both ships.

While you're in the area, take the elevator to the top of the World Trade Center for a view of the Baltimore Maritime Museum, the harbor area and indeed the entire city. The panoramic gallery is called the Top of the World, and it affords one of the best views in Baltimore. Telescopes and detailed maps help you pinpoint the city's main attractions. The World Trade Center at Pier 2 is the tallest pentagonal building in the United States. It is open 10:00 A.M. to 5:00 P.M. and admission is charged.

Directions: The two ships of the Baltimore Maritime Museum are docked at Pier 4 next to the National Aquarium at the Inner Harbor.

Baltimore's Municipal Markets

To Market, To Market. . .

Baltimore's markets could be called moveable feasts—you do the moving and they provide the feast. This market system is the oldest institution in the city. It was set up in 1765 when the Maryland General Assembly approved a lease for the Commissioners of Baltimore Town to establish and regulate a market. This was before the establishment of a Mayor's office, Health Department or other city agencies.

In 1752 Baltimore was a community of roughly 250 residents, with 25 homes, two taverns and one church. These townfolk needed a market where they could purchase fresh produce. The oldest market in Baltimore (indeed, the oldest continuously operated market in the country) is the **Lexington Market,** established in 1782 when General John Eager Howard donated some of his land so that outlying farmers could meet there and sell their wares. Conestoga wagons and farm carts rumbled to market with harvested crops, fresh meat, fowl and even seafood. General Howard named the market Lexington, after the Revolutionary battle.

By 1803 sheds appeared; more and more were added until the market spread onto another block. The reputation of Lexington Market also spread, and colonial leaders stopped here, including George Washington and Thomas Jefferson. Baltimore, too, was growing. In the mid-1800s it was the second largest city in the country, and the markets were where the crowds congregated to shop and gossip. More than 600 wagons from Maryland, Virginia and Pennsylvania rolled into the city on Saturday mornings to serve a crowd of 50,000. Oliver Wendell Holmes paid a visit to Lexington Market in 1859; its size and selection so impressed him he dubbed Baltimore The Gastronomic Capital of the Universe.

On March 25, 1949, a six-alarm fire destroyed Lexington Market. It was rebuilt, re-opening in 1952 even bigger than before with three block-long sheds sheltering more than 130 merchant stalls. Fresh meats and produce, a complete seafood spread including a raw bar, and home-baked goods are augmented by 22 ethnic eateries in a glass-enclosed market arcade. The Lexington Market at Lexington and Eutaw streets is open Monday to Saturday 8:30 A.M. to 6:00 P.M.

Although Lexington is the most well-known market in the city—it claims to be "world famous"—six other markets provide old-fashioned shopping experiences in neighborhood settings. These are not tourist markets but the daily stop of in-town natives. Because the original Lexington Market burned to the ground, the oldest market structure in the city is the more than 200-year-old **Broadway Market** at 1640–41 Aliceanna Street, originally constructed in 1785. This hub at Fell's Point (see selection) is set among newly refurbished shops, pubs, fashionable restaurants and ethnic eateries. It's a neighborhood that maintains its maritime ties.

Broadway Market's two buildings have stalls selling meat, poultry, seafood, bakery goods, spices, plants and flowers, as well as fresh fruit and vegetables. Market stalls were the goal of European immigrants to Baltimore who wanted to move up from a streetside produce cart. Descendants of these early immigrants still own stalls in the city markets. The Broadway Market is open Monday through Thursday 7:00 A.M. to 6:00 P.M., Friday and Saturday 6:00 A.M. to 6:00 P.M.

There are two other East Baltimore neighborhood markets, the **Northeast Market** and the **Belair Market**. The former is located at 2101 East Monument Street, near the Johns Hopkins Medical Institutions. Northeast Market was originally built in 1885. Today, in addition to fresh produce, you'll also find lunch counters, a delicatessen and a bakery here. It is open Monday through Thursday 7:00 A.M. to 6:00 P.M., Friday and Saturday 6:00 A.M. to 6:00 P.M. Operating during the same hours is the Belair Market, built in 1835, at Gay and Forest Streets in the **Oldtown Mall**. It is an unglorified neighborhood market selling food staples and baked goods.

Visitors can enjoy the chance to mingle with the hometown crowd at **Cross Street Market,** easy to reach via trolley from the

Inner Harbor. Cross Street Market, built in 1845, is at 1065 S. Charles Street. It's the neighborhood market for Federal Hill and South Baltimore. The food here is not pre-packaged; you'll find a wide selection of fresh meat, poultry and fish. The raw bar is a popular meeting spot and the stalls sell everything from hand-dipped chocolate to European cheeses. As in all the markets, specialization means better selection and better service. The butcher cuts the meats to order and can advise just how much you'll need for dinner guests, while the cottage cheese is scooped per request and the steamed crabs can be packaged to go. Cross Street Market is open Monday through Thursday 7:00 A.M. to 6:00 P.M., Friday and Saturday 6:00 A.M. to 6:00 P.M.

These markets with all their ethnic input epitomize the melting pot in operation; they even provide the produce for the pot. One well-known Baltimore resident who habitually haunted West Baltimore's **Hollins Market** was H.L. Mencken (see Mencken House). Mencken shopped at the market near his home and often rhapsodized in his column on "the whole incomparable repertoire of Maryland Masterpieces—beaten biscuits, soft crabs, oysters, fried chicken and blackberries." Hollins Market still carries all this and more; it's open Tuesday through Thursday 7:00 A.M. to 6:00 P.M., Friday and Saturday 6:00 A.M. to 6:00 P.M.

The last of the municipal markets is **Lafayette Market,** 1700 Pennsylvania Avenue. It too serves West Baltimore residents. It was originally built in 1869 and has served discriminating natives over the years. Hours are Monday through Thursday 7:00 A.M. to 6:00 P.M., Friday and Saturday 6:00 A.M. to 6:00 P.M.

The city has one additional market that is not part of the municipal system but does offer fresh produce from nearby farmers. It's the **Farmers' Market** at Holiday and Saratoga streets beneath the Jones Falls Expressway. From late June through mid-December, farmers from Maryland and Pennsylvania sell their goods on Sunday mornings from 7:00 A.M. until they sell out. Thus they continue a practice that began in the late 1700s, producing not decades but centuries of satisfied customers that have shopped at Baltimore's markets.

Directions: To help you plan your marketing pick up a city map at the Baltimore Office of Promotion and Tourism, located at 34 Market Place, north of Pratt Street at the Inner Harbor.

The Baltimore Museum of Art

Old Masters Are Waiting in the Wings

Have you ever wondered what it would be like to live amid the splendor of great art? In the newly renovated and expanded Cone Wing of **The Baltimore Museum of Art,** two rooms from Claribel and Etta Cone's Marlborough Apartments have been replicated and filled with paintings by Henri Matisse. The furnishings look like those Matisse used in his work, so the feeling in these rooms is not only of being around the art—it's as if you are actually in it.

The Cone sisters began seriously collecting art in 1901 under the tutelage of their friend Gertrude Stein and her brother Leo. The Cones amassed a stunning selection of early 20th-century French art—works by Picasso (in addition to several oils, they collected 113 of his works on paper), Cezanne, Gauguin, Van Gogh, Renoir and Matisse. Etta met Henri Matisse in 1906 and they became lifelong friends. This special relationship developed a passion in the sisters for Matisse's art, and they acquired an outstanding collection of his works—42 oils, including one for each year starting in 1917 and going to 1940; plus 18 sculptures, 36 drawings, 155 prints and seven illustrated books.

The Cone Wing alone makes a visit to the Baltimore Museum of Art rewarding. In fact, William Rubin, Director of Painting and Sculpture of New York's Museum of Modern Art, said, "Seeing the Cone Collection is one of the truly great experiences available to the public for modern art." The museum, however, is known as a "collection of collections," and the Cone sisters are just two of several art devotees who have donated substantial holdings. Numerous Baltimore collectors have contributed works by Mondrian, Miro, O'Keefe, Pollock, de Kooning, Rauschenberg and others that hang in the post–World War II collection in the Hooper wing.

For those who prefer the Old Masters there is the Jacobs Wing, with works by Botticelli, Titian, Rembrandt, Frans Hals, Fragonard, Van Dyck and Raphael. There are also the fabled Antioch Mosaics, dating from the early Roman Empire. These mosaics were part of a group of stone pavements excavated at Antioch-on-the-Orontes in Northern Syria.

The American Wing encompasses galleries on three floors and includes landscapes, portrait work, a study section for Maryland decorative arts from 1730–1840 and a comprehensive array of American furniture. All these arts are combined in the nine period rooms, which include a room from 18th-century Eltonhead Manor, a Baltimore Federal parlor from Waterloo Row, the Weston Bed Chamber and a 1771 room from the Abbey, or Ringgold House, in Chestertown.

There are also galleries filled with the art of diverse cultures form Africa, the Americas and Oceania. Many of the items were used in ritual ceremonies marking harvests, funerals, coronations, coming of age rites and marriages. African masks, miniature stone carvings, mortuary carvings, intricately detailed household items, woven baskets, jewelry and other objects are displayed in large glass cabinets that offer a 360-degree perspective.

Because there is so much to savor, you'll want to spend several hours exploring. In 1982 the museum added a café, which is open 11:00 A.M. to 10:00 P.M. Tuesday and Wednesday, 11:00 A.M. to 11:00 P.M. Thursday through Saturday and 11:00 A.M. to 9:00 P.M. on Sunday. It is closed on Mondays. The café overlooks the Wurtzburger Sculpture Garden, and during the summer you can eat outside on the garden patio. The fountain and reflecting pool provide a cool oasis on the hottest day.

The Baltimore Museum of Art is open Tuesday through Friday 10:00 A.M. to 4:00 P.M., Saturday and Sunday from 11:00 A.M. to 6:00 P.M.; selected galleries are open on Thursday and Friday evenings from 5:00 to 9:00 P.M. Closed on Monday and major holidays. Admission is charged except on Thursday and in the evenings.

Directions: From downtown Baltimore take Charles Street north and turn left on 29th Street. Go right on Art Museum Drive. The Baltimore Museum of Art is three miles north of the Inner Harbor at North Charles Street and 31st Street. Parking is available on Art Museum Drive.

Baltimore Museum of Industry

A Working Museum for a Working City

If to you industry means only steel and smokestacks and workers in overalls, a visit to this museum will be a delightful surprise. You'll find it fascinating and full of hands-on fun.

The **Baltimore Museum of Industry** is appropriately located on the working side of Baltimore's harbor in an old oyster cannery, the 1865 Platt Packing Company. The weekday bustle of the Baltimore–Locust Point Industrial District is matched by the weekend bustle within the museum's three work areas.

The turn-of-the-century machine shop still turns out replacement parts for the museum's antique industrial equipment. Huge belts extending from floor to ceiling turn the big flywheels that power the machine tools. If you are familiar with Rube Goldberg's cartoon contraptions, you'll recognize these machines as the real thing.

The second work area is an old-time print shop where visitors can help "pull the devil's tail." The heavy lever on the vintage printing press is indeed a devil to pull, and after one try you'll understand why so many printers developed muscular arms. You'll also have the opportunity to work the 1900 Poco Proof Press and print your own souvenir that reads: "I Printed This." Several American expressions may have evolved from these early printing methods. A printer had to "mind his Ps and Qs" as he picked the correct type from his composite case. (Another explanation for this phrase involves bartenders carefully pouring pints and quarts.) The expression "hot off the press" makes sense when you learn printers dried the wet ink on the freshly printed pages by holding them over a candle flame.

The garment workshop also lets you get the feel of the job. You can try your hand—and your foot—working the 80- to 100-year-old treadle sewing machines. Many young girls spent all their daylight hours in Baltimore lofts working these machines, some of which were quite specialized for the day: a belt looper, for example, a large and small basting machine and a hand-operated button sewer.

Other museum displays remind visitors of Baltimore's canning and shipping industry. You'll also learn that this was the first city in the country to have a gas company, which used the gas lamp, or "ring of fire," invented by painter Rembrandt Peale. A re-created tinsmith's shop is lit and powered by gas. There is also an 1895 Baltimore drugstore that once stood on the corner of Eastern Avenue and Conkling Street, and an elaborate electric repair shop full of old-fashioned household appliances.

Moored at the dock just outside the museum is the historic 1906 S.S. *Baltimore,* one of the last steam engine tugboats on the East Coast. Recovered from the bottom of the Sassafras River, this boat is in the process of being repaired. The museum is also restoring the Glenn L. Martin Company's 1937 *Tadpole Clipper,* a prototype seaplane. You can watch the restoration work in the museum's back gallery.

The Baltimore Museum of Industry is open on Saturday 10:00 A.M. to 5:00 P.M. and Sunday noon to 5:00 P.M. Admission is charged.

Directions: In downtown Baltimore go south past Harborplace on Light Street. Make a left on Key Highway; the museum is on the left at 1415 Key Highway. From I-95, get off at Key Highway Exit. Turn left at light, go under the underpass, turn left on Key Highway. Museum is immediately on your right.

Baltimore Public Works Museum

Down Under

Day and night, all year round, there is a working world beneath the city streets; that's what the **Baltimore Public Works Museum** is all about. Located on the eastern fringe of the Inner Harbor, this unusual facility—the only one of its kind in the country and free to boot—faces glitzy competition from the National Aquarium and Harborplace. It can easily be included on a day trip to its more well-known neighbors. The museum provides a behind-the-scenes—and even under them—glimpse of how a large city provides the utilities services its citizens need.

Youngsters are immediately attracted to the museum's outdoor **Streetscape** sculpture. This gives you a look down under, beneath the streets. You'll see the connections for street lights, phone lines, conduits, storm drains as well as a network of pipes for water, sanitation and gas.

The museum is housed in the Eastern Avenue Pumping Station, built in 1912 as part of Baltimore's sewage system. Despite its utilitarian purpose, the building has a number of architectural embellishments, including a copper-trimmed roof and decorative gables and cupola. Visitors are reminded that civic pride is not a new commodity in Baltimore.

Many people have only a fuzzy idea of what constitutes public works. The museum's exhibits acquaint visitors with such diverse services as street lighting, road maintenance, sewer service, trash removal and water service. A 15-minute slide presentation encapsulates the history of public works in Baltimore, and rotating video shows correspond to current exhibits. These presentations are socially, rather than technically, oriented; you don't learn how a pump works, you learn how it influences your life.

The Baltimore Public Works Museum is open Wednesday through Sunday 11:00 A.M. to 5:00 P.M.

While you're in the area with pipes on your mind, you may want to visit the **B. Olive Cole Pharmacy Museum** and see how folks got their plumbing, among other things, fixed the old-fashioned way. Those interested in medicine will appreciate the museum's collection of early pharmaceutical paraphernalia. Old medicine bottles, pill crushers, prescription scales and a selection of 19th- and 20th-century mortars and pestles fill the shelves. Downstairs there is a complete turn-of-the-century pharmacy, its cabinets still stocked with vintage potions and its prescription book yellowing. This museum is in the Kelly Memorial Building at 650 West Lombard Street on the Baltimore campus of the University of Maryland. Hours are 10:00 A.M. to 4:00 P.M.; there is no charge.

Directions: In downtown Baltimore take Pratt Street past the Inner Harbor and turn right on East Falls Avenue. The entrance to the Baltimore Public Works Museum is on East Falls Avenue, at the corner of Eastern Avenue, across the pedestrian bridge from Pier 6. It is adjacent to Baltimore's Little Italy, where you will find the popular Sabatino's Restaurant at 901 Fawn Street. (It's is said Anthony Quinn visited Sabatino's seven times when he was in Baltimore for a two-week run of *Zorba the Greek*. Frank Sinatra, who ought to know Italian food, has also been a customer.)

Baltimore Zoo

Animal House

You may not think that 52 deer and a flock of purebred South-down sheep would be much of a draw, but back in 1876 that was pretty exciting. Baltimore's collection of captive animals at that time was only one of three zoos in the country (the others were in Philadelphia and Cincinnati). The Main Valley of the zoo has some of the original displays, but progress and innovation are slowly transforming the **Baltimore Zoo**.

The African Plains Lion exhibit area, which opened in 1981, is an example of the zoo's new look. The lions roam the perimeter of their large grassy enclosure. One sector is separated from visitors by a heavy stockade fence with a picture window. The window provides nose-to-nose confrontations that leave visitors wondering about the strength of the glass.

Though not majestic like the king of the beasts, the prairie dogs, whose new home was also added in 1981, seem to enjoy playing king of the mountain as they chase one another around their hillside homes. There is also a new 3½-acre naturalistic enclosure for the zoo's four African elephants, and an outdoor pool and yard for the Nile hippos.

The Baltimore Zoo has more than 1,200 birds, reptiles and mammals spread out along wandering paths in the 150-acre Druid Hill Park. The picturesque setting makes an outing to the zoo a pleasant contrast to the city's downtown.

A 1988 addition is the new Children's Zoo, a comprehensive educational playground with 48 animal exhibits and a variety of activities designed to give youngsters a new perspective on nature. These include a groundhog exhibit, where children burrow right next to the animals, and a submerged plexiglass tunnel for underwater exploration. There is also a simulated beaver lodge, a giant turtle shell for youngsters to climb in, a walk-through flight cage and a huge man-made tree kids enter through the roots and climb from the inside. Climbers will also enjoy playing on the jungle gym shaped like a woolly mammoth's rib cage. A barnyard petting area and creative displays on Maryland's eco-systems are a part of this special zoo, too.

The zoo is divided into 14 major animal exhibit areas. When you enter you'll get a park map with an explanation of the symbols used at each exhibit. These symbols provide a wealth of information about each animal. You'll learn their native habitat, their diet, the hours they are most active and how they live with others of their species in the wild.

The Baltimore Zoo is open daily 10:00 A.M. to 4:20 P.M. Summer Sunday hours are 11:00 A.M. to 5:20 P.M. Though admission is usually charged, every Saturday from 10:00 A.M. to noon entrance is free.

Directions: From downtown Baltimore take Martin Luther King Boulevard north. Turn left on McCulloh Street to Druid Hill Park. Follow signs for the Baltimore Zoo. From north of Baltimore take the Jones Falls Expressway (I-83) south to Exit 9, Cold Spring Lane, and head west to Greenspring Avenue and then follow zoo signs.

Carroll Mansion and Shot Tower

Hot Shot

There were a number of well-known Charles Carrolls in Maryland, but the one who attended the Continental Congress, Charles Carroll of Carrollton, stood apart, both at home and at the Congress.

He was the only Roman Catholic delegate. He had also attended the First Continental Congress but only as an observer because Catholics weren't often included in the councils of government. Charles Carroll's wealth and influence in Maryland plus his dedication to the cause of independence resulted in his appointment to the Board of War, as well as his being chosen as a Maryland delegate to the Second Continental Congress.

Carroll was one of the wealthiest men to sign the revolutionary Declaration. It was said that one couldn't cross Maryland without traveling on Carroll land. He owned 80,000 acres and amassed a fortune estimated at two million dollars.

Ironically, Charles Carroll of Carrollton never actually lived at Carrollton. This estate was given to him by his father on the occasion of his marriage in 1768, but the newlyweds moved instead to Annapolis, where Charles attended Maryland Assembly sessions. Carroll served concurrently in the Maryland Assembly and as Maryland's senator in the U.S. Congress, which met in New York at that time.

His real home was the family estate, Doughoregan Manor, 40 miles from Baltimore. Doughoregan is a Gaelic word meaning "house of kings," not altogether an appropriate name for the house of such an ardent supporter of independence. Although Doughoregan was to be Carroll's home throughout his life, his last 12 winters were spent at his daughter Mary's house on Lombard Street in Baltimore. The Howard County estate is now owned by an eighth-generation descendant. Of the two homes, only the Baltimore townhouse is open to the public.

Richard and Mary Caton, Carroll's son-in-law and daughter, moved to this Lombard Street house so they could accommodate her father. He joined them in the fall of each year with his furniture, silver and paintings. When Thomas Jefferson and John Adams died in 1826, Carroll became the sole surviving signer of the Declaration of Independence. A living legend, he received visitors by the score. In 1828 he laid the foundation for the Baltimore & Ohio Railroad and the cornerstone for Shot Tower. He continued to play a role in the development of the new nation and was active and alert until just before his death on November 14, 1832.

The **Carroll Mansion,** built about 1808, is considered the finest Baltimore townhouse to have survived from this early era. Although there are no records that tell how the rooms were used, nine have been furnished to suggest their appearance when Carroll was in residence.

The first floor, like most 18th and early 19th-century houses, was used for business. The only merchant townhouse still standing in Baltimore, it has a counting room to the left of the front door. An exhibit provides fascinating information on Carroll and the business he conducted here.

The winding staircase to the second floor is the most interesting architectural feature in the house. It leads to the formal rooms; the grand salon, or parlor, is decorated in the Empire fashion popular in 1820. Even when new, this furniture style, copying the classical designs of Greece and Rome, was considered antique. The library, with titles brought from Carroll's Doughoregan library, is furnished in the height of style for 1825, while the formal dining room and music room reflect the fashions of 1830.

The third floor has the private bedchambers. Carroll died in bed at this townhouse in 1832; his bedroom is furnished with pieces that match those listed in his estate inventory. One item that always captures attention is the Mexican chair, a comfortable chair for its day. Also upstairs is a lady's bedroom with the colors and styles of the 1820s.

The Carroll Mansion, a part of the Baltimore City Life Museums, is open at no charge Tuesday through Saturday from 10:00 A.M. to 5:00 P.M. and Sunday noon to 5:00 P.M. During the winter months it closes at 4:00 P.M. It is closed on Mondays and major holidays.

Just two blocks north of Carroll Mansion is the **Shot Tower,** for which Carroll, at the age of 91, laid the cornerstone. The tower was built using 1,100,000 handmade bricks. No exterior scaffolding was used as the tower gradually extended up for 246 feet. The wall is four feet six inches thick at its base, narrowing to 20 inches at the top.

From the outside the tower resembles a smoke stack. Inside you'll find an innovative audio-visual presentation that explains how musket balls were made at Shot Tower. There are no guides, so visitors are requested to start the presentation themselves by pushing a button, the lights then dim and a disembodied voice explains the drop method. You'll see what looks like hot lead falling from the tower top; kids squeal and parents have to resist the impulse to pull them out of what appears to be harm's way. Musket balls were formed when hot lead was dropped from stations at various heights in the tower; the higher the station, the bigger the ball. As the lead fell it became cylindrical, passing through a perforated iron ladle at the bottom of the tower, then cooling in the water cistern. From there it went into a dryer and a polishing cask. Each year until the tower closed in 1892 approximately 500,000 25-pound bags of shot were turned out. You can visit the Shot Tower at no charge 10:00 A.M. to 4:00 P.M. daily.

Directions: Take Pratt Street past the Inner Harbor area. Turn left on High Street at Little Italy. Continue up one block to East Lombard. The Carroll Mansion is to your left at 800 East Lombard Street. For Shot Tower continue up High Street and turn left on Fayette Street. Shot Tower is on your left.

Churches of Baltimore

Freedom of Choice

Baltimore, celebrated for its baseball team, ethnic restaurants and colorful Inner Harbor, is also known as the "city of 1,000 spires." A tour of the churches of Baltimore provides an overview of the development of various religious denominations and a wide range of outstanding examples of ecclesiastical architecture. The Mother Churches of American Methodism and Catholicism are found in Baltimore as is the third oldest synagogue in the country and an early Lutheran and Episcopalian church.

The **Lovely Lane Methodist Church and Museum** is an architectural gem, listed on the National Register of Historic Places as the first church designed by Stanford White. A leading architectural scholar calls it "a national treasure." Leaving aside for a moment its religious significance, this Romanesque church with Etruscan detailing is a fascinating place to explore. The massive grey stone walls and 186-foot tower built of Fort Deposit granite loom impressively over St. Paul Street.

Interior interest focuses on the vaulted ceiling above the sanctuary. It was painted to show the heavens, complete with 719 planets and major stars, as they were at 3:00 A.M. on November 6, 1887, when the church was dedicated. The sky was charted by Dr. Simon Newcomb, the first professor of astronomy at Johns Hopkins University. The beautiful wooden staircases and doors, the Tiffany glass in the chapel and the organ especially captivate visitors. If you are lucky enough to hear the organ, you will understand why a music critic called the sanctuary "the finest small concert hall in the area."

The Lovely Lane Museum in the church basement traces the history of American Methodism from the founding Christmas Conference, which took place at the Lovely Lane Meeting House in 1784. The present church was built as a centennial symbol of that meeting. Lovely Lane is open Monday through Friday from 10:00 A.M. until 4:00 P.M. and there are Sunday tours at noon. The address is 2200 St. Paul Street.

The **Basilica of the Assumption** is the Mother Church of Roman Catholicism in the United States. Begun in 1806, this church was designed by Benjamin H. Latrobe as the first classic-revival church in the country. One architectural historian, Nicholas Pevsner, calls it "North America's most beautiful church." Its interior spaciousness is much admired, as is the central dome supported by segmented vaults. It, like many of Baltimore's churches, features stained-glass windows, which add luminous color to the interior on sunny days. The Basilica, at Cathedral and Mulberry Streets, is open daily from 7:00 A.M. to 6:30 P.M. Tours are given at 1:30 P.M. on the second and fourth Sunday of the month.

The first synagogue built in Maryland (the third oldest in the nation) was erected in 1845 at 11 Lloyd Street in Baltimore. Now restored as a museum and historic site, the **Lloyd Street Synagogue** is noted for its Star of David window and matzoh oven. The architect, Robert Cary Long, Jr., built it in a Greek classical style at a time when the classical revival in Baltimore was ending. The synagogue is open year-round Monday through Thursday from 11:00 A.M. to 2:30 P.M. (guided tour at 1:00 P.M.) and Sundays 1:30 to 4:00 P.M. (guided tours at 2:00 and 3:00 P.M.).

The **Zion Lutheran Church** at Holiday and Lexington Streets is one of Baltimore's first Lutheran churches. It was built in 1807. The stained-glass windows make this worth visiting. It is interesting to compare these windows with those you will see at the Basilica.

Baltimore's first Episcopal Parish was established in 1692, and **Saint Paul's Parish and Church** at Charles and Saratoga streets was begun in 1854. It was designed in an Italian Romanesque basilica style to replace an earlier church that burned to the ground. This church is noted for its Tiffany stained-glass windows, exterior bas-relief panels and the garden. The church is open Monday through Friday from 8:15 A.M. to 5:15 P.M. and on Sunday from 8:00 A.M. until 11:00 P.M.

These five only skim the surface of the many houses of worship to be seen in Baltimore. On another visit you may want to see the **Old Otterbein United Methodist Church** at Sharp and Conway streets, which is the oldest church in continuous use in

128

Baltimore. The **Mother Seton House** at 600 North Pratt Street can be seen by appointment. The beautiful **Cathedral of Mary Our Queen** at 5200 North Charles Street has a series of lovely stained-glass windows.

Directions: In order to help you plan your own church tour you may wish to pick up a city map available free at the Baltimore Office of Promotion and Tourism, located at 34 Market Place, just north of Pratt Street at the Inner Harbor.

Cylburn Arboretum and Sherwood Gardens

Floral Double Feature

Those who complain about alternately freezing and sweltering during Maryland winters and summers can take some comfort from knowing those same variations make it possible to grow flowers indigenous to both cold and warm climates. Maryland's cornucopia includes a rich array of wildflowers whose small, delicate blossoms are too often overlooked amid the color of spring.

Cylburn's wildflower preserve, which peaks in April and May, is just one part of the 167-acre **Cylburn Arboretum**. Nature's bounty can be enjoyed on the trails as well as in the more formal gardens near the Cylburn Mansion, built in 1863 by Jess Tyson. Benches provide resting spots and vantage points from which to savor the sights, sounds and smells of the forest, field and gardens. Flowers and trees are labeled, but you'll need a field guide to identify the more than 150 species of birds that have been observed at Cylburn, a designated bird sanctuary.

There are several formal gardens planted with perennials; these are particularly appealing in June. Cylburn also has a vegetable garden, an herb garden, several small specialty gardens and an All-American Display Garden. The Display Garden is one of 105 across the country heralding new varieties of flowers and vegetables not yet ready for marketing. A Garden of the Senses is designed for those in wheelchairs and the visually impaired. Plants are chosen for their scent and texture, and the plants are labeled in print and in Braille. Cylburn Arboretum is open daily 6:00 A.M. to 9:00 P.M. at no charge. Like all parks the rule is, "Take nothing but photographs, leave nothing but footprints." The Cylburn Mansion, purchased by the City of Baltimore in 1942, is open periodically for special events and garden shows.

Not more than a 15-minute drive from Cylburn in the elegant Guilford section of Baltimore is the seven-acre, privately developed **Sherwood Gardens** (open free to the public). In mid-May it's worth combining these two floral attractions. Sherwood is a riot of colors when the 5,000 azaleas and 100,000 tulips bloom. Pansies, dogwoods and flowering spring trees add to its charm.

Directions: From the Baltimore Beltway, (I-695) take the Jones Falls Expressway (I-83) south and then take Northern Parkway west. Turn left onto Cylburn Avenue. Proceed to the left for Greenspring Avenue and immediately turn left into the Cylburn Arboretum at 4915 Greenspring Avenue. For Sherwood Gardens take Greenspring Avenue south to Cold Spring Lane and follow it east across Jones Falls Expressway. Approximately two miles past the expressway turn right onto Underwood Road and then right onto Stratford Road and the gardens will be on your left.

Edgar Allan Poe House

Mythic and Mysterious

"Ill-fated and mysterious man!—bewildered in the brilliancy of thine own imagination, and fallen in the flames of thine own youth!" Edgar Allan Poe could well have been speaking of himself in this passage from his story "The Assignation." He apparently could not confine his extraordinary imagination to the poetry and stories that have since established him as one of America's greatest writers. His tales of his heroic defenses of freedom in Greece and Russia, for example, were picked as fact in the early accounts of his life. Later biographical research revealed that he had never traveled to these countries. Poe even gave a false name—Edgar Perry—to the U.S. Army. For Poe mystery was a way of life.

Several cities in the Mid-Atlantic lay claim to Poe; Philadelphia and Richmond both have houses associated with him. Poe's link with Baltimore is perhaps stronger, however, because he lived and died here. His years in Baltimore were not happy, despite the fact that it was during this period he met and courted his young cousin, Virginia Clemm.

Although Poe romanticized his forebears, he was without family support from a young age. His parents were itinerant actors and his father deserted while Poe was still an infant. His mother died when he was two. Poe was raised by the Allans, a Richmond family. Poe's gambling ways, the death of his foster mother and the remarriage of his foster father all contributed to the severing of ties between him and Allan. From the age of 22 Poe was completely on his own—and for the most part constantly in debt and struggling to eke out a living.

When Poe left West Point in 1831 he went to Baltimore to live with his father's sister, Mrs. Maria Poe Clemm, and her daughter Virginia. Previously he had published two volumes of poetry, and now he began writing prose stories. From Baltimore Poe

Edgar Allan Poe lived here as a struggling poet with his aunt, grandmother and cousin from 1831 to 1835. He married the cousin in Richmond in 1836 when she was but 13.

wrote to Allan that he feared debtor's prison, but he received no help. He stayed in Baltimore until 1835 when he moved to Richmond to edit the *Southern Literary Messenger*. Just 13, Virginia lied about her age and married him in Richmond in 1836.

The Baltimore house where Poe lived and struggled from 1831 to 1835 is still in a struggling neighborhood; during Poe's era it was virtual country, on the western edge of the city. Poe, who had rarely seen his blood relations, was now surrounded by family; in addition to Maria and Virginia, his grandmother lived in the house. The family welcomed the addition of the $240 annual widow's pension his grandmother received from the government because of her husband's service in the Revolution and the War of 1812. Poe's grandmother died in the upstairs bedroom.

The house is small and the upstairs barely more than a garret. There is not much furniture and none is original. The kitchen is furnished to represent the 1820s. You'll be able to watch video presentations of Poe's poems and stories. The **Edgar Allan Poe House** at 203 N. Amity Street is open Wednesday through Saturday from noon to 4:00 P.M. During July, August and September hours are Saturday only noon to 4:00 P.M. The Poe House is closed January, February and March. A nominal admission is charged.

At the time of his death, Poe was en route from Richmond to New York and had stopped off in Baltimore. He did not, as some stories would have it, die in a gutter. He was found in a doorway violently delirious and taken to a hospital where he died on October 7, 1849. Although rumors intimated he was under the influence of drugs or alcohol, later research indicates the probability of diabetes and pneumonia. The condition of his body and his clothes also suggest that he had been beaten and robbed.

Poe was buried in Baltimore's Westminster Cemetery. The church is on the National Register of Historic Places and can be toured by appointment; call (301)328-2070. Poe was not even buried in peace. Biographers disagree about his funeral, some claiming that only a few attended services and others reporting that hundreds followed his cortege. After the first burial, his remains were reburied in 1875 in a more prominent position at the front of Westminster Churchyard, a position that can be seen from the street.

Directions: In downtown Baltimore take Paca Street north to Fayette Street, where you turn left. (Poe's grave is at the corner of Fayette and Greene streets.) Proceed west on Fayette Street and turn right at Schroeder Street. Go two blocks and turn right at Saratoga Street and turn right again almost immediately at Amity Street. The Poe House is at the far left end of Amity Street.

Fell's Point

Point Worth Taking

Fell's Point is unique; it is the only one of the three colonial settlements that made up Baltimore Town that has survived. It is also one of the East Coast's few remaining original urban waterfront communities. A visitor can easily sense the early American flavor of this seaport that contributed so much to Baltimore's growth during the Revolutionary War. The architecture and physical characteristics have changed very little over the years.

Edward Fell, a Quaker shipbuilder, purchased this point on the Patapsco River in 1731. The Fell family divided the land into building lots. By 1763 these lots, with their deepwater frontage, were in great demand. By 1804 there were more than 20 shipyards at Fell's Point. Among the ships built and launched here were the historic frigate *Constellation* (see selection) and many of the classic Baltimore Clippers. Sailors, settlers and European immigrants filled the taverns, restaurants, streets and docks.

There are 350 residential structures from the American Federal architectural period. But only the **Robert Long House** is restored to its 18th-century appearance and open to the public. Long purchased three lots from Edward Fell in 1765. On his waterfront lot Long built a four-story brick warehouse. He built his home on the Ann Street lot, now 812 S. Ann Street.

The house that Long built was not typical of 18th-century Baltimore architecture. In fact, no other surviving home is designed in a similar style. Long's house follows the Quaker floor plan, two-and-one-half stories with a pent-roof across the second floor front. The interior design is simple, and the small rooms are furnished to reflect occupancy by the Longs from 1765–81. The Robert Long House is open Thursday from 10:00 A.M. to 4:00 P.M. Groups may arrange tours by appointment; call (301)675-6750.

You can obtain a walking tour guide to Fell's Point from Baltimore's Visitors Information Center at the Brokerage on Water Street between Market Place and Frederick Streets (open year-round Monday through Thursday 10:00 A.M. to 6:00 P.M. and Friday through Sunday 11:00 A.M. to 7:00 P.M.). The Fell's Point brochure provides information on the buildings you will pass as you stroll around the historic neighborhood. Be sure to stop at the Broadway Market (see selection), where you'll be tempted by the array of deli items that can make up a picnic lunch. Or you might want to try one of the ethnic cafés or bistros so popular with Baltimoreans.

One lunchtime or overnight option is The Admiral Fell Inn at 888 South Broadway (call (301)522-7377). This was once a hotel for seafarers but now is an elegantly decorated inn. Each room has a distinctive style. . .and a jacuzzi.

The specialty shops scattered around Fell's Point are yet another attraction. One of the popular spots is The China Sea Marine Trading Co., Inc., at 1724 Thames Street. The shop, an old stable and rope establishment, carries a wide range of maritime curiosities. Fell's Point also has an old book shop, antique emporiums, art galleries and boutiques. A brochure listing the restaurants and stores is available in any of the shops.

Directions: Fell's Point is in downtown Baltimore east of the Inner Harbor and south of Pratt Street. From Pratt Street, turn right on Broadway for this quaint neighborhood.

Fort McHenry

A Real Star

The play of history is often sensed best in the places where our forebears lived and fought. At **Fort McHenry** there have been a number of occurrences that not only bring back the past but also suggest the presence of past inhabitants. A shadowy figure has been spotted on the Civil War battery walls, noisy footsteps have been heard, furniture has been rearranged, windows raised and lowered, lights turned on and off and a presence felt in a guardhouse cell. There are those who believe the spirit of Lieutenant Levi Clagett, killed during the 25-hour British bombardment during the Battle of Baltimore, is responsible for at least some of these phenomena.

The 13th of September, 1814, was a dark and stormy night for Lt. Clagett and the 1,000 other soldiers and sailors manning Fort McHenry. Their job was to defend the fort and save Baltimore from the fiery fate suffered by Washington when the British captured that city. Rain made it difficult for the British to keep their powder dry, but the Americans had a greater problem—their guns could not reach the British ships. The British were in range to bombard the fort with their guns and the new Congreve rocket; they fired between 1,500 and 1,800 bombs, rockets and shells. It is amazing that the heavy barrage resulted in only four deaths and 24 men wounded. Despite the strength of their firing position, the British could not subdue the fort, and thus the attack on Baltimore failed.

The gallant defense of the fort is captured in a 16-minute film that is shown at the Fort McHenry Visitor Center. The film packs an emotional wallop: It ends with a stirring rendition of the national anthem as the window curtain is slowly withdrawn to reveal the oversize flag still flying over the fort.

134

At Fort McHenry, an honor guard and a park ranger lower a replica of the flag that flew during the War of 1812 when Francis Scott Key wrote the words to the national anthem.

You'll get more out of your walk around the fort if you see the film. The fort you will see is not the first to stand on this pivotal ground guarding the approach to Baltimore. Fort Whetstone protected the city during the American Revolution. The star-shaped fort you'll explore was built between 1798 and 1803. The design was chosen to make surprise attacks impossible, each point of the star being visible from the points on either side.

As you explore the star fort you'll notice along the base of the walls the remains of the dry moat that once encircled it. The fort is entered through an arched doorway, or sally port, which is flanked by bombproof underground rooms built immediately following the bombardment. Across from the sally port is a ravelin, consisting of angled embankments used to protect the powder from enemy attack. Guardhouses, barracks and junior commanding officers' quarters have been re-created.

During the summer months members of the Fort McHenry Guard, in replica U.S. uniforms of 1812, perform drills and military demonstrations in the fort.

Fort McHenry is open daily at a nominal charge from 8:00 A.M. to 5:00 P.M. (in the summer it is open until 8:00 P.M.). Closed Christmas and New Year's Day. From mid-June through Labor Day ranger-guided activities are offered daily. Check the directory board behind the information desk in the Visitor Center for the schedule. On most Sundays in July and August at 6:30 P.M. military tattoos (programs of music and drill) are performed. Each September there is a Defenders' Day Program to celebrate the anniversary of the Battle of Baltimore with a mock bombardment, military drills, music and fireworks.

Those who want a different perspective on Fort McHenry should take the *Baltimore Patriot* when it sails from the *Constellation* dock at the Inner Harbor (see selection). The 1½-hour narrated boat tour lets you see the fort from the vantage point of the British ships anchored off Baltimore. Boat tours are given spring, summer and fall. The schedule for mid-April through May and October is 11:00 A.M., 1:00 and 3:30 P.M. From June through September boats depart hourly 11:00 A.M. to 4:00 P.M. During the summer two additional boats, the *Defender* and the *Guardian*, also sail from the Inner Harbor to Fort McHenry. For more information call (301)685-4288.

Directions: From the Inner Harbor area go south on Light Street. Proceed past the Light Street Pavilion and the Maryland Science Center and turn left on Key Highway. Take Key Highway for one mile then turn right on Lawrence Street. Take Lawrence Street to Fort Avenue and turn left and proceed to Fort McHenry National Monument. From I-95, take the Fort McHenry exit and follow the signs.

H.L. Mencken House

Genus Genius

"Injustice is relatively easy to bear; what stings is justice," said H.L. Mencken. What would really sting the acerbic Baltimore critic is seeing the public (the "booboisie" as he called it) wandering today through his inner sanctum, his home at 1524 Hollins Street.

Mencken moved with his family to this middle-class, 19th-century rowhouse when he was but three and ended up spending 67 of his 75 years here. He left it only to marry Sara Haardt, who died five years later.

In 1883, when Mencken's family moved to Hollins Street, the neighborhood was still rural. Then came a branch of the Enoch Pratt Free Library and Mencken obtained a library card before the age of nine. "I began to inhabit a world," he was later to write, "that was two-thirds letterpress and only one-third trees, fields, streets and people."

At the age of about eight, Mencken received a Christmas present that changed his life. He would write: "Other presents came and went, but there was never another that fetched and floored me like Dorman's Baltimore No. 10 Self-Inker Printing Press." His famous signature—H.L. Mencken—dates from this early apprenticeship. He smashed all the lower case r's, which meant he could not print his first name, Henry—hence H.L. Mencken.

As the eldest of three boys Henry was destined for his family's cigar business. But after his father's death on January 13, 1899, he left the family firm for newspaper work. It wouldn't work today, but Mencken simply showed up every night at the city room of Baltimore's *Morning Herald*. After a month he was sent out to cover a rural suburb, and he was on the beat. He would remain a newspaperman for the next 43 years. He also managed to write 30 books.

Mencken did a great deal of his writing in the bright second-floor front study overlooking Union Square Park. Photographic blow-ups show Mencken working at his rolltop desk. The original desk is here, but the 1888 Smith-Corona typewriter is a twin to the original, which is displayed in the Enoch Pratt Library's Mencken Room.

Downstairs in the Mencken House are the family rooms—the formal front parlor, dining room and sitting room where Henry and his brother, August, spent most of their time. At the Mencken House you're not kept behind obtrusive ropes. Visitors are invited to sit in the parlor and watch a 17-minute slide presentation on Mencken's life. The program describes Baltimore during the Mencken years, and there are numerous first-person remem-

In the parlor of H. L. Mencken's house, visitors are invited to view a slide show on the life of the colorful newspaperman and author. The house may be rented for dinner parties.

brances. When you look around the parlor, one of the first things that catches your eye is the baroque gilded pier mirror hanging between the floor-to-ceiling windows. The parlor was used by the family for formal entertainment, but it was the sitting room where Henry and August felt comfortable. There they enjoyed their evening glass of beer; in fact, a collection of beer mugs is displayed. Gin was another favorite. Mencken even brewed his own in the bathtub; he called it Hoax Brand.

Mencken buffs may rent the house for dinner parties, and guests are free to gather at Mencken's Hepplewhite table and take inspiration from the setting. Money from such parties helps to maintain the Mencken House.

Outside, Mencken's narrow garden has been carefully restored. There is a life-size blow-up of him beside the woodpile. The kindling has been colorfully painted as it was when August and Henry wiled away the time painting wood after Henry's stroke. Henry loved to putter in his garden. He built the brick walls and columns, embedding in them reliefs he collected from around the world. He also built a gazebo, where he and his brother enjoyed a drink on summer evenings.

Mencken suffered a cerebral thrombosis in 1948 and died on January 29, 1956. If your visit brings him to mind, then the great man left some instructions for you: "If, after I depart this vale, you ever remember me and have thoughts to please my ghost, forgive some sinner and wink your eye at a homely girl."

The **H.L. Mencken House** is open Wednesday through Sunday from 10:00 A.M. to 5:00 P.M. A nominal admission is charged.

Directions: From downtown Baltimore take Lombard Street west to Union Square. Hollins Street runs parallel to Lombard on the right side of Union Square. Coming into Baltimore on I-95 north, take I-395 and follow signs to Martin Luther King Boulevard. Take Martin Luther King Boulevard to Lombard Street exit. Turn left on Lombard Street and follow above directions.

Maryland Historical Society

Preserving the Heritage of the Free State

Where would you expect to find the original draft of the *Star Spangled Banner*? Appropriately, it is one of the prized possessions of the **Maryland Historical Society** Museum and Library of Maryland History in Baltimore. This is a museum for history buffs who want to be thorough in their coverage of Baltimore's historic sites.

The Maryland Historical Society's collection is the largest single repository of the state's cultural heritage. Begin exploring at the Radcliff Maritime Museum on the museum's basement level. There you'll see rigged models of Baltimore clippers, as well as paintings of steamboats and other Chesapeake Bay craft. A 13-minute audio-visual presentation delves into the life of Maryland's watermen and Maryland's maritime heritage. There's also an exhibit on ship chandlery and ship building.

On the first floor you'll see exhibits on Early Maryland. Artifacts are displayed from those who inhabited the land before European settlement. Contributions made by the first settlers are recognized. The newly renovated Darnell Children's Museum is also on the first floor.

On the museum's second floor more recent Maryland history is presented. Here you'll find the Library of Maryland History. The library includes more than 50,000 books plus manuscripts, maps, prints and photographs dealing with Maryland and its citizens from the earliest years to the present. You do not have to be engaged in academic research to consult this collection. Those researching their family genealogy and those simply interested in wiling away an afternoon reading for pleasure are welcome.

The museum, which has a fine collection of furniture built and designed in Maryland, is also linked to the adjacent 1847 Enoch Pratt House, which has 19th-century period rooms. In the Pratt House the rooms provide a complete picture of 19th-century life. In the bright orange parlor, mannequins wearing day dresses are arranged around the tea table. The front room mannequins wear visiting dresses. The upstairs bedrooms are not open to the public but the lower level has a collection of doll houses on display.

The Maryland Historical Society Museum is open Tuesday through Friday from 11:00 A.M. to 4:30 P.M., Saturday from 9:00 A.M. to 4:30 P.M. and Sunday from 1:00 to 5:00 P.M. from October through April. It is closed on holidays. Admission is charged.

Directions: The Maryland Historical Society is located at 201 West Monument Street in downtown Baltimore. From the Inner Harbor go north on Charles Street to the Washington Monument and then go west on Monument Street four blocks.

Maryland Science Center

Gee Whiz Kids

The innovative **Maryland Science Center**, at Baltimore's Inner Harbor, is one destination where children should bring friends or count on an active assist from parents, because it takes two to carry out many of the center's experiments.

This scientific wonderland, like Alice's, invites visitors to "Try this!" Easy-to-understand instructions help you get involved with science. After you try the various experiments, you'll learn their scientific significance in the "what's going on" message.

Plan to set aside a long morning or full afternoon because youngsters will not want to be hurried as they tackle the wide variety of participatory experiments, challenge the games in the computer center and marvel at the planetarium show. The admission is roughly that of an afternoon at the movies, with an extra charge for the IMAX theater and the planetarium. Both are well worth the extra time and money.

There are three floors to explore, with changing exhibits and permanent displays. The latter include a look at "Your World, Maryland"; energy; computers; optical illusions; probability; fish and the Chesapeake Bay. In the "Something Fishy" exhibit, parents are relieved to learn that neither the pirhana nor the boa constrictor are hands-on items. And who says Maryland doesn't have slot machines? There's one here that asks questions about the Bay. The Maryland Science Center is without a doubt one of the best ways to introduce children to science—it's educational and never boring.

Talking with a slot machine will seem tame compared to the effects created in the Science Arcade on the third floor. This educational fun house has a room of distortion with a slanted floor and mind-confusing optical illusions that change visitors into midgets and giants. Special lenses, telescopes, lights, sound and optics turn science into a game.

Youngsters enjoy video games in the Computer Company, also on the third floor. The technology of the computer is explained so that terms like binary counter, logic gate and memory bank become more than the unfathomable jargon of a new age. The games continue in Energy Place where a metric tic-tac-toe game lets you convert from one form of energy to another.

Staff members of the Maryland Science Center present live demonstrations throughout the day. One of the presentations focuses on energy as the center's Van de Graff Generator produces one million volts of electricity. In another, a staff member pulls a tablecloth from beneath a stack of dishes to illustrate Newton's first law of motion. In addition to these and other popular live demonstrations, there are science films and shows in the Boyd Theatre.

Finally, no visit to the Maryland Science Center should be considered complete unless it includes the Davis Planetarium's multimedia presentation. Although you can measure this 144-seat theater's dimensions—50 feet in diameter and 32 feet high—when the lights dim it seems to encompass all of space. The illusion is enhanced by the 125 projectors and four-channel sound system. A laser projection system permits exciting laser graphics. Topics covered include Halley's Comet, the earth's weather, light and the space telescope. Traditional astronomy shows are also offered. During a typical 30 to 35 minute show, 500 to 700 visual effects are used and might include a star-filled universe, flaring comets, falling meteors and spinning galaxies. The effects are all brilliantly employed to tell a scientific story.

In 1987 an IMAX motion picture theater was added, making the Science Center one of a handful of theaters in the country presenting IMAX films. For those not familiar with the term, it is the name for the world's biggest motion picture system. Screens are over 55 feet high and 75 feet wide, more than five times the width of the average movie screen. Viewers have the vivid sensation of being in the picture as astronauts blast into space, divers probe the ocean's depths and explorers cover the far corners of the globe.

During the winter, spring and fall the Maryland Science Center is open Monday through Friday from 10:00 A.M. to 5:00 P.M., Saturday 10:00 A.M. to 6:00 P.M. and Sunday noon to 6:00 P.M.

The IMAX performances are Monday through Friday at noon, 1:00 and 3:00 P.M., Saturday on the hour from 11:00 A.M. to 5:00 P.M. and Sunday on the hour from 1:00 to 5:00 P.M. The planetarium schedule is Monday through Friday at 2:00 P.M., Saturday at 11:00 A.M., 1:00, 2:00, 3:00, 4:00 and 6:00 P.M. and Sunday on the hour from 1:00 to 5:00 P.M. From mid-June through Labor Day weekend the Science Center hours are 10:00 A.M. to 9:00 P.M. daily, with planetarium and IMAX performances on the hour from 11:00 A.M. to 8:00 P.M. There is a special K.I.D.S. (Key Into the Discovery of Science) Room to encourage children ages four to seven to get involved with science. It is open during the summer daily, noon to 4:00 P.M. For additional information call the Science Center at (301)685-2370.

Directions: In downtown Baltimore take Light Street south past Harborplace; the Maryland Science Center is on the left at 601 Light Street. You can park in the adjacent hotel parking lot or at Piers 5 and 6 near Harborplace.

Mother Seton House

The Bells of St. Mary's

The austere simplicity of the small house on North Paca Street in downtown Baltimore reflects the lifestyle of its most significant tenant, Elizabeth Ann Seton, the first American-born canonized Roman Catholic saint. She lived here for one pivotal year in her life, arriving on the very day, June 16, 1808, that the Old Saint Mary's Seminary Chapel was dedicated.

The future saint, raised a non-Catholic, married William Seton when she was 19 and they had five children. His declining health prompted the family to seek a cure in Europe. The trip was to no avail, and Seton died in 1803. Elizabeth and her daughter, Anna, who had accompanied her parents, were left in Italy without funds but not without friends. The Filicchi family, devout Catholics and old acquaintances, invited Elizabeth to stay with them and to bring over her other four children, who were being cared for by relatives in New York. Elizabeth declined their generous offer. It was while she waited to return to New York, under the wing of the Filicchi family, that Elizabeth became interested in the Catholic faith. She converted in 1805.

Elizabeth Seton's first efforts to establish a nonsectarian school in New York were not successful. Then Father Dubourg of the Sulpician Fathers in Baltimore, the religious order that established the first Catholic seminary in the United States, invited Mrs. Seton to set up a Catholic girls' grade school.

With the help of several young women, Seton established the school. She took her first vows of poverty, charity and obedience in St. Mary's Lower Chapel on March 25, 1809. Archbishop John Carroll conferred on Elizabeth Seton the title "Mother." The other young women who joined Elizabeth took their vows in Emmitsburg in Western Maryland. They formed the nucleus of the Sisters of St. Joseph.

For the year that Mother Seton lived and worked in Baltimore, the bells of St. Mary's framed her day. Angelus bells rang at 5:30 A.M. before she attended morning service; they rang again at midday and then at 7:45 P.M. In a letter to a friend, she described the chapel as "the most elegant chapel in America open from daylight till nine at night." When you visit her home be sure to include a stop at this historic church, included on the National Park Service list of national landmarks.

When Mother Seton was offered property in Emmitsburg (see Seton Shrine selection), she and her young teachers took their young boarders with them. Her inclusion of parish children in her school led to the establishment of the first parochial school in the country.

When you tour the **Mother Seton House** you'll see that it reflects the period but not the specific residency of Mother Seton. There are no original furnishings here, although there are some at the Emmitsburg house. Family pictures do cover one wall, and upstairs you will see a lap trunk that belonged to Seton. In the bedroom closet there is a copy of the black habit, short black cape and white and black bonnets that Mother Seton and other Sisters of St. Joseph wore. The house also has a relic of Mother Seton.

You can visit without charge on Saturday and Sunday from 1:00 to 4:00 P.M. At other times you may visit by appointment. Call (301)323-7272.

Directions: The Mother Seton House is at 600 N. Paca Street in downtown Baltimore. It is one short block north (right) off Route 40W (Franklin Street) at Paca or two blocks north (left) off Route 40E (Mulberry Street) at Paca.

National Aquarium

5,000 Fish to Lure You

More people visited the Inner Harbor last year than Epcot at Disney World. While at the Inner Harbor most visitors included a stop at the **National Aquarium.** Since opening on August 8, 1981, the aquarium has quickly become the premier paid tourist attraction in the state, drawing upwards from 1.3 million visitors a year.

The aquarium is a big water wonderland—the entire living collection includes 5,000 marine and freshwater animals—and you'll want to allow plenty of time for exploration. Most visits take two hours, but you can easily stay longer, especially if you watch the feedings.

Five feeding presentations, scheduled throughout the day, take place in the central Marine Mammal Tray, Level 1, on the self-guided tour. Anore and Illama, the belugas, or white whales, frolic in this pool. These female belugas arrived at the aquarium November 20, 1985, after being collected at Churchill, Canada, above the Hudson Bay. If you watch one of the feeding sessions, which for the belugas are also training sessions, you'll quickly realize why belugas are nicknamed "canaries." They have 11 different calls, including barks, whistles, squawks, chirps and clicking sounds. The whales are being taught skills that will aid the staff in keeping them fit and healthy. At sessions in the morning and afternoon the staff gets into the water with their pupils, leading to some playful interaction. Anore has a jealous nature and never wants to be ignored, whereas Illama may go off and play on her own. Check the times of these sessions when you arrive so you won't miss the action.

The self-guided tour of the aquarium is arranged as a one-way trip. The objective is to give visitors an awareness of the importance of the aquatic environment. Level 2, Maryland Mountains to the Sea, starts with a mountain pool and traces the various water habitats of Maryland. An eight-minute film focuses on environmental problems of the Chesapeake Bay. The killdeers you'll see in the Coastal Beach section stand so still it's always startling when they move, but records show that these birds are indeed active. They've raised two chicks in their glassed-in home. That's nothing compared with the gray-necked wood-rails, who have reared 56 offspring!

On Level 3, some very exotic animals help demonstrate various facets of adaptation. You're not likely to forget the yellowhead jawfish, featherduster or red-backed cleaning shrimp in the section on "evolving." In the "feeding" exhibit visitors are delighted with the striking color of the clownfish, who attract prey for their host plant, the sea anemone.

One exhibit that challenges the staff is the live coral display. Growing these delicate sea creatures in an aquarium is extremely difficult. Coral requires sunlight, wave action, a precise temperature range and shallow depth.

The first exhibit you'll see on Level 4, the Sea Cliffs with puffins, murres and razorbills, has microphones that enable you to hear the birds. It's fascinating to watch the puffins' underwater swimming. Also on this floor is the Children's Cove. In the Cove's North American Tidal Pools youngsters can handle live specimens, such as hermit and horseshoe crabs and starfish. Volunteers are on hand to help youngsters dip into the experience.

You reach the heights at Level 5, the glass-roofed South American Rain Forest. On a cold winter's day its warmth, colorful feathered inhabitants, and constant activity prompt visitors to linger, enjoying this bit of the tropics. Try to spot the lizard that walks on water and the brilliant orange and black bird known as the Andean cock-of-the-rock. The large iguana periodically tumbles down from its precarious roost, causing momentary consternation among passing visitors. It's fun to stand on the observation deck, which affords a bird's eye view of the Inner Harbor, and try to spy the numerous birds residing in the rain forest.

Exiting the rain forest you'll see the tiny and colorful poison arrow frogs whose brilliant hues warn enemies of their venom. The aquarium, with 11 species, has one of the world's most comprehensive collections of these reptiles.

As you begin your descent back to Level 1, remember you can always retrace your steps or get your hand stamped and return later in the day. On the way down you will come to the Atlantic Coral Reef, one of the aquarium's best exhibits. This multilevel, 335,000-gallon donut-shaped tank provides a diver's view of the denizens of the reefs. Their placid circular progress is interrupted three times daily when a diver enters the tank to feed the fish. They are hand fed to prevent the more aggressive fish from consuming all the food.

In the first five years of operation, the Aquarium's fish have consumed more than 65 tons of cut mix, which is a combination of squid, shrimp, smelt, clams and krill, plus more than 550 cases of produce, including lettuce and broccoli. The fish consume 50 pounds of food daily. Volunteer divers not only feed the fish, they also "do" windows, keeping them clean to provide maximum visibility.

Beneath the coral reef is the 200,000 gallon Open Ocean ring. Here you can have a close encounter with four varieties of sharks—lemons, sand tigers, sandbars and nurses—plus six rays and a number of large game fish (the number of game fish changes when the larger predators occasionally eat their fellow tank mates). This is just one of the tanks that together contain 92 million gallons of city water the aquarium has transformed into sea water by the addition of 1.4 million pounds of Instant Ocean, a product containing a blend of more than a dozen synthetic sea salts.

On the pier level there is an outdoor seal pool and the Aquarium Café. Look for the new Marine Mammal Exhibit Pavilion with its 1,300-seat amphitheater, a large central pool, satellite pools, and holding pools for dolphin and small whales.

Although the admission is steep, it is certainly good value for dollar spent, and various discount opportunities are available. For example, from mid-September through mid-May on Fridays

145

after 5:00 P.M. there is a substantial reduction in admission. For information call (301)576-3810. Hours mid-May through mid-September are Monday through Thursday 9:00 A.M. to 5:00 P.M., Friday through Sunday 9:00 A.M. to 8:00 P.M. From mid-September to mid-May hours are Saturday through Thursday 10:00 A.M. to 5:00 P.M. and Friday 10:00 A.M. to 8:00 P.M.

During the summer and on weekends there is often a long waiting line for aquarium admission tickets. This wait can be avoided by purchasing advance tickets through Ticket Center outlets. There is a nominal charge for this service. In Baltimore call (301)792-4001, in Washington call (202)432-0200 and elsewhere call (800)448-9009. On the day you plan to visit you can also purchase coupons for specific entry times from the aquarium's outdoor reservation booth.

Directions: In downtown Baltimore take Pratt Street to Pier 3. Parking is available for a fee at Pier 5 and 6 and at the Inner Harbor Center Garage on Pratt Street across from the Aquarium.

Peale Museum

Peek at the Peale

Inner city Baltimore architecture strikes the unobservant as street after street of repetitious rowhouses. Nothing could be farther from the truth, as the **Peale Museum** points out in a fascinating and different exhibit called "Rowhouses: A Baltimore Style of Living." Once you are aware of the wide range of architectural styles and details, your trips through Baltimore will take on a new dimension. You can play the "rowhouse game" and try spotting the five different styles used from the early 1800s to the mid 1900s.

It isn't just visitors to the city who are captivated by the authenticity of the Peale's rowhouse exhibit. Many long-time residents, who have spent their lives in such old houses, are amazed to see them in a museum context with individual rooms carefully re-assembled.

There is a 1933 kitchen from one of the "daylight" rowhouses, the name given to the homes built from 1915 to 1955. These houses were two rooms deep and two rooms wide, giving each room a window to let in the daylight. The 1933 kitchen is remarkably thorough in its depiction of that era. Food lines the shelves and fills the refrigerator. Household supplies of that era stock the cabinets, and there is even a mousetrap to complete the picture.

Other re-created rooms include an 1875 "alley" house kitchen, a Victorian parlor, an 1840 parlor of a workingman's home, an 1890 bedroom that would likely have been rented to one of the city's immigrant laborers, a 1911 bathroom and a 1917 dining room.

The Peale Museum is itself a Baltimore landmark. It is claimed to be America's oldest museum building. Rembrandt Peale opened the museum in 1814, the year of the Battle of Baltimore, a pivotal encounter during the War of 1812. Peale was a noted portrait painter and a tinkerer. He constructed a gas light, and this museum was the first building in the city to be illuminated by gas. The Peale became the city's history museum in 1931. Now it is a part of the Baltimore City Life Museums, which include the H.L. Mencken House, the Carroll Mansion, the Center for Urban Archaeology and the 1840 House (see selections).

The Peale Museum is open 10:00 A.M. to 5:00 P.M. Tuesday through Saturday and noon to 5:00 P.M. on Sunday. Admission is charged. The Peale is at 225 North Holliday Street.

Directions: The Peale Museum is six blocks north of Pratt Street and Harborplace in downtown Baltimore. Go north from Pratt on Gay Street and turn left on Saratoga. Take Saratoga for one block and make a left on Holliday; the Peale Museum will be on your left.

Star-Spangled Banner Flag House

Spirits That Never Flagged

Oh, say can you see by the dawn's early light,
What so proudly we hailed at the twilight's last gleaming?
Whose broad stripes and bright stars, thro' the perilous fight,
O'er the ramparts we watched were so gallantly streaming?
And the rockets' red glare, the bombs bursting in air,
Gave proof thro' the night that our flag was still there,
Oh, say does that star-spangled banner yet wave
O'er the land of the free and the home of the brave?

On September 14, 1814, Francis Scott Key wrote these stirring words that became the first stanza of our national anthem. Key was trying to negotiate the release of his friend, Dr. William Beane, who was taken hostage after the British burned Washington during the War of 1812. From his position aboard an American truce ship anchored outside Baltimore's harbor, Key witnessed the British attack on Fort McHenry, and he anxiously awaited the coming of dawn to see if the flag still flew and the fort still held.

The flag he searched for had been designed with visibility very much in mind. Major Armistead, Commandant of Fort McHenry, had wanted a giant flag so big "that the British will have no difficulty in seeing it from a distance." He commissioned Mary

147

Pickersgill to fashion the oversize flag. Mary, with some help from her teenage daughter and niece, worked for ten hours a day for six weeks to make the 30- by 42-foot flag. It was the largest battle flag ever designed and weighed 80 pounds. Eleven men were needed to raise it.

Mary Pickersgill, a young widow, had moved from Philadelphia in 1807 to this rowhouse at 844 East Pratt Street with her seven-year-old daughter, Caroline, and her mother, Rebecca Young, also widowed. Mrs. Young had worked as a flag and banner maker in Philadelphia and had made the first flag of the Revolution at the request of George Washington. That flag, the Grand Union, was raised with the Continental colors by General Washington on January 1, 1776, at Cambridge, Massachusetts.

The furnishings in Mary Pickersgill's home are from the Federal period, popular when she lived here. In the parlor there is a Charles Willson Peale portrait of Mary's uncle, Colonel Flower, who was George Washington's Commissary General. The upstairs front bedroom is where Mary and her daughter and niece spent hours working on the giant flag. Keeping it all in the family, the material they used was probably purchased at the Fells Point dry goods store of Captain Jesse Fearson, Mary's brother-in-law. It was Mary's military connections and her mother's reputation as a flag maker that prompted Major Armistead to choose her to make the Fort McHenry flag.

Visitors enter the **Star-Spangled Banner Flag House** by way of a small building, which is both a gift shop and a small 1812 War Military Museum. A short audio-visual program serves as a background for understanding the War of 1812 and the part played by Mrs. Pickersgill's flag: a symbol of defiance to the British and a source of inspiration for Francis Scott Key. Guided tours of the house are given after the program.

Mary Pickersgill's tattered flag is displayed at the Smithsonian Institution's National Museum of American History in Washington. A replica may be seen at Fort McHenry (see selection). Mrs. Pickersgill's receipt for the flag is owned by the Flag House; a photostatic copy is on display. She received $405.90.

The Flag House and Museum is open Monday through Saturday from 10:00 A.M. to 4:00 P.M. and Sunday from 1:00 to 4:00 P.M. It is closed on Sundays during the winter months. A nominal admission is charged.

Directions: Take Pratt Street east past the Inner Harbor to the 800 block. The Star Spangled Banner House is on the left at the corner of Pratt and Albemarle streets. A large sign for Little Italy on the left provides a landmark for locating the Flag House. There is an adjacent parking lot.

U.S. Frigate *Constellation*

Sea-Link with History

Britannia indeed ruled the waves during the War of 1812. When the newly established United States Navy challenged her sea it was akin to David attacking Goliath. England had some 400 large warships, 350 of which were outfitted with 50 or more cannon. She also had smaller brigs, sloops, schooners and cutters. Against this the United States had three 44-gun frigates: the *Constitution*, the *President* and the *United States*; and four frigates with between 32 and 38 guns. Among the latter was the 38-gun *Constellation*, the first official ship of the U.S. Navy, which had been launched from Baltimore's Fells Point on September 7, 1797.

The *Constellation* was a seasoned veteran by the time the young country became involved in the War of 1812. She had the distinction of being the first U.S. Navy ship to engage and defeat a man-of-war from Europe. In 1799, the *Constellation*, reacting to attacks on American ships by French privateers and men-of-war, triumphed over the French frigate *L'Insurgente* off Nevis in the Caribbean. She had also engaged the Barbary pirates (and would continue to do so after the war). Unfortunately she was unable to contribute during the War of 1812 because the Yankee Race Horse, as she was called, was penned up in Hampton Roads, Virginia, for the duration of the conflict by a seven-ship British fleet under Admiral George Cockburn.

The *Constellation* was to achieve other distinctions. It was aboard this ship that the U.S. Navy signal book was written by the ship's first captain, Thomas Truxtun. The signals and regulations he wrote still serve as basic operating guides. Later in the *Constellation's* service, while circumnavigating the globe in 1842, she became the first U.S. ship-of-war to enter China's inland waters.

The *Constellation* is one of the only surviving American warships that saw action in the Civil War. Recognizing the *Constellation's* historic significance, President Franklin Roosevelt ordered her back to active duty during World War II as the flagship of the U.S. Atlantic Fleet. It was the only sailing ship to hold this honor. Fleet Admiral Chester Nimitz called the *Constellation* "perhaps the most important link that the United States Navy and the American people have with our early historic efforts to preserve our liberty."

The *Constellation's* long career means that she has the longest record of service of any U.S. warship. She is also the oldest ship in the world that has been continuously afloat. Purists may argue that the extensive rebuilding undermines this distinction, but

U.S.F. Constellation at Pier 1, the first official ship of the U.S. Navy, launched from Fells Point in 1797, became the flagship of the U.S. Atlantic Fleet in World War II.

most Americans are grateful that this historic link with our past has been saved.

The *Constellation* may be visited mid-June to Labor Day from 10:00 A.M. to 8:00 P.M.; Labor Day to mid-October 10:00 A.M. to 6:00 P.M.; mid-October to mid-May 10:00 A.M. to 4:00 P.M.; and mid-May to mid-June 10:00 A.M. to 6:00 P.M. Admission is charged.

Directions: The U.S.F. *Constellation* is docked at Pier 1 off Pratt Street at the Inner Harbor.

Walters Art Gallery and Evergreen House

Art of the Ages

It isn't surprising that the young William Walters, who claimed he spent the fist five dollars he earned on a painting, should go on to amass one of 19th-century America's most eclectic art collections. Thomas Hoving, former director of the Metropolitan Museum of Art, lists William Walters and his son Henry among the top five private collectors in the country's history.

The Walters, père and fils, are lauded not so much for the number of works they acquired as for the breathtaking diversity of their collection. A day spent at the **Walters Art Gallery** provides the same scope as a semester-long course in art appreciation. In addition to European art, the collection includes Tibetan reliquaries, Persian rugs, Chinese porcelains, Egyptian mummies, Japanese armor, Indian illuminated manuscripts and Russian icons.

Sheer breadth of range is no guarantee of a collection's quality, but among the Walters's 30,000 pieces there are numerous acknowledged masterpieces. The impressionist works *At the Café* by Manet and Monet's pastel-hued *Springtime* are but two of the great paintings. More somber is the ivory sculpture *The Virgin with the Standing Christ Child*, carved around 1400. The Walters's Raphael *Madonna of the Candelabra* is a prized Renaissance canvas; the 5th-century Rubens Vase, exquisitely carved from a single piece of agate, is another treasure. You should be sure to see the magnificent K'ang Hsi Peach Bloom Vase.

Ferreting out these art works can be something of an adventure. The five-story wing added in 1974 has circles within circles for you to explore. To direct you, there is an explanatory floor plan guide that gives information on the art to be found; also a marvelous series of children's guides can be found on each floor. Ignore the age limit and pick up one or all of these. You can choose *Looking for Lions, Hunting for Horses* or *Watching for Wings*. These engaging guides help you focus your visit, providing fascinating background on a variety of art forms as you search for the unifying motif.

It's been a long time since the Walters Art Gallery has looked as good as it does now. A total renovation of the original galleries is newly completed. The Renaissance sculpture court, modeled on the Palazzo Balbi in Genoa, Italy, has state-of-the-art lighting; and the walls of the ornate galleries are covered with rich brocade. Art is displayed as it was for the Renaissance princes, with paintings, furniture, sculpture and decorative pieces combined for total visual pleasure.

The gallery's attention turns next to the adjacent Hackerman House, which John Russell called "the epitome of the mid-nineteenth-century American town house." The gallery plans to display its Asian collection, much of which has remained in storage since it was acquired, in this new exhibit area scheduled to open in 1989.

"The most important privately assembled general museum in the U.S.," in the opinion of art authority M.S. Young, the Walters Art Gallery is open Tuesday through Sunday from 11:00 A.M. to 5:00 P.M. The gallery hosts ongoing special exhibitions and has a full schedule of public programs, including family days, lectures, films and concerts. Admission is charged, except on Wednesdays when, as a public service, it is free.

The home of another Baltimore collector, Alice Warden Garrett, and her husband, John Work Garrett, is also open to the public. Their home, **Evergreen House,** was bequeathed to Johns Hopkins University and is the location of many university functions. It was the scene of many glittering social events during the first half of this century, when the Garretts entertained the political and artistic elite. Mrs. Garrett dabbled in the arts (her paintings are hung at Evergreen), but she also acquired a number of outstanding works that have never been exhibited elsewhere. The walls of Evergreen House display the works of Picasso, Utrillo, Dufy, Modigliani, Vuillard, Bonnard and Rivera. Alice's collection of paintings by her friend Raoul Dufy—17 watercolors and two oils—is perhaps the largest private collection of Dufy's work in the United States.

Art aside, the house is worth touring because it affords a glimpse of the lifestyle of the rich and famous. There is a Victorian bedchamber, an ornate gold bathroom, a library that could well serve as a set for Masterpiece Theater, as well as a marvelous private theater designed for Mrs. Garrett by Leon Bakst, set designer for the Ballet Russe de Monte Carlo, who also designed the dining room.

The house is open the second Tuesday of each month. Tours are given at 10:00 and 11:00 A.M. and 2:00 and 3:00 P.M. at no charge. Do call before visiting to make sure the renovation work is finished, (301)338-7641.

Directions: The Walters Art Gallery is at 600 North Charles Street at Centre Street, one block south of the Washington Monument. Evergreen House, farther north, is at 4545 North Charles Street.

1840 House

Dated Drama

In the 1840s the city of Baltimore encompassed four square miles with a population of approximately 100,000. A typical family of that era was the Hutchinsons, who lived at 50 Albemarle Street in one of the growing number of middle-class rowhouses. With nine people residing in this small city home there was a lot of activity. There's still a lot of activity; it's all part of the dynamic living history program that brings the Hutchinson household vividly to life.

John Hutchinson was a wheelwright, and his wife, Mary Ann, ran a grocery store from their house. The Hutchinsons had three children and took in John's sister Margaret and Thomas Ward as boarders. The latter was an abolitionist by principle and a journeyman wheelwright. Working for this crowded household was Sarah West, a free black, who lived in the basement with her young child.

When you visit the **1840 House** an interpreter portraying one of these historical persons will take you around, your tour integrated with a natural series of chores. For example, Sarah West may have to sweep the floor after a meal in the dining area, dust the parlor table, fluff the upstairs beds, or get a head start in the basement kitchen on the next day's meals. The furniture appears authentic, but most of the pieces are actually period reproductions. This means you can touch and use them. You'll be invited to "sit a spell" in the parlor, help out in the kitchen or, like Goldilocks, try the various beds.

Since its opening, the 1840 House has hosted a popular annual program, "Steps in Time: Scenes from 1840 Baltimore." From mid-February through late May, this entertaining and educational production is performed hourly on Saturday afternoons and Tuesday through Friday for school tours. Theater students from Baltimore's School for the Arts bring to life the Hutchinson household as they move from room to room. The program deals with important issues of the times—racial and ethnic relations, class differences, health concerns and a variety of needed reforms.

The 1840 House is part of the Baltimore City Life Museums project, which also includes the adjacent Carroll Mansion, the Baltimore Center for Urban Archeology and the Courtyard Exhibition Center (see selections). The Peale Museum and the H.L. Mencken House (see selections) are also administered by the City Life office.

Tours of the 1840 House are given Tuesday through Saturday from 10:00 A.M. to 4:00 P.M. (5:00 P.M. during daylight saving time) and Sundays noon to 4:00 P.M. (or 5:00 P.M. during daylight saving time). Call (301)396-3277 for tour reservations.

Directions: The 1840 House is at the corner of Albemarle and Lombard streets, just east of the Inner Harbor. Enter through the Carroll Mansion Courtyard on Front Street.

Maryland's Capital
Diversion

MONTGOMERY COUNTY

Brookside Gardens at Wheaton Regional Park

A Bloomin' Retreat

Once discovered, **Brookside Gardens** in Wheaton Regional Park is a destination you'll return to any time during the year. It is close enough to the suburbs of Baltimore and Washington to be an easy drive, and diverse enough to be consistently interesting.

From early spring through late fall the many specialty areas of the 50-acre garden complex are in flower, and in the coldest months the blossoming continues in the conservatories. Evergreen plants in the glass-enclosed gardens provide a backdrop for the seasonal displays that flank a meandering path along an indoor stream. Young visitors enjoy the stepping-stone path across the water, and camera buffs appreciate the wooden footbridge for pictures.

The big Christmas display lasts well into January—glorious poinsettias, cyclamen, Jerusalem cherries and many other winter flowering plants. The next major exhibit is the winter/spring extravaganza of lilies, azaleas, fuchsias, hydrangeas and forced bulbs. By late March the spring bulbs begin to bloom outdoors, peaking in late April with an outstanding display of 15,000 tulips. During the azalea season the paths of Brookside are lined with brilliantly colored shrubs. In June more than 60 varieties of roses reach their peak, continuing their bloom until the first hard frost. Rose fanciers can get an advance look at the subsequent year's All-America Rose Selections at Brookside. New varieties of annuals can also be seen in the trial garden where hybrids are tested and evaluated. All summer long there is a riot of colorful annuals in the gardens and a wide selection of herbs in the Fragrance Gardens.

In the fall the outdoor display garden makes a final burst with chrysanthemums, then in November the show moves indoors with the chrysanthemum conservatory exhibit. This is a real winner; multiple varieties of chrysanthemums grow in cascades, upright columns and even miniature trees.

Brookside Gardens in Wheaton Regional Park offers floral extravaganzas every day of the year except Christmas. The park has a steam train for children and Old MacDonald's Farm.

One of the most charming areas at Brookside is the Japanese-style garden. It is worth exploring even on mild winter days. A gazebo sits amid tranquil ponds, surrounded by attractive trees, shrubs and ornamental gates.

There are wheelchair routes at Brookside Gardens, also a horticulture library and horticultural information sheets. Guided tours are given and educational classes are offered. No pets, food or drinks are permitted.

The Wheaton Regional Park's Brookside Nature Center is only a short walk along a path from the conservatory parking lot. Here you can learn about the flora and fauna of the surrounding forest through exhibits, films and guided walks.

Families with young children will want to stop at the park's Old MacDonald's Farm to see the pigs, cows, sheep and chickens. Behind the farm is the well-stocked 5-acre Pine Lake, where fishermen of all ages can try their luck catching bass, bluegill, crappie and catfish.

Youngsters enjoy riding the Wheaton Line Railroad, a 24-gauge reproduction of an 1865 steam train. The two-mile track travels over the meadow and through the woods before arriving back at the station. The park's carousel is also a hit.

Wheaton Regional Park has hiking and riding trails and an innovative playground area. The park is open at no charge 9:00 A.M. to 5:00 P.M. Brookside Gardens is closed on Christmas Day.

Directions: From Baltimore take I-95 south to the Washington Beltway (I-495) and go west to Exit 31A (Georgia Avenue). Go north on Georgia Avenue to Randolph Road and turn right. Then make a right on Glenallen Avenue for Brookside Gardens and Brookside Nature Center. The playground, carousel, farm and train station can all be reached by turning right off Georgia Avenue onto Shorefield Road.

Clara Barton National Historic Site and Glen Echo Park

The Angel of the Battlefield

Clara Barton gave this account of her experiences at Antietam: "A man lying upon the ground asked for drink—I stooped to give it, and having raised him with my right hand, was holding the cup to his lips with my left, when I felt a sudden twitch of the loose sleeve of my dress—the poor fellow sprang from my hands and fell back quivering in the agonies of death—a ball had passed between my body—and the right arm which supported him—cutting through the sleeve, and passing through his chest from shoulder to shoulder." (See Antietam selection.)

Barton was working as a clerk in the Washington, D.C., patent office immediately before the Civil War. With the outbreak of hostilities she devoted her time to aiding injured soldiers. Filling wagons with needed supplies—bandages, linens, anesthetics and oil lanterns—she worked with the field surgeons at the battles of 2nd Manassas, Antietam, Fredericksburg, the Wilderness and Spotsylvania (1861–65).

After the war the Angel of the Battlefield made it her mission to locate and identify soldiers the U.S. Army had listed as missing. Civil War casualties numbered 359,528, with only 172,400 identified. In four years of grueling work Barton located and identified 22,000 missing soldiers. She was instrumental in having the burial grounds of the infamous Andersonville prison in Georgia declared a national cemetery in 1865. It contained the graves of 14,000 Union soldiers.

Such work took its toll and Barton suffered an emotional breakdown. She went to Europe to recover, but rather than rest she became involved in the great cause of her life, the International Red Cross. Barton's supposed convalescence included duty with the Red Cross in the Franco-Prussian War. She returned to the United States and devoted herself to establishing the American Red Cross, of which she served as president from 1882 to 1904. Barton significantly expanded the scope of Red Cross relief work by involving the organization in peacetime aid, such as the Johnstown Flood of 1889 and the Galveston Hurricane in 1901.

On a hilltop overlooking the C&O Canal and Potomac River, Barton built a 35-room house in 1891. Now a National Historic Site, this Victorian house is architecturally intriguing. From the main hallway you look up to railed galleries on the second and third floors, the latter gallery seemingly suspended over the floors below. A top floor bedroom seems to hang from the sides of the house with no visible means of support, a delightful structural oddity.

One thing this house doesn't lack is closets—there are 38 of them. These storage areas were used for disaster supplies. Two rooms are re-creations of the home offices Barton used from 1897 to 1904, and the house is complete with her furniture. She spent the last 15 years of her life in this house and died at Glen Echo on April 12, 1912, at age 90.

Barton was not without her flaws. She was ousted from her position with the Red Cross not only because members felt she was too old but because they found her disorganized and unbusinesslike. There was even talk of a congressional investigation of her financial records before her resignation in 1904.

The heroism and the flaws of this remarkable woman are presented during a guided tour of the house. The Clara Barton National Historic Site is open daily at no charge from 10:00 A.M. to

5:00 P.M. Closed on federal holidays. Throughout the year there are many special weekend programs. Call (301)492-6245 for details.

Barton picked Glen Echo for her home because she was interested in the Chautauqua self-improvement movement, which used facilities at Glen Echo. She was considerbly less enthusiastic about the amusement park built here after 1899. The only reminder of the artistic Chautauqua years is Glen Echo's old stone tower, now an art gallery, which was used for Chautauqua gatherings in 1891. However, the spirit of the Chautauqua does remain; Glen Echo again offers workshops and classes in the arts. Artists create, teach, demonstrate and sell their work on the grounds.

The only working reminder of the amusement park era is the hand-carved Dentzel Carousel, which is considered by folk art specialists to be one of the finest carousels in America. There is always a rush to ride the carousel animals that go up and down while the music plays on and on. You can hop on your favorite on Wednesday, Saturday or Sunday from May through September. In addition to carousel rides, summer activities include performances for children by the Adventure Theatre (301)320-5331 and other cultural events. For general information on Glen Echo call (301)492-6282.

Directions: From the Baltimore Beltway, take I-95 south to the Washington Beltway (I-495). Head west on I-495 to Exit 40, for the Cabin John Parkway to Glen Echo. Exit from the parkway at MacArthur Boulevard and turn left. Proceed on MacArthur Boulevard to Glen Echo Park on your left; signs will indicate the parking lot for the Clara Barton National Historic Site.

Doctor's Museum, Beall-Dawson House and Strathmore Hall Arts Center

Rockville Trio

When you see the medical instruments at the **Doctor's Museum** in Rockville, you'll be glad the doctor isn't in. In fact, this is one collection that certainly doesn't evoke nostalgia for the good ol' days.

Some of the medical tools on display here were put to gruesome uses, and look it. There are sharp blades for amputation and devices for bleeding. There is also a collection of drugs that certainly helped patients forget their problems even if they didn't cure them. Many of the old nostrums included a considerable amount of opiates.

Doctors in the early 19th century did not have the benefit of autopsies to determine the causes of diseases. Instead, they used a "physiological manikin" like the one displayed here. It is a full-scale diagram of the human form, with sectional cutouts displaying arteries and organs. The museum's skeleton is a favorite with the younger set.

This museum was once the office of Dr. Edward E. Stonestreet, who practiced medicine in the Rockville area from 1852–1903. During the Civil War, Dr. Stonestreet was an Examining Surgeon for local Maryland draftees. A photograph of the doctor, his wife and their six daughters hangs in the museum. His saddlebags and boots still hang behind the door. He kept them in the office to be used on his frequent house calls. Dr. Stonestreet's office sits on the grounds of the **Beall-Dawson House**. Tours are given at both sites Tuesday through Saturday from noon to 4:00 P.M. and on the first Sunday of the month from 2:00 to 5:00 P.M. Admission covers both sites.

Upton Beall, son of Maryland tobacco merchant Brooke Beall, built his Rockville "mansion house" around 1815. The exact date is not known, but a Beall family legend says that the lumber Upton Beall acquired for construction of his house was used instead by American troops retreating through Rockville in 1814, during the War of 1812. Tax records for 1820 valued the house Beall built at $1,500. When Beall was a 40-year-old widower he married 17-year-old Jane Neil Robb, daughter of a prominent Rockville tavern keeper. Upton and Jane Beall had five children. Three of the girls lived but none married, so this Rockville house remained their home.

After the Civil War, when death claimed two of the sisters, Margaret Beall invited her cousin, Amelia Holliday Somerville, to live with her. When Amelia married John Dawson the newlyweds made their home with Miss Margaret, a condition she demanded before giving her permission to their union. Margaret Beall died in 1901 at the age of 84. The house was inherited by the Dawsons and did not pass from the Dawson family until 1946.

This Federal-style brick house is now the headquarters of the Montgomery County Historical Society. It has been restored to its 19th-century appearance. The downstairs rooms are furnished to represent the years Upton and Jane Beall were in residence, 1815 to 1847. About six pieces actually belonged to the Bealls, other pieces duplicate items listed on the inventory of Upton Beall (1827) and Jane Beall (1847). Over the parlor mantle there is a portrait of Upton Beall. The parlor also has a piano that Margaret Dawson, one of Amelia and John Dawson's nine children, used when she gave tap-dancing lessons to Rockville youngsters. The piano was bought for Margaret Beall in 1834.

Several of the upstairs rooms are used to display the Historical Society's collection of textiles, period clothes, kitchen and farm utensils and old books. Many of the Society's books are in the adjacent frame library, built in the late 1940s. The library can be used by genealogical and local history researchers. Hours are the same as for the Beall-Dawson House and the Doctor's Museum. For more information call (301)762-1492 or (301)340-9853.

If you are in Rockville on a Wednesday, plan to include afternoon high tea at the **Strathmore Hall Arts Center**. This elegant English Georgian country mansion serves as a showcase for the visual, literary and performing arts. At the weekly tea, given from 1:00 to 3:00 P.M. September to May, there are chamber music, fashion shows and literary readings. This is a delightful addition to a day spent exploring historic Rockville or shopping at White Flint Mall. Strathmore serves its own blend of teas with scones and other light refreshments. Gallery walls display changing art exhibits. Hours at the gallery are Monday through Friday from 10:00 A.M. to 4:00 P.M. and Saturday 10:00 A.M. to 3:00 P.M. For information on upcoming programs or reservations for the always popular teas, call (301)530-0540.

Directions: From Baltimore take I-95 south to the Washington Beltway (I-495) and head west to Exit 34N (Rockville Pike, Route 355). Strathmore Hall is on your right just past the Grosvenor Metro Stop at 10701 Rockville Pike. For the Beall-Dawson House continue out Rockville Pike about four miles to Middle Lane, across from the Rockville Metro Stop. Turn left on Middle Lane, go two blocks then turn left on Adams Street and right on West Montgomery Avenue. The Beall-Dawson House is at 103 West Montgomery Avenue.

Great Falls, Chesapeake & Ohio Canal (Lower) and Seneca

On the Rocks

On sunny afternoons the rocky promontories at **Great Falls** become a rookery of sunbathers, with people perched all along the great boulders. The dramatic churning water provides a fascinating natural attraction, even without the availability of the trail to the major falls, which washed out in the flooding following Hurricane Agnes in 1972 and has yet to be repaired. You have to visit the Virginia side to view the full scope of the Great Falls of the Potomac. (Visitors should be cautious exploring these rocks because they are dangerous. From 1975 to the early 1980s nine people drowned in the Potomac while rock hopping and sunbathing.)

Great Falls, Maryland, is part of the **Chesapeake & Ohio Canal National Historical Park**. The Great Falls Tavern Visitors Center is housed in a large white building erected in 1830, and you can

161

catch a short movie on the history of the canal almost any time during the day. The exhibits are not without their humorous touches; the sign under the mule bells explains that they "satisfy the mule's sense of style."

The best way to experience canal life is to take a boat ride on the *Canal Clipper*, a barge that plies the narrow waterway from mid-April through mid-October. Right after you board the boat the captain blows the giant lock horn and begins the "locking through" maneuver designed to bring the boat up to a higher water level. The barge enters a lock and then a valve is opened, raising the water level eight feet in five minutes. In 1870 there were 74 of these lift-locks on the 185.5 miles of canal stretching from Georgetown to Cumberland.

Once the boat is locked through, mules are hitched up and the 1½-hour canal voyage begins. The barges usually covered only four miles an hour, the speed limit imposed by the Canal Company so that the wake of the boats would not erode the sides of the canal. It took about ten minutes for each locking through maneuver; with 74 locks that meant a minimum of 12 hours to pass all of the canal's locks. If a boat traveled at the maximum allowable speed of four miles per hour for ten hours a day, it could travel the distance from Cumberland to Georgetown in about six days.

On quiet evenings the boat captain, who often traveled with his entire family, would pull out his harmonica or Jew's harp, and passengers and crew alike would join a sing-along. You will be invited to help re-create these songfests on your boat ride.

In the spring and fall the boat trips are weekends only at 10:30 A.M., 1:00 and 3:00 P.M. with an added trip on Sundays at 5:00 P.M. From mid-June through mid-September boat rides leave Wednesday through Friday at 10:30 A.M., 1:00 and 3:00 P.M. Boat tickets go on sale two hours before each departure. On weekends they are quickly sold out. For more information call (301)299-2026. Boat rides are also given at the C&O Canal in Georgetown, and tickets for them are sold at the Foundry Mall. Call (202)472-4376 for information.

If this glimpse of life aboard the canal boats whets your appetite, you can easily extend your day and visit Riley's Lockhouse in **Seneca** at Lock #24. On weekends from 1:00 to 4:00 P.M. Girl Scouts conduct free tours of this small lockhouse overlooking Seneca Creek and the Potomac River. Youngsters will particularly enjoy this informal tour led by young girls in Victorian period dresses. The four-room lockhouse is furnished to represent the period 1870–85. John Riley tended the lock from 1892–1924, and he lived in this small house with his wife and their seven children. Different Girl Scout troops sponsor different activities at the lockhouse. Some act out scenes of family life;

162

others engage in demonstrations of crafts and skills. Among other activities, they wash clothes, pop corn, whittle, weave, sing, dance, crochet, garden, sew quilts, make cornhusk dolls, churn butter and play old-time games.

After your tour, if you hike a short way up the canal you'll pass the ruins of the Seneca Red Sandstone cutting mill. The Smithsonian Castle was built from these distinctive stones. You'll also see the turning basin where canal boats were manuevered to make the return trip to Georgetown.

Directions: From Baltimore take I-95 south to the Washington Beltway (I-495) and head west to River Road, Exit 39W. Take River Road (Route 190) three miles out to Potomac and turn left on Falls Road (Route 189), which leads directly to Great Falls and the C&O Canal National Historical Park. For Seneca just continue for about 15 minutes on River Road to Riley Lock Road and make a left.

John Poole House, White's Ferry and Seneca Schoolhouse

Medley Historic Triple

In 1793 when John Poole II built a single-room log store with an overhead sleeping loft, at the crossing of two plantation roads, he never imagined a town would grow around his modest establishment. But this enterprising 24-year-old divided part of the 15 acres given to him by his father into lots. Other merchants purchased the lots, set up stores, and formed the nucleus of the town of Poolesville.

The sign over the door of Poolesville's oldest building reads, "General Merchandise, John Poole, Jr." Though the merchandise has changed in the two centuries since John Poole served his customers, hand-crafted items are still for sale. The knit sweaters, colorful quilts, pottery and baskets are mixed with a few authentic reminders of the items sold from 1793 to 1820. You'll see leather hides, leaf tobacco, slabs of bacon and old tools.

Not long after John Poole built his home and business, a lean-to kitchen and second fireplace were added. Between the two huge stone chimneys there is a pent, a rarely seen colonial storage area. Because the stone walls made this one of the only areas of the house not at risk from fires, the family stored their valuables here.

Just outside the kitchen of the **John Poole House** you get a glimpse of the Arboretum; you'll want to explore it before departing. Started in 1976, it features plants indigenous to this part of Maryland before 1850. Plants and herbs are sold at the John Poole Store. In the Herb Garden are annual and perennial culinary herbs, medicinal plants, a dyer's garden and a fragrance garden. An arboretum map and guide helps identify and locate the various specimens.

In addition to the original section of the house, there are frame additions built in 1810 and 1866. The upstairs has an original bedroom and a museum area. In the bedroom is a poplar thistle bed with rope webbing. The mattress is feather ticking, and it is covered with a signed quilt made in 1834 by John Poole II's daughter-in-law, Evalyna W. Hyde.

The museum area has a Civil War collection, much of which was found in and around Poolesville. The town's proximity to Washington made it a major communication link with the capital. By October 15, 1861, roughly 15,000 Union soldiers were camped in the fields around Poolesville. On sale are copies of a town map drawn by a Union soldier on December 29, 1863, to show his parents where he was living. His map shows gun placements, but they are not shown on the walking tour guide of Poolesville. The churches and many of the houses on the 1863 map still stand.

In September 1862, General Lee wanted to capitalize on the Confederate victory at the Second Battle of Bull Run by carrying the war into the north. Lee staged his first large-scale invasion of the north by crossing the Potomac River at White's Ford. After your tour of the John Poole House, open Saturday 10:00 A.M. to 5:00 P.M. and Sunday noon to 5:00 P.M., continue down Route 107 to **White's Ferry**.

At this crossing the *Jubal A. Early*, the only ferry still operating on the Potomac River, journeys back and forth throughout the day. It runs daily 6:00 A.M. to 11:00 P.M., in winter service stops at 8:00 P.M. The fare is $3.50 round-trip, or $2 one-way. The ferry is named for General Jubal Early, who took command of Stonewall Jackson's 13,000-man force after Jackson's death following the Battle of Chancellorsville in May 1863. General Early led his men across the Potomac River just below the ferry landing on July 14, 1864. General Early's was the only Confederate force to come within striking distance of the capital, prompting President Lincoln to have a steamboat standing by on the Potomac in case he needed to evacuate.

In addition to its historical significance the area around White's Ferry is popular with fishermen, canoeists, bicyclers, hikers and picnickers (though there is a $1.50 charge for the use of the picnic tables). You can rent boats here or use the available boat ramps. Fish found include bass, catfish, perch, crappie and carp. For $2 you can get from a Vend-a-Bait machine minnows, crayfish, night crawlers or (!) blood balls. Live bait, tackle and licenses are available at White's Ferry Store, also canoes and bicycles to rent.

When John Poole II built his single-room log store in 1793 he had no idea it would become the nucleus of the town of Poolesville. Nowadays craft items and plants are sold in the store.

Poolesville and White's Ferry are part of the Medley Historic District, one of Maryland's early voting districts, where ballots were cast at Mr. Medley's tavern. In the same area, at 16800 River Road, is the **Seneca Schoolhouse**, the only one-room schoolhouse built of stone in Montgomery County. It is open Sundays noon to 4:00 P.M. from March 15 to December 15. Upton Darby, a miller in Seneca, collected money from his neighbors in 1865 to build it, and the red stones were quarried nearby (see C&O Canal National Historical Park selection).

Inside, the old double desks are still lined up. The boys sat on one side of the room and the girls on the other. In the center is the bench on which the youngsters sat to recite their lessons. Children 6 to 16 attended grades 1 through 7. The desks used by the older students have inkwells; those in the front rows do not. There's a pot-belly stove like the one that warmed the school, but there are no lights. On severely overcast days students were simply dismissed. Classes were taught here from 1866 until 1910 in such subjects as reading, writing, grammar, geography, history, arithmetic, good behavior and orthography. Every Friday afternoon Seneca School had a spelling bee.

A small gift shop sells copies of McGuffy Readers, slates, penny candy that costs 5 cents, cornhusk dolls and a charming children's novel, *Country School Boy*, by Bess Paterson Shipe. Included with the novel is a personal recollection from a former student at Seneca Schoolhouse.

Directions: From Baltimore take I-70 west. At the Route 27 exit, head south. You'll turn left on Route 355 and go just a short way to Route 118 where you continue south to the intersection with Route 28 (Darnestown Road). Turn right on Route 28 and continue west. Take a left fork at Route 107 and continue into Poolesville. Signs will indicate the John Poole House on the right at 19923 Fisher Avenue. For White's Ferry continue west on Route 107. For Seneca Schoolhouse go east on Route 107 to Partnership Road and turn right, which leads to River Road. Turn left on River Road and proceed for just a short distance to the Seneca Schoolhouse on the right at 16800 River Road.

National Capital Trolley Museum

Trolleys Hold the Line

The first trolleys in the nation's capital were horse cars that traversed the city during the tumultuous presidency of Abraham Lincoln. The last were electric streamliners that transported passengers during John F. Kennedy's administration a century later. The era of trolleys in Washington ended on January 28, 1962, but some of the streetcars are still running at the **National Capital Trolley Museum** in Wheaton, Maryland.

The man who saved the cars, transit company vice-president A.E. Savage, literally hid some of the streetcars in the Navy Yard Car House so they wouldn't be junked for scrap. Nostalgia buffs who enjoy riding old No. 766, the car that made the District's last run, can thank Mr. Savage and the volunteers who repair, maintain and operate the cars at this trolley museum.

The museum's roster of equipment includes three cars from Austria and two from Germany. The 1924 gray and white Berlin car was operated during flower festivals in Karlsruhe, Germany. It still looks festive with its red and white parlor curtains and shiny brass fittings. The red, white and black Vienna car has wooden seats and bell-shaped lights. From the U.S. there are cars from New York and Pennsylvania and six from Washington. A car long-time residents of the area may recognize is car No. 1101, Washington's first PCC streamliner, which entered service in 1937 and celebrated its 50th birthday in 1987.

Most of the streetcars are in the car barns and are brought out only for trolley festivals held on the third Sunday of April (or a week later if this is Easter Sunday) and September. Rides are

The National Capital Trolley Museum displays one of the finest collections of American and European antique trolley cars. Rides are available on some of them.

offered on several cars during museum hours, which are 12:00 to 5:00 P.M. on weekends year-round as well as on Memorial Day, July 4 and Labor Day. During July and August the museum is also open from 1:00 to 4:00 P.M. on Wednesday. It's closed December 15 to January 1.

Purchase your ride ticket, at a nominal fee, from the Visitors Center, built to resemble an old-time railroad station. Streetcars leave the station every half-hour. (While waiting, you can check out the model trolley exhibit.) The conductor rings the trolley bell, punches the tickets and reminisces about the days when a person could travel anywhere in Washington by streetcar. These gentle rides are a pleasant respite from today's gridlocked beltway scene.

The trolley museum hosts special programs, antique car exhibits and trolley parades, plus movies and lectures. For details call (301)384-6088.

Directions: From Baltimore take I-95 to the Washington Beltway, I-495, and proceed west to Exit 28 (New Hampshire Avenue). Take New Hampshire Avenue north for 5.4 miles and turn left on Bonifant Road. The museum is at 1313 Bonifant Road in the Northwest Branch Regional Park.

Woodend

Towhees or Vireos, Anyone?

The regional Audubon Naturalist Society, which predates the National Audubon Society, was formed in 1897 to protect the country's bird population. One of its earliest and most influential members, President Theodore Roosevelt, prepared a list for the Society of all the birds he had seen in and around Washington. He also established the Forest Service, five national parks, 51 bird sanctuaries and four game reserves.

Roosevelt would have loved **Woodend**, a 40-acre wildlife sanctuary that serves as headquarters for the Society. Bordering Rock Creek Park in northwest Washington, it is home for roughly 30 species of birds, including towhees, indigo buntings, woodpeckers, red-eyed vireos and yellowthroats. These species are augmented by migratory birds that use Woodend as a resting stop. The Main Trail and Explorer Trail wind through fields, thickets and woods, then pass a stream and pond. If you want to spot the birds and resident mammals (gray squirrels, cottontail rabbits, opposums, raccoons, woodchucks and foxes), tread quietly and slowly. Sometimes you have to stop and watch to discover the birds hidden among the foliage or the shy animals in the underbrush.

Be sure to pick up a nature trail guide that identifies the 22 numbered points of interest along the Main Trail. Woodend is noted for its diverse native and ornamental trees. The gardens that once graced this estate are no longer maintained as such, yet you'll still see year-round blooms. Even in winter you'll spot snowdrops and aconite, also known as wolfsbane or monkshood. In the spring, flowering trees and wildflowers join with garden favorites to tint Woodend with pastel hues. Day lilies abound in summer, but the trails are at their most colorful in the autumn when fallen leaves carpet your path.

Nature is not alone in filling the calendar at Woodend. The members and staff arrange a full schedule of natural history films, lectures, wildlife photography workshops, nature study classes, art exhibits and conservation forums. One of their biggest annual events is the Spring Open House and Plant Sale held in late April. For information on their schedule call (301)652-9188.

These events are held in the Georgian Revival mansion built in the 1920s for Captain and Mrs. Chester Wells. Mrs. Wells wanted her home patterned after her family estate in Australia. The house was designed by John Russell Pope, architect of the National Gallery of Art and the Jefferson Memorial. Mrs. Wells bequeathed her estate to the Audubon Naturalist Society to be preserved as a wildlife sanctuary. The grounds are open daily

dawn to dusk. The mansion is open Monday through Friday from
9:00 A.M. to 5:00 P.M. as well as during spring Sunday open
houses. They have a well-stocked bookshop that specializes in
optical equipment and wildlife art in addition to books on natural
history (they have a second bookshop in Georgetown). The bookshop is open Monday through Friday 10:00 A.M. to 5:00 P.M. and
Sundays from mid-March to mid-April (excepting Easter) from
1:00 to 5:00 P.M.

Directions: From Baltimore take I-95 south to the Washington
Beltway (I-495) and go west to Exit 33 (Connecticut Avenue). Go
south on Connecticut Avenue towards Chevy Chase for ¾ mile.
Turn left on Manor Road and then make a right on Jones Bridge
Road. Go left at the "T" on Jones Mill Road. Woodend entrance
is at 8940 Jones Mill Road on the left.

PRINCE GEORGE'S COUNTY

Belair Mansion and Stables Museum

Good Blood Lines

Most fathers hope the man their daughter marries will provide
an appropriate house; Benjamin Tasker made sure his did. He
supervised (though he did not pay for) the construction of his
daughter and son-in-law's country house, **Belair Mansion.** At
least that is the legend that persists despite historians' efforts to
debunk it. But then the union between 18-year-old Anne Tasker
and 47-year-old Provincial Governor Samuel Ogle was hardly a
tale of youthful exuberance. The match raised eyebrows among
Annapolis society; even in colonial times the disparity in age
was considered excessive.

Samuel Ogle had requested that, upon his death in 1752, Belair
be sold to pay for his son's education. It was not. Benjamin
Tasker, Jr., brother of Anne Ogle, took over the estate. He planted
the handsome avenue of tulip trees that still graces the property.
Other aspects of this early concern for landscaping can be appreciated by modern visitors as well. The grounds of Belair contain a number of horticultural state champions, among them
Maryland's largest cucumber tree (*Magnolis acuminata*). A brochure available at the estate will help you identify it and other
tree specimens on the grounds.

Visitors to Belair Mansion should not expect to see a fully
restored and furnished colonial estate. This five-part Georgian
mansion is noted for its historical links, not for its current con-

dition. Three early Maryland governors owned this property, but only the architectural features of their house remain to impress today's guests. The house will need a complete face-lift before it looks as it did in its heyday. Free house tours are given on the second Sunday of each month from 2:00 to 4:00 P.M. and on Wednesdays from 10:00 A.M. to 1:00 P.M.

Maryland's first families are not the only ones to have roots at Belair; the blood lines of some of horse racing's most valuable horses can also be traced to Belair. The stables are called the Cradle of American Racing, and you can retrace 200 years of racing history during your free tour. Samuel Ogle returned from his honeymoon in England with two of the most famous horses of his day—Spark and Queen Mab. The stallion, Spark, had been given to Charles Calvert, fifth Lord Baltimore, by Frederick, Prince of Wales and father of George III. Calvert in turn gave the stallion to Ogle, who had also acquired the filly Queen Mab.

Belair's second owner, like its first, was governor of Maryland. Benjamin Tasker, Jr. was also interested in acquiring horse flesh, and he imported the mare Selima, from England. A later owner of Belair, William Woodward, enshrined the mare's name in racing history by establishing the Selima Stakes. Woodward also added a plaque to the stable wall of his country home honoring Selima and her famous offspring, Selim.

During the Woodward era, there were three great horses stabled at Belair—Gallant Fox, Omaha and Nashua. The first two won the Triple Crown, and Nashua collected over a million dollars in prize money, making him the greatest money winner of his day.

Belair Stables Museum exhibits the white and red silks of the Belair Stables. The colors had been used by the Marquis of Zetland in England as early as 1763. The silks are still used by descendants of William Woodward. You can explore the Belair Stables Museum Sundays from 1:00 to 4:00 P.M. during May, June, September and October.

While in the Bowie area, if time permits, stop at scenic Allan Pond. A paved walkway extends along the pond edge to a hilltop gazebo. Swallows glide through the wooden gazebo while ducks and geese float serenely on the pond. In the spring and fall migratory birds frequently rest at the pond. Youngsters can fish from the pond banks, and during the summer, canoes and rowboats can be rented.

Directions: From Baltimore take Route 3 south to the intersection with Route 450 in Bowie. Turn right on Route 450 and continue to Bowie High School. Make a left on Belair Drive. Continue for 8/10 of a mile. The stables are on the left. Turn right on Tulip Drive for Belair Mansion, which will be on your left at 12207 Tulip Grove Drive. Allan Pond is south off Route 197 just past the Route 50 overpass. Turn right off Route 197 at Northview Drive.

Beltsville Agricultural Research Center

Uncle Sam as Jolly Green Giant

Crop monitoring via satellite, cloning apple trees and developing machine-harvestable fruits are just a few of the 3,000 ongoing projects that keep employees busy at the **Beltsville Agricultural Research Center**.

You can arrange a guided tour of the 7,250-acre facility by calling (301)344-2483. This is a spot where you need a knowledgeable guide, and the background imparted by the tour leaders is fascinating. For instance, it is hard to get excited about the concrete cattle feed lot until the guide begins his story about experiments on alternative livestock diets. Visitors are amazed to learn that the cattle here once ate newspapers and phone directories, but couldn't tolerate the comics or yellow pages. The dye was bad for them. This paper feed was part of a test developed to see if cattle could be fed without competing with people for scarce food crops. And why a concrete feed lot? By being crowded onto this small area the cattle are unable to exercise; thus the meat is more tender.

Then there are the pigs. Considered the smartest animals on the farm, they are also invaluable for medical research because they metabolize food as humans do. The sow (mother pig) is not to be underestimated. She will fiercely defend her young even from employees she recognizes.

If you want to see the animals at their best, plan a spring visit when lambs, calves and piglets gambol in the Beltsville fields and paddocks. This is not a petting farm, however. One of the firm rules at Beltsville is that visitors should never touch the animals; they are all under preventive quarantine. That doesn't mean they are sick—just the opposite. Animals often contract illnesses from humans. These are disease-free and the staff would like to keep them that way.

Cute newborns and longtime residents are only part of the picture at this agricultural research center, the largest such facility in the world. During the summer months, employees conduct plant research in the extensive fields. For more than 30 years they have been studying turf grasses. Horticultural collections include blueberries, strawberries, thornless blackberries and dwarf fruit trees. You'll also see fields of soybeans, alfalfa, sunflowers and day lilies.

Beltsville also has a large greenhouse area divided into four sections: fruits and vegetables, ornamental flowers and shrubs, major economic crops and an area devoted to testing pesticides. Anyone interested in agricultural research can use the National Agricultural Library, which contains 1.7 million volumes. The research center's slogan is Agriculture Makes Tomorrow Better. At Beltsville they keep working to realize that goal.

Tours of the facility take 1½ hours and are given between 8:00 A.M. and 4:00 P.M. Monday through Friday.

Directions: From Baltimore take I-95 south to Exit 29 (Powder Mill Road, Route 212). Go east on Powder Mill Road. You will enter the grounds of the Beltsville Agricultural Research Center after you cross U.S. 1, about 2.5 miles. The Visitors Center will be on your left.

College Park Airport Museum

The Cradle of American Aviation

If you've been to the National Air and Space Museum in Washington, D.C., and long for the early days of flying, visit the **College Park Airport Museum** at the oldest continuously operated airport in the world.

After making the first motor-driven, heavier-than-air flight on December 17, 1903, Orville and Wilbur Wright were anxious to sell their flying machine to the U.S. Army. They brought their plane to Fort Myer, Virginia, for test flights. The Wright plane was well built, but many problems still needed to be worked out. This became evident during one of the tests at Fort Myer when the plane crashed and Orville broke his thigh (his passenger, Lt. Thomas E. Selfridge, died, becoming the first military aviation fatality). But the Army decided to accept the Wright plane anyway and on August 2, 1909, it became Signal Corps Airplane #1, on the condition that the Wrights would instruct two officers in the art of flying.

In October of that year the Army moved their operations to a field near the Maryland Agricultural College in College Park, and Wilbur began the training of the two Army officers. From the earliest days, a succession of dramatic aviation firsts occurred at the College Park Airfield. The first flights by Army and Navy officers and the first flight in the U.S. with a woman passenger kept College Park in the news. After Army specifications for the Wright plane had been met and the officers taught to fly, a minor accident damaged the machine. It was crated and sent to Fort Sam Houston, Texas. Money had not yet been appropriated by Congress for aviation, so Army activities at College Park's Airfield temporarily came to a halt with the departure of Signal Corps Airplane #1. However, civilian aviators have always kept the airfield busy, and it is now recognized as the world's oldest

172

continuously operated airport, the "Cradle of American Aviation."

One of the civilians working at College Park was Rexford Smith, who perfected one of the earliest biplanes. A private firm, National Aviation Company, began offering instruction at College Park on Wright, Curtiss and Bleriot airplanes. With the civilian aviation market expanding, the government finally appropriated money for aviation and in June 1911 a Signal Corps aviation school was established at College Park.

Records were again being made at the airport. It was here the first bomb-dropping devices were tried, the first mile-high flight was flown, and the first machine guns were fired from an airplane. This "aerodrome" was also the starting point for the first "long cross-country flight," from College Park, Maryland, to Frederick, Maryland. The two-man craft made it to Frederick all right, but the pilots couldn't find their way back; when they stopped to ask directions the plane stalled on take-off. The red-faced pilots ended up returning by train!

The U.S. Post Office air mail flights that began in 1918 had their share of problems, too. Although official mail flights began at College Park, test flights were carried out by the Army at Potomac Park in Washington. For the first delivery on May 15, 1918, which embarked from Potomac Park, President Wilson was watching. . .and watching! When the pilot started his takeoff, the plane wouldn't go. Officials paced while mechanics checked out the engine for 30 minutes. Someone finally thought to check the fuel tanks—they were empty. This was far from the only hitch; once under way the pilot, perhaps rattled by his rocky start, flew southeast instead of north to Philadelphia. He had followed the wrong railroad tracks. Stopping in Waldorf, Maryland, to ask directions, he broke the propeller during his landing. The 140 pounds of air mail was eventually delivered to Philadelphia by truck.

Another series of aviation experiments began at the airport in 1920, but these involved vertical aviation. The father and son team of Emile and Henry Berlin began testing a machine that could rise vertically. After several years of testing and experiments, in 1924 the machine made what many consider the first successful controlled flights by a helicopter. The Berliner helicopter is currently on exhibit at the Paul E. Garber Facility (see selection).

Yet another government agency became active at College Park between 1927 and 1935. Those were the years the Bureau of Standards ran experiments on "blind," or instrument, landings. This led to the development of the first radio navigational gear and all blind landing equipment that today is standard equipment.

At the College Park Airport Museum you'll see photo displays on these and other aviation firsts, aviation equipment, aviation memorabilia from the earliest flying years, field aviation films and a collection of early air mail items and photographs. There is no charge to visit this museum open Friday, Saturday and Sunday from noon to 4:00 P.M.

You may want to plan lunch at the adjacent 94th Aero Squadron Restaurant, which looks like a French farm used by American forces during World War I. Adding to the atmosphere are the tables that overlook the action on the still-active runways at College Park Airport. Some tables even have hook-ups so you can listen to the cockpit conversations.

Directions: From Baltimore take Route 295, the Baltimore-Washington Parkway, to Greenbelt Road. Take Greenbelt Road toward College Park, then make a left on Kenilworth Avenue. Head south on Kenilworth to the intersection with Calvert Road. Make a right turn onto Calvert Road and then turn right immediately before the railroad tracks on Cpl. Frank Scott Drive for the College Park Airport Museum. The entrance for the 94th Aero Squadron is also off Calvert Road just before the museum entrance.

Cosca Regional Park and Cedarville State Forest

Au Naturel

A garden for butterflies, paddleboats on a quiet lake, a tram train, innovative play equipment plus hands-on science games at the Nature Center make the Louise F. **Cosca Regional Park** a many-optioned outing.

The summer of '86 saw the addition of the Prince George's County Butterfly Garden, a quarter-acre plot filled with flowers favored by indigenous butterflies. Bright red zinnias, yellow black-eyed Susans and purple flowering butterfly bushes are among the 35 varieties that attract an almost equal number of butterflies. According to the park naturalist, the best time to spot these colorful flutterbys is during July and August in the heat of the day, between 10:00 A.M. and 3:00 P.M.

You'll also want to explore the Clearwater Nature Center's Herb Garden. This 48- by 15-foot garden is not ornamental but rather a collection of "edible wild plants." Like those in the nearby Sensory Garden, many of the herbs and wildflowers are highly aromatic. Although the plants are billed as edible, it is never advisable to taste a leaf or berry unless you are on a guided nature walk. The herb garden is right behind the Nature Center, which is open Tuesday through Saturday from 9:00 A.M. to 4:00 P.M. and

174

Sunday 11:00 A.M. to 4:00 P.M. (except November through March, when it is closed on both Sunday and Monday). Naturalists are available to answer questions about both the Butterfly Garden and the Herb Garden.

The naturalists also schedule guided walks through the Suitland Bog. A cool-climate bog located at the southern limit of its range, this bog is a rare ecosystem. Its fragile environment is now protected by a high fence and can only be observed under the watchful eye of the naturalists. But it is only with the help of a trained specialist that the unique carnivorous plants can be spotted. The best time to see the bog is in the late spring and early summer; for dates of guided walks call ahead, (301)297-4575, or stop at the Clearwater Nature Center and pick up a schedule of activities. The Nature Center is well worth a visit, particularly for families with elementary-age children. The center has a number of live specimens—a large tank in the middle of the room has several varieties of fish and turtles. There is also a rabbit, several snakes and some incredibly huge cockroaches.

The exhibit hall has a number of participatory activities. Children can reconstruct the skeleton of a white-tailed deer, crawl through the mole tunnel, dial-a-bird, listen to distinctive insect calls, dig through the trash treasure in the history room and play matching games with animals and their fur and habitats.

Science is so much fun at the Clearwater Nature Center that youngsters need no additional incentive, but Cosca also has a variety of innovative play equipment. On the hillside overlooking Lake Louise there is a perfect area to play cowboys and Indians. An outline of a fort has wagons, platforms, cannons and telescopes. Nearby are the colorful teepees of an Indian village.

During the summer months and on spring and fall weekends you can rent rowboats and paddleboats or take a 15-minute train ride around the park. There are hiking and riding trails (no stables), a campground, picnic areas, tennis courts and athletic fields. You can even fish in the 15-acre lake, but a license is required for those over 16. The lake is stocked with bass, bluegill and catfish.

There is no charge for Prince George's and Montgomery County residents, but others pay a parking fee from Memorial Day through Labor Day.

If the fish aren't biting at Lake Louise you can head over to **Cedarville State Forest,** just about 15 minutes from Cosca. Here you'll find a stocked four-acre pond as well as five trails, campgrounds, a picnic area and playground. The shortest trail, just two miles, is one of the most interesting because it passes through the headwaters of the Zekiah Swamp, Maryland's largest freshwater swamp. John Wilkes Booth fled through this swamp in April 1864, after assassinating Lincoln. The three-mile, white-blazed Birdwatcher's Trail follows Wolf Den Branch Creek. Little has changed along this trail since the days when the Piscataway Indians made their winter camp here.

If you want to recapture bygone days, try your skill with a bow and arrow during dove season (mid-October to February). One hundred acres at Cedarville are open on Wednesday and Saturday for dove hunting. In addition to the bow and arrow, hunters can use shotguns and muzzle-loading black-powder rifles. A Maryland hunting license is required.

Directions: From Baltimore take I-95 south to Washington Beltway and continue south on I-95 toward Andrews Air Force Base. At Exit 7A (Route 5, Branch Avenue) head south toward Waldorf. Go straight for several miles and turn right onto Route 223, Woodyard Road. At the second light, turn left onto Brandywine Road, Route 381. Go about 1½ miles on Route 381 and then make a right turn onto Thrift Road. Go two miles (following the signs) to the Clearwater Nature Center. For Cedarville State Forest take Route 5 to Route 301 and go south on Route 301 to Cedarville Road and turn left. It is just three miles east of the intersection of Route 301 and Route 5, roughly 55 miles south of Baltimore.

Fort Washington

On the Ramparts

In 1794 George Washington selected this bluff overlooking the Potomac River as the site of the first fort to be built to protect the country's new capital. Fort Warburton, as it was called, was unheroically destroyed only five years after its completion, during the War of 1812. Twelve years later its replacement, the present Fort Washington, began a much longer life as capital defender and military post.

The destruction of Fort Warburton becomes even more ignoble when you learn that no shots were fired at an enemy. So how did it meet its fate? That's what the army asked fort commander Captain Samuel Dyson before he was stripped of his commission. Dyson's orders were to destroy the fort if it came under land attack from British troops during the War of 1812. The United States government did not want Fort Warburton to fall into enemy hands. But it was from the Potomac River that the threat was posed on August 27, 1814. A British fleet of seven ships under Captain Gordon had with great difficulty—they ran aground 22 times—made its way up the Potomac. Positioned off Fort Warburton, the ships opened fire. Dyson panicked and blew up his own powder magazine, then abandoned the fort. It was not America's finest hour.

The British threat prompted quick action, and barely 12 days after the fort was destroyed Secretary of War James Monroe commissioned Major Pierre L'Enfant, architect of the nation's capital, to rebuild it. The French engineer ordered 200,000 bricks and a large quantity of stone and lumber. But work proceeded slowly, so slowly that after the Treaty of Ghent ending the war was signed on February 13, 1815, the need for defense was tempered by the desire for economy.

L'Enfant was insulted when requested to submit reports on the work in progress and his plans for the fort's construction. He simply ignored the request. Work was then halted, and he was eventually dismissed. On September 6, 1815, Lt. Col. Walker K. Armistead took over. When Fort Washington, as the new fort was called, was finally completed on October 2, 1824, the total cost was more than $426,000.

Little has changed since 1824, as you will see when you cross the drawbridge over the dry moat and enter the walled fort. From the sally port entrance there is a panoramic view of the construction design, which incorporates three levels of defensive positions. The lowest level is the V-shaped water battery, positioned 60 feet below the main fortifications. This battery was started under L'Enfant's direction. Next are the casemate positions, bombproof gun sites from which defending soldiers could fire upon ships on the Potomac. From the high ramparts two half-bastions commanded the river above and below the fort.

Uniformed guides will explain the advantages and disadvantages of these three-gun positions. On Sunday afternoons costumed volunteers re-create military life of the mid-1800s. The men will show you around the offices and soliders' barracks. On selected occasions a cannon is fired on the parade ground. To obtain more background on the fort, stop at the Visitor Center, located in the historic Commanding Officer's House.

A different perspective is gained by touring Fort Washington during the Torchlight Tattoo ceremonies. These are presented several times each summer on Saturday evenings (call (301)763-4600 for schedule and information). You'll be briefed before the ceremony begins; then the clock is turned back to the tense Civil War days. You will be treated as visiting Washingtonians anxious about southern attacks on the capital. In January 1861, Fort Washington, the sole fort protecting Washington, was manned by only 40 marines. By February units of the Regular Army and Militia took over. When Fort Foote was built on the Maryland side of the Potomac in 1864, the military significance of Fort Washington was eliminated. The masonry fort was closed in 1872, but the reservation was an active military post until 1945.

Fort Washington is open daily year-round from 8:30 A.M. to 5:00 P.M. Picknicking is encouraged.

Directions: From Baltimore take I-95 south to the Washington Beltway and proceed south (still on I-95) to Exit 3A (Route 210, Indian Head Highway). Take Indian Head Highway south for four miles to Fort Washington Road. Turn right and go three miles to the fort.

Montpelier Cultural Arts Center and Mansion

Elegant Quakers

The **Montpelier Cultural Arts Center** has something in common with the mythical phoenix, having arisen from the ashes of a 1976 fire that destroyed the old barn on the Montpelier estate previously earmarked for the arts center. The blaze reduced all but the cylindrical glazed-block silo to rubble.

A state grant and hard work salvaged the project, and the Montpelier Cultural Arts Center opened in August 1979. Artists and craftsmen display their work in the center's three galleries, and anywhere from 20 to 30 artists rent studios. Painters, sculptors, printmakers, photographers, cabinetmakers, basketweavers and ceramists all work and display at Montpelier. Classes, workshops and performances are regularly scheduled; for information call (301)953-1993. Visitors are welcome to drop in between 10:00 A.M. and 5:00 P.M. daily, except holidays.

If you visit on Sunday from noon to 4:00 P.M., you can include a tour of the 18th-century Montpelier Mansion, which was built by Thomas and Ann Snowdon around 1783. When Thomas and Ann married in 1774, their combined wealth was so great that they were forbidden to attend Quaker services until they divested themselves of a portion of their bounty. They sold 100 slaves to satisfy the Quaker requirements.

At Montpelier you will see indications of the Snowdon wealth in the gracious and lavish Georgian architecture and indications of their religious commitment in the interior and exterior design. The door design suggests a wooden cross, with the bottom panels representing Bible pages.

The religious motif is continued in the garden, where the boxwood is shaped like a cross. The boxwood allée, or path, leads to the only surviving 18th-century belvedere, or summer house, in Maryland. Indeed, it is one of the few to survive from this early period in all America.

Directions: From the Washington Beltway take Exit 22, the Baltimore-Washington Parkway, to the Laurel exit, Route 197. Proceed north toward Laurel for a short distance to the Montpelier Shopping Center on your right. There will be a light and you will turn left on Muirkirk Road and then right into the parking lot for the Montpelier Cultural Arts Center and the Montpelier Mansion.

NASA's Goddard Visitor Center and Museum

Neighborly NASA

As a Trivial Pursuit question it would be a guaranteed puzzler: when, where and who launched the first successful rocket? The answer: March 16, 1926, in Auburn, Massachusetts, by Robert Hutchings Goddard. The flight of Goddard's liquid fuel rocket, though only a brief 2½ seconds, prepared the way for man's ventures into space.

You'll see a full-scale sculpture of Dr. Goddard and his rocket as you enter **NASA's Goddard Visitor Center** in Greenbelt. The facility named in honor of the Father of Modern Rocketry was established by the National Aeronautics and Space Administration. As you would expect from a space-age agency, the technology at the Visitor Center is state-of-the-art, with some refreshingly humorous exceptions. Families will want to bring a camera to get a shot of young space enthusiasts with their heads stuck in a space-suit cutout, more carnival than Canaveral.

Push-button audio-visual exhibits along with some incredible photography will answer questions such as: How do we explore space? Why do we need a space station? How can life be sustained on long space trips? The answer to the latter is by an EcoSphere, such as one exhibited here, whose sealed environment contains algae, shrimp, bacteria and sea water.

Space shuttles, we learn, carry both astronauts and huge payloads into space. But they also transport small Get Away Specials (GAS). You'll see examples of these self-contained experiments sealed in 2½ to 5 cubic feet metal containers. Some future space mission may carry your name into space if you sign one of the guest books.

Two exciting visual exhibits are virtually on top of each other. One is the three mock-up telescopes offering three views of planets, gallaxies and star clusters. The first glimpse of each is a naked-eye view, the second is of an earth-based telescope, while the third is what each would look like through the Hubble Space Telescope. A model of the space telescope is on display, but you should keep in mind that the real telescope is "roughly the size of a Greyhound bus," to quote a staff person at the Visitor Center orientation desk.

On a wraparound screen above the telescopes, a continuous visual presentation explores the earth, sun and stars through a series of stunning photographs. The Visitor Center also runs a

Among numerous mind-expanding exhibits at NASA's Visitor Center is a sculpture of the liquid fuel rocket and its inventor who prepared the way for man's ventures into space.

series of movies and short subjects on the hour and half-hour about space and NASA's ever-increasing technology.

Surrounding the Visitor Center are numerous sounding rockets, used in direct research measurement. NASA annually launches roughly 50 sounding rockets with payloads weighing from 12 to 2,500 pounds. There are Nike-Tomahawk sounding rockets, the earliest Iris, the large Javelin and the two-stage Nike-Black Brant. You'll also see a full-scale model of an Apollo space craft and an early Delta Launch Vehicle.

If you want to see rockets launched, stop by on the first and third Sunday of each month at 1:00 P.M., when model rockets are fired from the hilltop behind the Goddard Visitor Center. Another special program is the weekly grounds tour given on Thursday at 2:00 P.M. No advance reservation is required; just arrive at the Visitor Center before 2:00 P.M. The hour-long tour takes visitors to the Control Center, Building 14, the computer and communication nerve center for NASA's satellites.

Goddard Visitor Center is open at no charge Wednesday through Sunday from 10:00 A.M. to 4:00 P.M.

Directions: From the Washington Beltway take Exit 22 (well-marked for NASA/Goddard). Bear to the right for Greenbelt Road. Head down Greenbelt Road past the main entrance to Goddard Space Flight Facility; signs will indicate route for Visitor Center. Turn left on Conservation Road and then left again onto the Goddard grounds and into the parking lot for the Visitor Center.

National Colonial Farm

Harvesting Your Roots

In the early days of television there was a program called *You Are There* that put the viewer into pivotal moments in history. You get a similar sense of being part of America's continuum when you visit the **National Colonial Farm** in Accokeek.

Imagine standing along the farm's Potomac River bank in March 1634, watching the first Maryland settlers sail past on the *Dove*. Governor Leonard Calvert was on his way to meet the "Emperor of the Piscataway" to obtain his "permission" to settle in Maryland. This exchange marked the beginning of European settlement and the beginning of the end for the Piscataway tribe.

Move the clock forward to March 1799, the last year of George Washington's life. If you were standing on this farm looking through powerful field glasses, you might spot George relaxing on the porch of Mount Vernon. What is amazing is that the farm Washington would have seen across the river from his home has remained unchanged through all the subsequent years. What he saw then and what you see today is an 18th-century freeholder's farm.

Colonially garbed workers till the fields and prepare food in the rustic out-kitchen using handmade tools and implements. Many of the kitchen tools are carved from gourds that, like the ingredients for the meals, are grown at the farm. A few steps away from the kitchen is the Rosamonde Biere Herb Garden. Be sure to get a guided tour of this re-created kitchen garden, circa 1750–75. Like their colonial counterparts, the National Colonial Farm staff have experimented with the herbs. Both they and their forebears suffered rashes and allergies before discovering which plants served medicinal and which served culinary purposes.

Escorted walks give you a chance to learn about the uses of the various herbs. You'll also have the opportunity to smell, taste and touch these plants, something you should never do on your own because many plants have poisonous properties. More than 50 herbs are grown here, and the guide will recount the legends and lore associated with many of them. If you want to try some, stop at the Herb Shop where they sell dried herbs and herbal products.

The fields at this farm are planted, tended and harvested as they would have been during colonial days. One departure from bygone days is that some animals, once allowed to roam, are now penned. Tobacco was the cash crop but corn and wheat were, and are, also planted. An orchard, like the one you'll see, provided fruit for wine and juice (the colonists did not drink the water).

If time permits, take the farm's nature trail that leads through the woods along the Potomac shore. You'll see Mount Vernon across the river. Walking this trail is indeed walking back into history. Archeologists have found reminders of five prehistoric groups who criss-crossed this land. The Piscataway Indians settled here in a town Captain John Smith called Moyaone.

You can explore the National Colonial Farm Tuesday through Sunday from 10:00 A.M. to 5:00 P.M. A nominal admission is charged. The farm frequently hosts special weekend craft and cooking demonstrations.

Directions: From Baltimore take I-95 south to the Washington Beltway and proceed south (still on I-95) to Maryland Exit 3, Indian Head Highway. Go south on Indian Head Highway for ten miles. At the light for Bryan Point Road turn right and proceed four miles to the road's end for the National Colonial Farm.

National Colonial Farm Museum in Accokeek, across from Mount Vernon, provides settings for exhibits and demonstrations of women's and men's work on 18th century Tidewater farms.

Oxon Hill Farm

Your Kids Will Love These Kids
and Piglets, Too

The bib overalls and long cotton work dresses worn by the staff of **Oxon Hill Farm** help establish a late 1890s time frame. The farming methods they use also reflect that era. This living-history farm encourages both young and old to find out more about America's rural past by looking, touching and doing.

Visitors help with the milking, if they want. Youngsters are often amazed when they discover that milk comes from cows, not cartons. Of course, this milk is not pasteurized and is fed only to the pigs.

And speaking of pigs, they are the brains of the barnyard. Those in residence at Oxon Hill have learned to turn on the water spigot to get a drink. You won't find the cows or goats doing that. Spring is the best time to see the young animals, although family planning is not foolproof on the farm, and you will see some kids and piglets at other times. Traditionally the sheep get a haircut each May. Farm visitors just watch this tricky maneuver. The sheep look naked without their winter coats.

While the farm animals are of greatest interest to young visitors, they can learn a lot about the food they eat by examining the well-marked rows of vegetables. Youngsters can play "I spy" as they spot ripening tomatoes, squash, eggplants, peppers, peas and beans on the healthy plants. Another reason excursions to Oxon Hill are so popular with young visitors is that on weekends they often provide wagon rides and youngsters can get on one of the good-natured horses.

As with any operating farm, there is something happening at Oxon Hill year-round. The sorghum cane-cutting in the fall is particularly interesting to watch. Once cut, the cane is stripped and mashed, then the runoff is boiled to make sweet syrup. Winter, the slowest time of year, is when tools are repaired and fences mended. There are many special programs at the farm, including square dancing. To get up-to-date information on their schedule, call (301)839-1176. There is no charge to visit Oxon Hill Farm, which is open daily 8:30 A.M. to 5:00 P.M.

Directions: From Baltimore take I-95 south to the Washington Beltway, I-95/495. Take the beltway (I-95) south to Exit 3A, Indian Head Highway south. From Exit 3A, bear right immediately onto Oxon Hill Road and right again after about 100 yards onto the farm road.

Patuxent River Park and Merkle Wildlife Refuge

Walk on the Wild Side

Tucked out of the way in Prince Georges County's rolling farm country is Jug Bay Natural Area's 2,000 acres of undeveloped wilderness. This is just one of 11 limited-use areas that comprise **Patuxent River Park**. The park was established to allow visitation and use of the river without disturbing the natural environment. To achieve this objective, special-use permits for activities like hunting and fishing are issued, and advance reservations are necessary for many planned activities (call (301)627-6074). The park, however, is always open to first-time visitors who wish to discover the diverse activities and appeal of this marvelous natural area.

Nature study and environmental education take place in an outdoor classroom, the Black Walnut Creek Area, under the learned eye of a park naturalist. Boardwalks allow hikers to cross the marshy wetlands as well as penetrate the surrounding forest. The free 45-minute guided hikes must be pre-arranged.

Not everyone comes empty handed to the wilderness. Bird watchers never visit without their binoculars; and camera-laden photographers appreciate the marshland blind at the river's edge, a vantage point for nature shots.

For those who want to get out on the river there are 50-minute pontoon ecology tours. The pontoon program runs from mid-April to mid-October. Trips highlight various aspects of the ecology; one focuses on aquatic life while another is designed for bird watchers. The Possum and Muskrat trips are normally scheduled for groups, but families can often be added to pre-existing parties. Children must be over 13 for these tours.

A less structured way to see the river is by renting a canoe and exploring Mattaponi Creek and the Jug Bay area (do call ahead and check on availability). There are also scheduled downriver canoe trips that give you a chance to see the river's transition from woodland stream to tidal wetlands.

Other recreational options at Patuxent Park include eight miles of horseback riding trails (though there are no horses for hire), two fishing areas, six miles of hiking trails, two boat ramps, a primitive campsite for backpackers and a group campsite.

The river has historical as well as ecological significance. It has contributed to the social history of Prince Georges County for more than 300 years. The park's Patuxent Village shows what it was like to live along the river a hundred years ago. You'll see a rough-hewn log cabin. With old tools, park naturalists demonstrate pioneer skills, scoring the logs with a broad ax and finishing them with the adze. Patuxent Village contains a smoke-house, hunting and trapping shed, and a packing house with a tobacco prise. (See Tobacco Prise selection.)

Those interested in old tools should be sure to pre-arrange a visit to the W. Henry Duvall Memorial Tool Collection, which is open on Sunday afternoons from 1:00 to 4:00 P.M. Mr. Duvall collected more than 1,200 antique tools and farm implements; obviously the two buildings at Patuxent can only exhibit a small portion of them. Tools of the trade surround a carpenter's work-bench, and cobblers' and wheelwrights' tools are also displayed. The cumbersome implements of a country dentist illustrate just how far we've progressed in that field. One entire building is devoted to agricultural tools.

Your visit to Patuxent Park should be combined with a stop at the nearby **Merkle Wildlife Refuge**, where a Visitors Center and observation deck have recently been added. Merkle is best visited during the spring and autumn migratory seasons. If your timing is right, you will see the fields crowded with visiting Canada geese. Birds of prey and a wide variety of waterfowl stop here on their north-south journeys. Unlike the eastern shore wild-life refuges, Merkle is close enough to allow visiting in the early morning before the birds begin their day's foraging or at dusk when they return.

Directions: From Baltimore take Route 3 and Route 301 south to Upper Marlboro. Four miles south of Route 4 make a left turn on Croom Road (Route 382), and follow to Croom Airport Road where you turn left (there will be a sign for Patuxent River Park). For Merkle, continue on down Croom Road to St. Thomas Church Road and turn left. Follow St. Thomas Church Road for 2.8 miles to Merkle Wildlife Refuge sign and turn right.

Paul E. Garber Facility

The Right Stuff

Aircraft conservators responsible for taking old planes apart prior to restoration at the Smithsonian's **Paul E. Garber Facility** have discovered some unusual messages from the past.

Staffers working on the Enola Gay, the B-29 that dropped the uranium bomb on Hiroshima, found one of the three original arming plugs behind a piece of heavy equipment. In a Chance-Vought F4U Corsair, the U.S. Navy carrier–based fighter plane that first exceeded 400 mph, a conservator was dismantling the engine when he found a faded scrap—probably placed there by a fun-loving crew chief during a 1940s maintenance check. It read: "What in the hell are you looking for in here, you silly. . .?"

At the Paul Garber Facility you can readily see what it is they're looking for in these old planes—the blueprints of past designs. In the five buildings at Silver Hill that are open to the public, the Smithsonian has roughly 140 aircraft on display, as compared with 75 at the Mall museum in downtown Washington. The remainder of the 322 aircraft in the collection are on loan, in storage or undergoing restoration. In an average year two or three aircraft are restored, each requiring between 5,000 and 13,000 manhours of labor.

Touring the Garber warehouses gives you an inside look at the world of aviation. A typical tour group of 15 to 30 will consist mainly of pilots or aviation buffs. The conversation tends to sound like Hollywood outtakes with talk of "augering in," the "outside of the envelope" and "hangar queens." No two tours are exactly alike because the docents tailor the 2½- to 3-hour tours to the participants.

Grown men become enthusiastic youngsters as they crowd around vintage biplanes and one-of-a-kind experimental models. A frequently asked question is "Can these planes fly?" Many can, but none do. Once the Smithsonian acquires a plane it is grounded to prevent additional damage.

As you tour the workshop you'll see planes still unrestored and wonder how they return what in some cases is boxed rubble to mint condition. Providently, aviation developed simultaneously with photography, and there was always someone with a camera to rush out to the field when a barnstorming show came to town. Thus there is excellent photo documentation of even the earliest aircraft. All restorers need is one small piece clearly visible in a photo and the remainder can be drawn to scale. Another factor that helps restorers is that planes can be bisected with one side balancing the other, so if the parts on one side survive, the other can be duplicated.

At the Smithsonian the planes are restored exactly as they were; if the insignia had been painted on with a brush, a brush will be used, not a spray gun. On the Bellanca CF every screwhead on the wooden section has the slots lined up just as they once were. Such a lineup enabled the pilots to tell when a screw was loose. If restorers cannot locate an original part, it is made to match, then carefully labeled to indicate that it is not authentic. Oldtimers have come through the Garber Facility and commented that the planes here look better than the originals.

In addition to learning a good bit of aviation history, you'll discover why the early pilots wore flowing white scarves, why the Messerschmitt killed more friends than foes, what one airplane was on the military inventory the day WWII started and the day it ended, and why German fighter pilots had an edge over the WWII Lightning.

The Paul E. Garber Facility gives wings to Hemingway's words: "You love a lot of things if you live around them, but there isn't any woman ... or any horse ... that is as lovely as a great airplane."

After a visit you may agree with the Ernest Hemingway quote prominently displayed over a desk in the reception area, "You love a lot of things if you live around them, but there isn't any woman and there isn't any horse . . . that is as lovely as a great airplane."

To arrange a visit call (202)357-1400 weekdays between 9:00 A.M. and 5:00 P.M. Or write the Tour Scheduler, NASM, Smithsonian Institution, Washington, D.C. 20560. Free tours are given Monday through Friday at 10:00 A.M. and on weekends at 10:00 A.M. and 1:00 P.M. Wear comfortable walking shoes and note that the cavernous warehouses have neither heat nor air-conditioning.

Directions: From Baltimore take I-95 south to the Washington Beltway (I-495/95) and go south on I-95 to Exit 7B (Branch Avenue, Route 5, Silver Hill). After exiting make a left on Auth Road and proceed one block to the traffic light at the junction with Route 5. Make a right and follow Route 5 north for one mile to St. Barnabas Road, Route 414. Make a right on St. Barnabas and go ½ mile to the Paul Garber Facility on the right directly across the Silver Hill Road intersection.

The Surratt House

Marriage Parlor Turned Rebel Spy Nest

Solemnly the wedding party walks beneath the soldiers' arch of bayoneted rifles. The groom leads, proudly wearing the uniform of the 42nd Virginia Volunteer Infantry. The bride follows, her hooped skirt swaying as she glides beneath the guns. The time is June 1861 and the first real battle of the Civil War is still a month away.

The parents of the bride invite one and all to a Victorian Wedding at the **Surratt House** in Clinton. This yearly June event is so realistic you'll hear the crowd whisper, "Are they really getting married?" A well-brought-up visitor once brought a present. Customarily at the Surratt House it's guests who are given presents—silk rosebud favors for the ladies.

Unlike most historical re-enactments, this one lets the audience partake of the food. Wedding feasts in the 1860s were not, alas, as lavish as in later eras. You'll be served punch, nuts, mints and a piece of the cake. The cake is prepared in a biscuit pan according to a 19th-century recipe that belonged to a Mississippi woman who earned spending money by baking cakes. Guests at the wedding are given the recipe along with a serving.

Unfortunately this happy mood is not ordinarily associated with the mid-Victorian home of Mary Surratt. It has a tragic history. Although the extent to which Mrs. Surratt was involved in the criminal conspiracy to assassinate Lincoln is still debated, it was sufficient for the government to execute her, the first of her sex to suffer that fate at the hands of the federal government.

Mary Surratt was widowed in 1862, ten years after her husband, John Surratt, built a house and tavern in Clinton. From the beginning the tavern served as a gathering spot for the community. As the country became ever more bitterly divided, Southern dissidents gathered here to repudiate Maryland's Northern alignment. When John Jr. left college to help his widowed mother run the family business, he quickly fell in with Confederate sympathizers and became a party to a scheme to kidnap President Abraham Lincoln.

The tavern also became a safe house for Southern agents. John Wilkes Booth was one such agent who knew he could find help here. As Booth made his way south after shooting the President, he stopped at the Surratt House to pick up his field glasses, left for him earlier in the day by Mary Surratt, and the "shooting irons" that had been hidden in the ceiling as part of the earlier kidnapping plot. His accomplice took one of the guns, but Booth's injured leg made it difficult for him to ride and he decided against carrying one. Testimony that Mary Surratt had indeed helped Booth in this way led to her conviction by a military court and her death by hanging on July 7, 1865. Two years later when her son, John Jr., was tried on similar charges in a civil court, the jury could not reach a verdict.

In the spring and fall the Surratt Society sponsors a full day's excursion along the route John Wilkes Booth took from Ford's Theatre to present-day Fort A.P. Hill where he was finally cornered and shot. To reserve a spot on the next tour write the Society at 9110 Brandywine Road, P.O. Box 427, Clinton, MD 20735, or call (301)868-1121.

The Mary Surratt House can be toured from March through mid-December on Thursday and Friday from 11:00 A.M. to 3:00 P.M. and Saturday and Sunday from noon to 4:00 P.M.

Directions:: From the Washington Beltway (I-95) take Exit 7A (Route 5, Branch Avenue) south to Woodyard Road (Route 223) in Clinton. Turn right on Woodyard Road and continue to second traffic light, where you turn left onto Brandywine Road. The Mary Surratt House is on the left at 9110 Brandywine Road.

Wild World

Wet 'n' Dry Fun for Everyone

If the rides at **Wild World** were to be ranked according to which produces the loudest screams from riders, the World's Sixth-Best Roller Coaster would surely get some votes. But first place would probably go to one of the numerous rides here that make thrill seekers literally hit the water. Those who want a "chilling" experience have a multitude of choices: Paradise Island's cannonball flumes, the precipitous 60-foot drop of the Sunstreaker slide, the four curlicued funnels of the Rainbow Zoom and the speeding slides that swoop from the 35-foot towers of the Rampage.

Wild World does not consider itself a theme park, rather a family entertainment park with an emphasis on water-related fun. The park, the only one of its kind in Maryland, appeals to all ages. Unlike some razzle-dazzle parks, Wild World has plenty of activities for the preteen set and a few for diapered visitors. Under a parent's watchful supervision, the young ones can splash in the Tad Pool, a kiddie pool with minislides, water cannons and sculpted sea creatures that squirt water.

There are two play areas for young children: Kiddie City, with its mechanical rides, and the participatory Playport. At Kiddie City there are a miniature roller coaster, ferris wheel and five other little thrillers. If you want to calm the kids, the adjacent Petting Zoo might afford some quiet moments. Kids can pet the docile llama, as well as more customary barnyard animals. Also in this part of the park is a theater presentation by the Kiddie City Characters.

In the vicinity of the water attractions you'll find Playport, with its eight different innovative areas. Parents are relegated to the role of observers as the kids have all the fun, hopping in the Bounce Back or rolling in the Ball Bath's 37,000 green balls. Older kids needn't turn green with envy—the park offers seven "big" thrills. The biggest is the 70-year-old, 98-foot-high wooden roller coaster from Paragon Park in Nantasket, Massachusetts. This survivor from the golden age of coasters is the East Coast's tallest. It was voted sixth best in the world by the American Coaster Enthusiasts, and USA Today in 1987 listed it among the ten best in the United States.

If the roller coaster is the most popular "dry" ride, the winner of the "wet" award has to be the Wild Wave pool, where the surf is always up. It's the world's largest wave pool, with surf running up to four feet high.

If that takes care of the young and young at heart, there is still plenty for the more sedentary visitor to enjoy. There are numerous on-going performances. Musical shows include a nostalgic look at the not-too-distant past—the 50s, 60s and 70s—and a country music show. There is also a high diving show and a puppet theater.

The park has food concessions, games of chance and a gift shop. Wild World opens at 10:00 A.M. and closes at 9:00 P.M. daily from Memorial Day to Labor Day weekend (unless Maryland public schools have opened in which case it reverts to weekends

191

Wild World's Sixth-Best Roller Coaster vies for generating most screams with the Sunstreaker slide, cannonball flumes and other rides that deliver thrillseekers right onto water.

only). The park is open on weekends from mid-May to Memorial Day and in September. Admission prices are scaled for adults, children ages 4 to 10, and seniors. Those under 2 are free.

Directions: From Baltimore take Route 3/301 south to Bowie and Route 214. Take Route 214 (Central Avenue) west and signs will indicate Wild World on your right.

Maryland's
═══Colonial Capital═══

ANNAPOLIS

Banneker-Douglass Museum of Afro-American Life and History

Maryland Roots

The **Banneker-Douglass Museum of Afro-American Life and History**, Maryland's official museum of Afro-American culture, is appropriately located in Mount Moriah A.M.E. Church, built in 1874 by the Macedonia African Methodist Episcopal Church. The congregation, many of whom had been freed from slavery only ten years earlier, were proud of their ability to build this small-scale Victorian Gothic Church. It served the community for 98 years before being sold to Anne Arundel County in 1971.

Scheduled for demolition, this historic church was saved by heroic efforts of local preservationists, who had it converted to a museum. They named it for two prominent black Marylanders—Benjamin Banneker (1731–1806), pioneer scientist and surveyor, and Fredrick Douglass (1818–1895), abolitionist, newspaper editor and civil libertarian.

The thrust of the museum's collections extends beyond the boundaries of Maryland. It includes work by black artists from America and Africa. In an effort to identify cultural heroes for young blacks, Hughie Lee-Smith of the Art Students League of New York painted the portraits of six famous black Marylanders: Banneker and Douglass, Supreme Court Justice Thurgood Marshall, Underground Railroad heroine Harriet Tubman, publisher John H. Murphy and Doctor Lillie Carroll Jackson.

The museum sponsors craft demonstrations, lectures and films and hosts special traveling exhibits. There is also a reference library on Afro-American history in Maryland. One of the permanent displays features explorer Herbert M. Frisby, the second black explorer to reach the North Pole. He followed in the footsteps of Matthew Henson, who was Admiral Peary's assistant. Henson was actually the first to set foot on the North Pole. He, too, was a Maryland-born Afro-American.

The Banneker-Douglass Museum at 84 Franklin Street is open Tuesday through Friday from 10:00 A.M. to 3:00 P.M. and Saturday noon to 4:00 P.M. No admission is charged but donations are welcome.

Directions: From Baltimore take Route 2 south to Route 50. Turn right on Route 50 to the Rowe Boulevard exit. Take Rowe Boulevard into Historic Annapolis and turn right on College Avenue to Church Circle. Turn right on Franklin Street off Church Circle and the museum will be in the church on your left.

Chase-Lloyd House and Hammond-Harwood House

Best Laid Plans

Two lovely Georgian homes sit on opposite sides of Annapolis's Maryland Avenue. Both begun by men whose dreams were never fulfilled, both were nevertheless beautifully built by master-builder William Buckland.

In the 1770s legal firebrand Samuel Chase, described by the Mayor of Annapolis as "an inflaming son of discord," wanted to build a dream house. It turned into a nightmare for Chase when business reverses forced him to sell the uncompleted house to wealthy Eastern Shore planter Colonel Edward Lloyd IV. Lloyd's opulent lifestyle earned him the nickname Edward the Magnificent, and when he acquired the unfinished Chase House, he employed William Buckland to oversee its completion. Buckland, too, had a sobriquet; he was called the Tastemaker of the Colonies for his influential style. The combination of Buckland's talent and Lloyd's wealth produced one of the finest 18th-century interiors in America.

The exterior of this three-story Flemish bond brick mansion has a decorative cornice, projecting pedimented pavilion and what is called a Venetian doorway. But it is the lavishly decorated interior that marks this as one of Buckland's finest achievements. It begins in the main hall, where you see graceful Ionic columns separating the entranceway from the grand staircase. On the first level of the stairway there is a Venetian window and the staircase divides, forming a much-photographed architectural delight.

The **Chase-Lloyd House** remained in the Lloyd family for 73 years and then ironically was purchased by Chase's descendants. The last surviving Chase niece arranged for the house to be preserved as a home for elderly ladies. It is, however, open to the public on afternoons from 2:00 to 4:00, except on Sundays and Mondays. A small entrance fee is charged to support the upkeep.

Chase's fortunes did not improve after he sold his Annapolis home. He went bankrupt in 1789. In 1805 his legal career ended in ignominy when he was impeached as an Associate Justice of the Supreme Court, though in the end he was not convicted.

If Chase's dreams foundered for financial reasons, Mathias Hammond's foundered on the shoals of unrequited love. The undocumented legend tells us that Hammond was jilted by the fiancée he tried so hard to please. It is said that he became so intensely preoccupied with the details of their home-to-be that he failed to pay sufficient suit to her and so was thrown over.

William Buckland was also the masterbuilder for this splendidly ornamented house. This was to be his last creation; he died before the house was finished. But it was also the first and only house he both designed and built. The house is a classic five-part Georgian mansion, considered by some experts the finest example of the style in America. Ionic pilasters, like those Buckland used in the interior of the Chase-Lloyd House, here flank the front door. The columns support an elaborately carved pediment and frieze.

Inside, a wealth of details embellish the formal rooms. The dining room and drawing room are particularly fine examples of Buckland's work; they reflect the culmination of years of craftsmanship. The **Hammond-Harwood House** is not a mere decorative shell, either. The house is exquisitely furnished with 18th-century pieces. Maryland craftsmen are well represented, and there are several portraits by Charles Willson Peale. Appropriately, there is a copy of his portrait of William Buckland that shows the drawings for this very house. There is also an original Peale portrait of Buckland's daughter.

The house came to be known as the Hammond-Harwood House after 1834, when it was given to the daughter of its second owner and her husband. The man she married was William Harwood, the great-grandson of William Buckland, the man whose vision and artistry had given birth to the beautiful house.

The Hammond-Harwood House is open April through October, Tuesday through Saturday from 10:00 A.M. to 5:00 P.M., and Sunday from 2:00 to 5:00 P.M. From November through March hours are Tuesday through Saturday from 10:00 A.M. to 4:00 P.M. and Sunday 1:00 to 4:00 P.M. Closed on Mondays and major holidays. Admission is charged.

Directions: From Baltimore take Route 2 south to the Annapolis area, then turn right onto Route 50/301 and cross the Severn River Bridge. Take the Historic Annapolis exit onto Route 70 (Rowe Boulevard) and head into Historic Annapolis. From Rowe Boulevard turn left on College Avenue, then right at the first light, King George Street. Proceed on King George Street to the first light and turn right on Maryland Avenue for both houses. Chase-Lloyd House is on the right corner and Hammond-Harwood on the left.

Maryland State House and Old Treasury Building

Stately Presence

When Francis Nicholson replaced Sir Lionel Copley as Royal Governor of Maryland in 1694, he immediately took steps to move the capital from St. Mary's to Arundel Towne (it was renamed Annapolis to honor Queen Anne) on the Severn River at Todds (now Spa) Creek. The town's designation as the provincial seat of government prompted Nicholson to choose a baroque town plan with streets radiating from two major circles, rather than the more common grid plan. The highest point of land was selected for Public Circle, now called State Circle, following Nicholson's directions to "survey and lay out in the most comodius [sic] and convenient part and place of the said town six acres of Land intire [sic] for the erecting of a Court House and other buildings as shall be thought necessary and convenient."

State Circle was never quite the six acres Nicholson ordered but it did become the visual and actual hub of the new town. The first **Maryland State House** was built between 1696 and 1698. When fire destroyed all but sections of the brick walls and foundations in 1704, it was rebuilt from the standing remains. The second State House, completed in 1707, was by 1772 so derelict it was described as an "emblem of public poverty."

The cornerstone of the third State House was laid in March 1772. Work was slow. When George Washington came to Annapolis in December 1783 for the Continental Congress, it was still unfinished. The state legislature had been meeting in the half-built edifice since 1779. It was eventually completed, and the colonial revival additions you see today were added between 1902 and 1906.

One of the first things you'll notice in the State House is the Shaw Flag, designed to welcome the President of Congress when that legislative body met here from November 26, 1783, to June 3, 1784. The flag was designed by John Shaw, chief mechanic, maintenance supervisor and carpenter of the State House.

In the last weeks of 1783, George Washington bade farewell to his Continental Army officers in New York and traveled to Annapolis to resign his commission before the Continental Congress. The evening prior to the ceremony, December 22, a lavish dinner was held for 200 guests. After 13 convivial toasts were drunk, the guests moved to the State House to dance by the light of eight pounds worth of candles, an expensive indulgence. It is said Washington danced with every lady present.

The next morning in full military uniform, Washington walked to the State House. In the Old Senate Chamber, he emotionally

The Maryland State House in Annapolis is the oldest state capitol building in continuous legislative use. It served as the Capitol of the U.S. from November 1783 to August 1784.

resigned the commission issued by the Congress on June 15, 1775. A mannequin now stands where he is thought to have stood for this dramatic leave-taking. A painting purporting to capture this moment shows Martha Washington watching from the Senate floor. Actually, women were not permitted on the floor, and Martha had remained at Mount Vernon. Washington left immediately to join her for the Christmas holiday.

Another moment of history occurring at the State House was the January 14, 1784, ratification of the Treaty of Paris by the Continental Congress. This treaty officially ended the American Revolution. In this, America's first peace treaty, Great Britain formally recognized the independence of her former colonies. This is worth remembering when you view the copy of the Declaration of Independence in the New Senate Chamber. Portraits of the Maryland signers grace the walls. Here, too, is the Edwin White painting of Washington's resignation.

The State House is open daily 9:00 A.M. to 5:00 P.M., closed Christmas. Twenty-minute guided tours are given daily, except on Thanksgiving and New Year's Day.

You may also want to stop in another of the Annapolis public buildings on State Circle, the State Treasury. It's the city's oldest surviving state building, erected between 1735 and 1737. Local designer Patrick Creagh planned the building to offer security for the money it later held in trust. There were iron bars on the windows, thick brick walls and even brick floors to reduce the risk of fire. Today you'll see a model of Annapolis in the **Old Treasury**, open daily 9:00 A.M. to 4:30 P.M. The building now houses the offices of Historic Annapolis, Inc., Tours. It is an excellent spot to pick up brochures on all the Annapolis attractions and from which to begin your walking tour.

Directions: From Baltimore take Route 2 south to the Annapolis area. At the intersection with Route 50 turn right and cross the Severn River Bridge. Exit onto Route 70 (Rowe Boulevard), and proceed into Historic Annapolis to Church Circle, then around to State Circle via School Street.

U.S. Naval Academy

Ship Shape

You'll be welcomed "aboard" at the **United States Naval Academy**, home of the Navy's undergraduate professional college since 1845. George Bancroft, President Polk's Secretary of the Navy, established this college at Fort Severn, an all but abandoned ten-acre army post. The fort had been built in 1808 to protect the thriving seaport of Annapolis from the dual threat of British and pirate attacks.

From this modest beginning the U.S. Naval Academy has grown to a 338-acre campus. The campus, or Yard, is best explored on an escorted walking tour, although with a self-guided brochure you can set off on your own. If you do, you'll miss all the fascinating history, legends and stories about the high-spirited traditions of the Academy. The school, which began with seven professors and 50 students (midshipmen) now has a 550-member faculty. They teach more than 500 courses to approximately 4,500 students.

The Academy is a National Historic Site with a mixture of turn-of-the-century Beaux Arts designs and modern architecture. Walking tours begin at Ricketts Hall, where the Visitor Information Center is located. Here you can pick up brochures, obtain tour information, have a quick lunch and buy souvenirs. The tour map provides information on 17 buildings and six monuments. One of the highlights is the world's largest single dormitory, Bancroft Hall (Site 7). Bancroft has 33 acres of floor space housing the entire student body, or brigade, as it is called. You can go in to see the rotunda, Memorial Hall, and an example of a midshipman's room. In front of Bancroft Hall during the academic year you can watch the Brigade Noon Formations. Brigade reports are given, the Drum and Bugle Corps performs and then the midshipmen march in to lunch. It's served in one of the world's largest dining rooms—65,000 square feet with 360 tables. But despite the room's size, lunch is always served within four minutes. Each day 13,000 hot meals are prepared and the students consume two tons of meat and 4,000 quarts of milk.

Also interesting is Preble Hall (#13 on your walking tour map), where 50,000 items are displayed in the Naval Academy Museum. Among these exhibits is the table from the mess deck of the U.S.S. Missouri on which the Japanese signed the surrender ending World War II. There is also a fascinating collection of sailing ship models and an extensive group of maritime and naval paintings. One display reviews the life and accomplishments of John Paul Jones, another covers the Navy's role in global conflicts.

The next to the last stop on the tour is the Naval Academy Chapel, a building that resembles Les Invalides in Paris. Its copper-green dome can be seen above all the other buildings on campus. The cornerstone was laid in 1904. The Tiffany stained-glass windows honor four sea heroes—Mason, Porter, Farragut and Sampson. A 12-foot model of a 15th-century Flemish sailing vessel hangs above the rear choir loft. Such models are traditional in churches serving communities of seafaring men.

Beneath the chapel is the crypt of American Revolutionary War hero John Paul Jones. Carved dolphins decorate the ark-like marble sarcophagus of the man who is called the father of the

United States Navy. The names of the ships commanded by Jones are inscribed on the deck encircling the crypt. Jones' battlecry, "I have not yet begun to fight!" is one of the few quotes most of us remember from high school history classes.

Before leaving the campus be sure to stop by the Robert Crown Sailing Center. The Academy's sailing program is one of the best in the world. The center has an impressive 120-craft fleet that ranges from ocean racers to windsurfers.

The Naval Academy Museum is open Monday through Saturday 9:00 A.M. to 4:45 P.M. and Sunday 11:00 A.M. to 4:45 P.M. One-hour escorted walks are given daily on the hour.

Directions: From Baltimore head south on Route 2 to the Annapolis area. At the intersection with Route 50 turn right and cross the Severn River Bridge. Take the Rowe Boulevard exit into Historic Annapolis and proceed to College Avenue. Make a left and drive two blocks to King George Street. Turn right. Go to the end of the street, through Gate #1 of the Academy. This is the Visitors Gate. Guards will direct you to the parking lot and the Visitor Information Center in Ricketts Hall.

Victualling Warehouse, Tobacco Prise House and the Barracks

Historic Annapolis's Trade and Troops

The Maritime Museum in the 18th-century **Victualling Warehouse** brings back the days when Annapolis was a bustling commercial center, the principal seaport of the upper Chesapeake Bay as well as one of Maryland's tobacco inspection centers. Victualling (pronounced vit-alling) simply means provisioning. The term first referred to stocking up with victuals, or food, but later encompassed the supplies, new sails, cordage and other equipment necessary for sailing. Annapolis was highly regarded for the quantity and quality of its ship chandlery, or provisioners. The museum has exhibits on trade goods; cooperage (barrel making); shipbuilding; iron; rope- and sailmaking, plus a corner that suggests a waterfront tavern.

The museum contains a triorama showing the waterfront, complete with shoppers, in its heyday—1751–91. Shoppers still ply the streets, and nine of the buildings you see today from the museum's windows present the same facade they did in the 18th century.

One of the buildings, saved by Historic Annapolis, is the **Tobacco Prise House** across City Dock from the museum. This warehouse is far smaller than the Victualling Warehouse and was used exclusively to pack and store tobacco. There were many similar small warehouses along Annapolis' waterfront.

Small farmers customarily processed their tobacco at these warehouses along the dock. Hogsheads (large barrels) were filled with tobacco and stored until sufficient cargo was assembled to warrant shipping. Large plantations shipped their crops from their own wharves. At the warehouse you'll see a prise, or wooden lever, that was used to compress the tobacco into the hogsheads. Each hogshead weighed between 750 and 1,400 pounds and was rolled, not carried, to the waiting ships. Port cities as well as large plantations had rolling roads for these large barrels.

Just up Pinkney Street is a mid-18th-century, gambrel-roofed house. Known as the **Barracks,** this carpenter's house was typical of the many small homes leased to the state for use as Continental soldier barracks during the American Revolution. Housing was so scarce that even such small dwellings were pressed into service. Records from that period indicate that neither side was happy with the enforced troop quartering. The soldiers complained of the meagerly furnished rooms and lack of firewood. They retaliated by burning what furniture there was as well as structural portions of the houses—to the dismay of their reluctant landlords.

At the Pinkney Street house you'll see an excellent example of an in-house basement kitchen. During the colonial period this was an unusual arrangement because most kitchens were separated from the main house to reduce the hazard of fire.

The Victualling Warehouse at 77 Main Street is open 11:00 A.M. to 4:30 P.M. daily. Closed Thanksgiving and Christmas. The Tobacco Prise House at 4 Pinkney Street and the Barracks at 43 Pinkney Street are open 11:00 A.M. to 4:30 P.M. on weekends from mid-May to mid-October. A nominal admission is charged to each or you can purchase a combination that includes the William Paca House and Gardens (see selection) from Historic Annapolis, Inc. The Tour Office is in the Old Treasury on State Circle or at the Victualling Warehouse at the City Dock.

Directions: From Baltimore take Route 2 south to Route 50. Take a right on Route 50 to Annapolis. Take Rowe Boulevard exit (MD 70) into Annapolis and continue to State Circle.

William Paca House and Pleasure Gardens

Picture Perfect

It is the colors you'll remember long after you visit the Annapolis home of William Paca (pronounced pay-ka). Five years of painstaking work peeled away 22 layers of paint and wallpaper to uncover the startling Prussian blue walls that have now been resplendently repainted. This sky-blue hue, so dramatically different from the muted Williamsburg shades that we think of as colonial, was the first commercially produced paint.

The restoration of the house was a remarkable achievement. The dramatic change can be seen in the before and after photographs displayed in the rear porch chamber. The additions made while the house was used as part of the Carvel Hall Hotel were all removed, and both the Georgian mansion and the 18th-century pleasure gardens were restored.

The house tour begins in the blue parlor, which, like the rest of the house, has been furnished to reflect fashions ten years before the American Revolution. Because the house did not remain in the family, the furniture is not original, although one chair and several pieces of silver did belong to the Paca family. Each room shows a popular activity that the family might have enjoyed during that era. There is a card game spread out on the parlor table. You'll next move to the hall, which, contrary to your expectation, is not a passageway but what we would call a family room, with the table set for tea. Again you'll see the bright blue, used here for trim. The table in the dining room is also set, but the guide explains that colonial families frequently had their meals served in whatever room they were using and only repaired to the dining room when entertaining company.

The back porch, not traditionally a part of Georgian homes, was added to the house by William Paca, who, it can be conjectured, wanted a room where he could enjoy the garden on which he lavished so much time. You'll get your best overview of the garden from the upstairs window. Note how the terraces lead down to the wilderness garden, which is highlighted by a two-story octagonal pavilion. This pavilion and the Chinese Chippendale trellis bridge were included in the background of the Charles Willson Peale portrait of Paca. The pleasure gardens look as though they haven't been touched since the days when the portrait was painted. They were all restored after detailed excavation work uncovered the old garden foundations.

Paca's interest in gardening is but one of many similarities between Paca and Thomas Jefferson, with whom he was often compared. Both were lawyers, both served in the Continental Congress and both signed the Declaration of Independence. Paca went on to help draft the Maryland Constitution and served as Governor of Maryland from 1782—85 (Jefferson served as Governor of Virginia). At Paca's death in 1799 he was serving as the first U.S. District Judge from Maryland, the position to which he was appointed by President Washington.

William Paca House and Pleasure Gardens are open for tours. Many visitors return to enjoy his gardens as they change with the seasons. There is a separate garden entrance and visitors center. The William Paca House is open Monday through Sat-

The William Paca House and Pleasure Gardens have been brilliantly restored to their original elegance of 1765. Paca is sometimes compared with his compeer, Thomas Jefferson.

urday from 10:00 A.M. to 4:00 P.M. and on Sunday noon to 4:00 P.M. The William Paca Garden is open the same days at the same hours except on Sundays, May through October, when it stays open an hour longer, until 5:00 P.M. Both house and gardens are closed Thanksgiving and Christmas Day.

Directions: From U.S. 50 take the Rowe Boulevard exit into Historic Annapolis. Turn left at the State House onto College Avenue, then make a right on King George Street, right again on East Street for one block to Prince George Street. Make a right on Prince George Street and you'll see the William Paca House at 186 Prince George Street. There is a garden entrance from Martin Street off East Street.

ANNE ARUNDEL COUNTY

London Town Publik House and Gardens

Public House & Public Figures

Doors as enormous as those at Edgewater's **London Town Publik House** seem built to accommodate giants. Fittingly, some historic giants did pass through these portals. George Washington, Thomas Jefferson and Francis Scott Key were among the well-known figures who noted in their diaries crossing on the ferry at London Town.

This once-bustling town on the South River was one of the major ferry stops for travelers between Williamsburg and Philadelphia. It was also a point of departure for Europe and, after 1683, the port of entry for tall-masted ships carrying cargoes of European and East Indian goods to the colonies and taking tobacco back to England.

A log tobacco barn built in 1790 on a Maryland plantation has been moved to the grounds of the London Town Publik House, but the publik house is the only town building to survive. Its extra thick walls were built to last. The bricks were laid in an all-header pattern, which you'll see on a number of colonial houses in nearby Annapolis. This pattern was costly, requiring far more bricks than the more traditional lengthwise pattern. The all-header pattern insured a greater depth and thus improved insulation. The publik house sits on a bluff overlooking the river, so it needed protection from the elements; as an additional deterrent to drafts each room was raised one step. All of the exterior doors, woodwork, hardware and even some windows are original. The sturdy furniture has been collected to reflect 18th-century styles.

According to records, the inn was built on land deeded to Col. William Burgess by Lord Baltimore in 1651. The publik house served as both an inn and post house. It was to the inn that town folk flocked for news. The innkeeper frequently had more than one job. From 1753 to 1781 William Brown ran the publik house, operated a cabinetmaking business, served as ferrykeeper and owned an upriver plantation.

The trees and flowers of London Town entice visitors to return to enjoy the city in different seasons. Spring is a particularly popular time to explore the eight-acre London Town gardens. There is a spring walk that features bleeding heart, Lenten rose, primrose, mayapple and phlox, with a separate area for azaleas and viburnums. The wildflower walk is also at its best in the spring.

During the summer months the day lilies provide the main attraction, but see the herb garden as well. Waterfowl, which can be seen at London Town's pond year-round, are abundant during their autumn migration. The winter garden features dwarf conifers.

The London Town Publik House and Gardens is a National Historic Landmark. Hours are Tuesday through Saturday from 10:00 A.M. to 4:00 P.M. and Sunday noon to 4:00 P.M. It is closed January and February. Admission is charged.

Directions: From Baltimore take Route 2 south to the Annapolis area. Go west on U.S. 50/301 to Parole and exit, following Route 2 south. At the second traffic signal past the South River (Veterans Memorial) Bridge turn left on Mayo Road, Route 253. Take Mayo Road for one mile and then turn left onto Londontown Road, which leads to the grounds of the London Town Publik House.

Sandy Point State Park

A Beach For All Seasons

Sandy Point State Park on the western shore overlooking the Chesapeake Bay Bridge, roughly 30 minutes from the Baltimore Beltway and 40 minutes from the Washington Beltway, is ideal for spontaneous beach outings any time of the year.

Summer is the most popular season but not necessarily the most interesting. Warm weather brings out the sun bathers, waders and swimmers. The calm Bay water is ideal for youngsters until the sea nettles arrive in mid-summer. Fishermen also flock to Sandy Point, where the catch includes perch, spot and bluefish. There are ramps to launch your own boats and a marina where you can rent boats and purchase bait and tackle. There is surf fishing and crabbing as well. During summer, naturalists are on hand at the park to conduct programs, give talks and lead walks.

It's fun to sit on the beach and watch the action on the Bay, and that too changes with the seasons. In summer pleasure crafts vie for attention with seagoing freighters. You will spot an occasional cruise ship bound for exotic ports.

During fall there are fewer recreational sailboats and more fishing boats as Maryland's oystermen, clammers and crabbers take to the water. Autumn brings the migratory birds to Sandy Point, one of the few spots on the Atlantic Flyway to be found on the western shore; another is Merkle Wildlife Refuge (see selection). Migratory geese and ducks can be seen in abundance, and there are also native shore and land birds in the park's marshland.

There's nothing quite like a walk along the beach to blow away the cares of winter. Children delight in an unexpected opportunity to play in the sand. The lapping water and rustling sea grass provide the perfect accompaniment to your walk, and white-sailed skipjacks can be seen on the Bay.

Waterfowl winter over at Sandy Point, but in spring the migratory birds leave for the north. The pleasure boats return to the Bay; any breezy day brings a colorful array of sails all tacking in the wind. The intrepid can wade and the anxious can get a head start on their tans.

There is a nominal admission to the park in the spring and fall; it's slightly higher during the summer season. From December through March there is no charge.

Directions: From Baltimore take Route 2 south. When it intersects with Route 50 head east on Route 50 to the Bay Bridge. Signs indicate the turn for Sandy Point State Park.

Southern
===Maryland===

CALVERT COUNTY

Battle Creek Cypress Swamp Sanctuary

Trees Knees and Bees

Urban adventurers seeking unfamiliar terrain should head for Calvert County's **Battle Creek Cypress Swamp Sanctuary**. Although this unusual 100-acre preserve was established by the Nature Conservancy more than 30 years ago, many daytrippers still have not discovered it.

The winding platform trail leads into the northernmost stand of bald cypress in North America. Bald cypress trees were found in the Chesapeake Bay Region some 120,000 years ago, but the current descendants of these primordial giants could not have been growing at Battle Creek for more than 5,000 to 10,000 years due to unfavorable climatic conditions. Walking beneath these trees, some as tall as 100 feet or more, you might easily get the feeling that you've walked back in time. Though the trees are of impressive size, the animals you'll see today—deer, muskrat and opposum—are smaller than the mammoths, prehistoric camels and scaly crocodiles that once roamed this land.

The trees are often called bald cypress because they shed their leaves each fall. Their most fascinating feature, however, is the rootlike protuberance at their base. These "knees" puzzle scientists. One explanation is that the knees stabilize the cypress in muddy terrain. Another theory is that the knees provide oxygen to the tree.

Spring is the best time to visit, when the swamp is bordered by a profusion of delicate wildflowers, and migratory warblers flit among the tree tops. If you are not equipped with field guides, the Nature Center staff is on hand to identify the flowers and birds for you. Throughout the year the center offers guided walks, lectures, nature films and field trips; you may call (301)535-5327 for information on upcoming programs. Children enjoy the live exhibits at the center. There is a glass beehive that lets you observe bees making honey from the nectar of a tulip poplar. Glass is all that separates you from yet another specimen that both frightens and fascinates spectators: the agile but nonvenomous black snake.

Battle Creek Cypress Swamp Sanctuary is open at no charge April through September, Tuesday through Saturday 10:00 A.M. to 5:00 P.M. and Sunday 1:00 to 5:00 P.M. From October through March the sanctuary closes at 4:30 P.M. It is closed on Mondays, Thanksgiving, Christmas and New Year's Day.

Directions: From Baltimore take Route 3/301 south to Route 4 in Upper Marlboro. Take Route 4 for approximately 23 miles to Prince Frederick. Make a right on Sixes Road and watch for Battle Creek Cypress Swamp Sanctuary signs. Make a left on Gray's Road. The sanctuary is a quarter of a mile down Gray's Road on the right.

Calvert Marine Museum and Calvert Cliffs

Maritime Memories

If you want to capture a heretofore unfamiliar Maryland memory, head down to Calvert County. All the way down, in Solomons Island, a quaint fishing town built around one of the world's deepest natural harbors, you'll find the **Calvert Marine Museum** designed to acquaint you with local maritime history, the paleontology of Calvert Cliffs and the estuarine biology of the Patuxent River and the Chesapeake Bay.

In a genuine shipbuilders' lean-to (part of the Maritime History), you'll see tools like those used in the three shipyards that prospered here more than 50 years ago. There is a re-created oyster-shucking room of the Sollors and Dowell Oyster Company and an audio-visual program on Patuxent River watermen. The crabbing area has net, pole and boat. This is just one of the many boats on display. The ship models include a bugeye, dory, sloop, schooner, skipjack, skiff and a log canoe once a common sight on the Bay. There's a point-by-point explanation of how to build a ship. On most weekends a master carver gives demonstrations throughout the day in the Woodcarving and Model Shop.

The Fossils of Calvert Cliffs Room interprets marine fossils dating back 12 to 19 million years to the Miocene Epoch. Youngsters are encouraged to reach out and touch these age-old reminders of both plant and animal life so different from that found in this region today. There is a 12-million-year-old whale vertebra and the jaw from a prehistoric crocodile that might have lived among the forebears of the giant cypress you can see at Battle Creek Cypress Swamp (see selection).

To acquaint visitors with the biology of the estuary (the mix of fresh water from the Patuxent River and salt water from the sea, via the Chesapeake Bay), there are two aquariums filled with aquatic life. To complete the picture the museum includes exhibits on military action on these waters during the War of 1812.

The coastline was defended by Joshua Barney's Chesapeake Flotilla until he had to scuttle his ships in the Patuxent River. Divers that explored this rich historical site used far more sophisticated equipment than "Jake," a hard-hat Navy diving suit from WWII days that the museum has on display.

There are several exhibits on the museum grounds. A small craft shed displays a gig, skiff, canoe and several work boats. The most picturesque and interesting outdoor exhibit is the 1883 Drum Point Lighthouse that once signaled the entrance to the Patuxent River. You can explore it on a 20-minute tour. This is one of only three remaining screwpile cottage-type lighthouses; at the turn of the century there were 45 of them protecting ships that plied the Bay waters.

Docked at the museum wharf is the *Wm. B. Tennison*, an oyster bugeye, built in 1899. This is the oldest certified passenger-carrying vessel on the Chesapeake Bay. A ride on this boat is an ideal way to end your visit. Call (301)326-2042 to get additional information about the hour-long cruise.

The Calvert Marine Museum is open May to October Monday through Friday from 10:00 A.M. to 5:00 P.M., Saturday and Sunday from noon to 5:00 P.M. From November to April the museum closes at 4:30 P.M. There is an admission for the oysterhouse and lighthouse but the museum exhibit building and the grounds are free.

While you are in southern Calvert County there is another significant lighthouse you might want to see, the Cove Point Lighthouse, the oldest tower lighthouse on the Chesapeake Bay. This, like Drum Point, is one of the last of its kind. It is an excellent vantage point from which to view the nearby Calvert Cliffs. On the National Register of Historic Places, this lighthouse can be visited from March through September from 8:00 to 11:00 A.M. and 1:00 to 4:00 P.M. It is closed on Monday and Thursday.

You can also visit **Calvert Cliffs State Park**. There is a trail down to the cliffs and a picnic and playground area. Watch out for ticks during the summer. You can't dig for fossils but you can scavenge on the beach for exposed fossils and shells. Nearby is the **Calvert Cliffs Nuclear Power Plant Visitors Center,** open daily from 9:00 A.M. to 5:00 P.M. except on major holidays. A converted tobacco barn has dioramas and audio-visual exhibits describing the fossils and the nuclear power plant that you see from an overlook. The phone number is (301)234-7484.

Directions: From Baltimore take Route 3/301 south to Route 4 which becomes Route 4/2 and go south to Solomons, about 44 miles. Make a left turn for the Calvert Marine Museum 200 yards before the Thomas Johnson Memorial Bridge at Solomons. For Cove Point Lighthouse turn off Route 4/2 at Route 497; signs on Route 4/2 will indicate the power plant.

Drum Point Lighthouse was a lookout for 80 years at the confluence of Patuxent River and western Chesapeake Bay. The lighthouse is now part of the Calvert Marine Museum.

Chesapeake Beach Railway Museum

Rail, Rod 'n' Reel

Things are pretty quiet around Chesapeake Beach these days, but in the early 1900s this was a popular resort with its own spur railroad line. Crowds flocked to the beach town by boat and train. Steamboats traveled from Baltimore and trains brought Washingtonians who boarded at Seat Pleasant for the 32-mile trip. Visitors stayed at the elegant Belvedere Hotel while enjoying the mile-long boardwalk, the ballroom, the carousel and the roller coaster extending out over the Bay.

The bayside beach's halcyon years are recalled at the **Chesapeake Beach Railway Museum**, housed in the original railroad station. The station was built between 1898 and 1899. The first train pulled into the Chesapeake Beach Station on June 9, 1900. The museum has photographs of both the early trains and the stations along the line: Seat Plesant, Marlboro, Owings and Chesapeake Beach. The railroad operated from March 21, 1899, to April 15, 1935. The trains heralded their own demise when they began transporting cars to destinations along their line.

Old railroad lanterns, steam whistles, schedules, tickets, handmade rail spikes and other memorabilia are part of the museum's still-growing collection. Also displayed is a 1914 Model T Ford Depot Hack. A carousel kangaroo reminds old-timers of the amusement park days when area families came down to picnic, swim in the saltwater pool and enjoy the rides. The amusement park closed in 1972. Behind the station, volunteers are working to restore Dolores, the line's only surviving railroad car.

The Chesapeake Beach Railway Museum is open Saturday and Sunday from 1:00 to 4:00 P.M. from October through April. It is open daily from 1:00 to 4:00 P.M. May through September.

Across the parking lot from the museum is the Rod 'n' Reel Restaurant. Large picture windows in the restaurant give you a ringside seat on the Bay action. Boats slowly make their way to the adjacent pier, and the white swans and geese are always in evidence. On sunny days it is a delightful spot to watch the sunset. The restaurant also operates an al fresco Boardwalk Café that extends out to the water's edge.

Directions: From Baltimore take Route 3 and Route 301 south to Route 4 in Upper Marlboro. Head east on Route 4 to Route 260. Turn left and take Route 260 to the beach. At the water's edge turn right on Route 261 and then make a left into the Rod 'n' Reel parking lot for the museum.

Patterson Park

Do You Dig It?

A number of worlds lie beneath the 512 acres of the **Jefferson Patterson Park and Museum**, one of Maryland's newest state parks. Although many of them have already been uncovered, there are still valuable historical treasures awaiting discovery by the park's enthusiastic archeologists and volunteers.

The goal at Patterson Park is to portray 12,000 years of change along the Patuxent River. When the park was officially opened on July 4, 1984, Governor Hughes turned over the first shovelful of dirt. It turned out to be rich in artifacts and yielded a 17th-century nail, a pipe stem, bone fragment, oyster shells and brick fragments. This sounds too good to be true until you have a look in the Visitor Center Museum at the rich yields workers discovered almost every day. The permanent exhibit covers the entire period of human occupation in the Chesapeake Bay area.

Excavations indicate that the King's Reach site was once a residence/plantation of a family of at least middling means. It had a main house plus typical 17th-century outbuildings. Archeologists have discovered trash-filled pits rich in artifacts and have reconstructed the foundations and fence lines. As their explorations and analyses continue, other exhibits will be added.

Underneath the King's Reach site, an Indian village of the late Woodland period was excavated in 1986. A small portion of the Indian village was occupied from 800 B.C. to 300 B.C., but most of the site dates from 1300 to 1500 A.D. In a large storage pit archeologists found evidence of Indian corn, the first found in the Maryland portion of the Chesapeake Bay. Charcoal found with the corn kernels was radio-carbon dated to 1459 A.D. The excavations suggest that this was a small farmstead occupied by one or several families of Indians. An Archeological Trail leads down from the Visitors Center to the King's Reach Site, then on to the Indian village dig.

As you watch the archeologists and volunteers at work you discover just how misleading the term "dig" can be. The first job is to remove eight to ten inches of dirt, painstakingly sift it, then slowly scrape it with a trowel. Watching such careful work makes you appreciate the effort involved in creating the exhibits you see in archeological museums.

Other exciting areas await attention. There are the battlement implacements from the Battle of St. Leonard Creek in the War of 1812 and the colonial town of Leonard that dates back to 1660–1706. These sites will fill gaps in Maryland's re-creation of her past. Currently there is no place in Maryland where you can see re-created the villages of Indians who once lived here. At Patterson Park the plan is eventually to reconstruct a part of the Indian village that stood along the Patuxent.

But history is only one thrust of this new park. There is already a one-mile Nature Trail, which one day will extend into five miles of trails. Marsh land, forest and river bank add to the scenic charm. Even now a pavilion for picnickers is finished. Jefferson Patterson Park is open April 15 to October 15, Wednesday through Sunday, from 10:00 A.M. to 5:00 P.M. There is no admission charged.

Directions: From Baltimore take Route 3 and Route 301 south to Route 4 in Upper Marlboro. Go south on Route 4 into Calvert County to Route 264, about four miles south of Prince Frederick, and turn right. Then make a left at Route 265; a sign indicates Patterson Park 5.5 miles down this road.

ST. MARY'S COUNTY

Chancellor's Point Natural History Center

You'll Get the Point

Visitors to the 66-acre **Chancellor's Point Natural History Center** interact with both river and woodlands hiking the meandering trails or perhaps fishing from the sandy shores of the St. Mary's River. Thus they become part of the continuing picture the center presents of man's use of this Tidewater area from prehistoric times to the present.

The center's 40-foot mural provides a visual time tunnel going back to the first Indians who lived along the river. The Indians, as you'll see, practiced a "slash and burn" technique to clear the underbrush and trap the wild deer. The European settlers are depicted next as they cleared and cultivated the land. The painting moves through the mechanization of farming to the present, represented by the very building in which the mural is housed. Kids are delighted to discover the mural even portrays the resident dog and cat they'll see at the center.

This nature study area encourages hands-on participation. Fossils and other artifacts uncovered along the river can give youngsters a sense of being in touch with the past. Wooden patterns that depict wildlife are used for rubbings, providing a chance to appreciate details of the surrounding natural world.

The park provides a map of the woodland trails. It will help you identify indigenous vegetation and the abundant shell fossils you'll see in the Miocene Marineland, one of the areas along the trail. It comes as a surprise to most visitors to learn that the

215

inland sea that covered this area extended as far as Washington, D.C.

From an overlook above St. Mary's River you'll see Priest Point where in 1637 the first Catholic Mission was established in British North America. Looking upriver you can see the site of a Yeocomico (or Yoacomico) Indian village.

To give you an idea of what life would have been like for the Indians at the time the European settlers arrived here, the center has re-created an aboriginal longhouse of the type constructed by Woodland Indians along the Chesapeake. The longhouse is two-thirds scale and was built using aboriginal tools. Hands-on learning experiences are planned to provide a feel for Indian life.

Annual events are hosted by almost all historic sites, but few reach back as far as Chancellor's Point Natural History Center's Aboriginal Life Day in mid-October. Where else can you try using a hunting bow, learn flintknapping, help scrape out a canoe, experience an Indian sweat lodge (a forerunner of the sauna), or taste such treats as raccoon stew and eels? Other special programs at the center focus on beekeeping, birdwatching, edible plants and stargazing.

The Chancellor's Point Natural History Center is open daily during the summer from 10:00 A.M. to 5:00 P.M. In the spring and fall it is open on weekends only. Visitors can walk in the parklands until dusk.

Directions: From the Washington Beltway (I-95) at Exit 7 take Route 5 south through Waldorf to St. Mary's, a total distance of approximately 60 miles. Once you arrive in St. Mary's, follow the signs to the Historic St. Mary's Visitor Center.

Godiah Spray Tobacco Plantation

The Past Is Present

Godiah Spray is the 17th-century equivalent of the 20th-century John Doe. The name is taken from the straw man of old English court records.

Though the **Godiah Spray Tobacco Plantation** at Historic St. Mary's City takes its name from England, it takes its characteristics from several authentic colonial American figures known to have lived in this area between 1650 and 1660. One settler, Robert Cole, unknowingly made an enormous contribution to this re-creation of a middling-income planter's life. Cole had a plantation 20 miles from St. Mary's between 1650 and 1662, and his ten-year account book was recovered from there. It provided invaluable assistance to the St. Mary's living history project.

Cole's detailed day-to-day record showed that although to-

At the Godiah Spray Tobacco Plantation, living history actors portray the Spray family. Here women are at work in the kitchen garden.

JOHN ENNIS

bacco was the cash crop, a limited amount of corn was grown. Corn was used primarily on the plantation, but some farmers did sell their excess. The yearly production of tobacco per man was three or four hogsheads (large barrels), or 1,300 to 1,500 pounds. To compute the value of this yield it helps to know that you could purchase a horse for roughly 500 pounds of tobacco, whereas a slave cost 5,000 pounds. The farmhouse where George Washington was born cost his father 5,000 pounds of tobacco.

The Godiah Spray Tobacco Plantation, as was typical of the period, has a kitchen garden close to the house. A picket fence encloses the vegetables and herbs to protect them from foraging livestock. In the Cole account he said he had 33 cows, 29 hogs, several horses and dunghill fowl, the old name for chickens.

The daily labor on a colonial farm was back breaking. Hoeing a roughly cleared forest land was a grueling chore, as you will see when you visit. If the men had to endure hours in the hot sun, the women had to endure equally long hours at the hot fireplace baking, boiling, roasting and frying their meals.

This plantation house is far removed from such gracious 18th-century plantations as Sotterley and Montpelier. This is the house of a "successful" Chesapeake Planter, meaning that he worked hard enough and lived long enough to be able to afford a few civilizing touches for his home. The house is of English design and has wood floors instead of dirt, windows with glass and lead panes and plastered walls. There is an old barn, also of English construction. It is heavily framed and elaborately jointed. The new barn and a freedman's cottage reveal the adaptation of carpentry from the old world to the new.

Throughout the summer months, from Memorial Day to Labor Day, living history unfolds for visitors at the Godiah Spray Tobacco Plantation from 10:00 A.M. to 5:00 P.M. From the last weekend in March (when Maryland Days are celebrated) to Memorial Day, and from Labor Day to the last weekend in November the plantation, along with the other Historic St. Mary's City exhibits, are open weekends only from 10:00 A.M. to 5:00 P.M. The Visitor Center, in 20th-century barns, is open daily, year-round, 10:00 A.M. to 5:00P.M. (except Thanksgiving, Christmas and New Year's). In addition to purchasing exhibit tickets you can watch a slide presentation at the Visitor Center and browse through the archeology display.

Directions: From the Washington Beltway (I-95) at Exit 7 take Route 5 south through Waldorf to St. Mary's, a total distance of about 60 miles. In St. Mary's turn right on Rosecroft Road and follow signs to the Visitor Center. A slightly longer but more scenic route is to turn left off Route 301 on Route 4 (it becomes Route 2/4) to the Governor Thomas Johnson Bridge at Solomons. Cross over to St. Mary's County and take Route 235 south to the sign for Historic St. Mary's City and follow the museum signs to the Visitor Center.

Maryland *Dove* and Old State House of 1676

Perils of the Pinnace

In 1634 Father White wrote the following description of his journey across the North Atlantic to Maryland, "The winde grew still lowder and lowder, makeing a boysterous sea, and about midnight we espied our pinnace with her two lights, as she had forewarned us, in the shroodes, from wch time till six weekes, we never see her more, thinkeing shee had assuredly beene foundred and lost in those hughe seas. . . Here we staied [the Barbadoes] from January 3 to the 24th by which meanes we came to enjoy againe our pinnace, wch not knowing of our comeing was guided, to our soe great comfort as if that day we had beene revived to life againe: for before we saw her in the harbour we gave her for lost in that hideous storme."

The ships of which Father White wrote, the *Ark* and the *Dove*, had sailed from Cowes on the Isle of Wight on November 22, 1633. On board were 18 British gentlemen, Father White and roughly 140 indentured servants. Leonard and George Calvert accompanied the group, representing their brother, Cecilius Calvert, the second Lord Baltimore. It fell to the two young Calverts to settle the province of Maryland.

The *Ark* was a 300-ton sailing ship, while the *Dove* was a 40-ton pinnace. The two ships had been used by the Calverts in an earlier attempt in 1627 to establish Avalon province on the island of Newfoundland, but both the climate and the soil proved inhospitable. George Calvert, the first Lord Baltimore, asked the king for a grant of land in a more southern climate and was given the Maryland province.

The journey of the *Ark* and *Dove* was hardly under way when the ships ran into a violent storm and became separated. The *Ark* "as strong as could be made of oak and iron" barely rode out the storm; those on board the *Ark* never thought they'd see the *Dove* again. So the arrival of the *Dove* at the harbor of Barbados in January was cause for celebration.

The ships arrived at Point Comfort, Virginia, on February 26, 1634, and in early March landed at St. Clement's Island (see selection). Leonard Calvert, Governor of the new colony, did not want to establish his first settlement on an island and so sailed on to Yeocomico. He purchased the Indian village there and changed its name to Saint Maries.

Soon thereafter the Ark sailed back to England. The Dove remained. Its small size meant it could easily negotiate the narrow inland rivers. The Dove was used to establish links with other areas. In August 1634, the Dove sailed to New England with a cargo of grain. In August of 1635 the Dove was loaded with beaver pelts and timber and set sail for England. She never arrived. Contradictory explanations are offered for her loss at sea with all hands aboard. According to Father White she was "much worme eaten." It is also thought she may have encountered a storm she could not ride out.

The Maryland Dove you'll see anchored at St. Mary's is not an exact reproduction of the original because no plans survived. It is, however, a reproduction of a typical 1634 pinnace like the smaller vessel that brought the first settlers to Maryland. The Dove had a crew of seven who lived in crowded quarters. They had to find sleeping space on the spare sails or even atop coils of rope. If they were lucky they had a hammock to rig from the beams. The master's "great cabin" wasn't all that great. He had a berth and a table that was used for the passengers' dining table as well as the navigation chart table and general work area. It was a spartan and small craft on which to brave the Atlantic.

Also reconstructed on the hilltop above the pier where the Dove is anchored is the **Old State House**. St. Mary's was the capital of the Maryland colony for 60 years, but for the first 41 years the colonial legislative body met in taverns and private homes. By 1674 the need for a permanent headquarters was apparent, and Maryland's first State House was finished in 1676. Eighteen years later the capital was moved to Annapolis. The State House was converted to a parish church. It was torn down in 1829.

The State House has been reconstructed, and within its brick walls 17th-century political drama is re-enacted. During the summer living history program, various trials are argued once again before the Calvert family and their allies. Costumed townspeople testify in colorful, but historically accurate, terms and visitors are drawn into the action as both jurors and witnesses. Their lines are supplied, but the sense of involvement is very much appreciated. These trials were far more boisterous than 20th-century trials. The entire community often attended and felt free to express their opinion of the proceedings, which sometimes developed into noisy free-for-alls.

As you watch the trial, or wander through the State House in quieter moments, be sure to look around this historic reconstruction. Imagine the early legislators trying to argue their case before the Royal Governor. They were merely an advisory body and could make no laws. In the upstairs area the Calverts kept many of the militia's guns. They were anxious to keep guns out of the hands of the Protestant settlers.

Historic St. Mary's City is open from 10:00 A.M. to 5:00 P.M. weekends from the last weekend in March through Memorial Day; seven days a week from Memorial Day through Labor Day; and on weekends only from Labor Day through the last weekend in November. Admission is charged. The Visitor Center and Museum Shop is open from 10:00 A.M. to 5:00 P.M. every day of the year except Thanksgiving, Christmas and New Year's Day.

Directions: From Baltimore take Route 3/301 south to the intersection with Route 4 in Upper Marlboro. Go south on Route 4. At Solomons cross Governor Thomas Johnson Bridge (Patuxent River) into St. Mary's County. Turn left onto Route 235 south and continue until you see the sign for Historic St. Mary's City and make a right onto Mattapany Road. Follow signs to the Visitor Center.

Patuxent Naval Air Test Center Museum

A-Ok

Young boys won't have to be dragooned into taking a family outing when the destination is the **Patuxent Naval Air Test Center Museum** in Lexington Park. It's the country's only museum devoted to this critical aspect of naval aviation. The collection includes planes, testing devices and displays that explain how planes are evaluated.

Outside the museum are five planes, a sidewinder missile and an MK-82 Snakeye bomb. The Salty Dog 100, the first "J" model F4 Phantom to arrive at the Naval Air Test Center, has been returned here after logging nearly 4,300 flight hours. Another hard-working plane on display is the Grumman S-2 Tracker. These trackers are among the safest planes in the Navy, and have collectively logged more than 7 million hours and made over 800,000 carrier landings with an accident rate a fraction of the overall Navy rate.

The first thing you'll see when you enter the museum is a model of the aircraft carrier escort USS *Commencement Bay*. You'll also see examples of Flight Test Instrumentation: a modular pulse code measurer, a frequency modulation system, an angle of attack indicator and a shielded total pressure instrument. Some of the larger pieces include an Askania Cine-Theodolite camera used during the 1940s to measure the motion and position of rapidly moving objects. With this tool the velocity of an aircraft could be measured and its behavior in dives and curved flights judged.

One of the roles of the Naval Air Test Center is to evaluate the feasibility of innovative and unusual aircraft. Among these experimental crafts on display are a portable helicopter, a parafoil and the Goodyear Inflatoplane. A slide program details the testing of the Inflatoplane.

This free museum is open year-round. July through September hours are Tuesday through Saturday 10:00 A.M. to 5:00 P.M. and Sundays noon to 5:00 P.M. If you visit on the first Sunday of the month, you might also want to drive through another St. Mary's County site, the **Seafarer's International Union/Harry Lundeberg School of Seamanship**. It's named for the founder and first president of the trade union for American seamen. At this training base is a small display of sailing vessels and the extensive fleet used for the U.S. Merchant Marine trainees. Visitors are welcome on the first Sunday of the month from 9:00 A.M. to 5:00 P.M.

Just down the road from Lexington Park is Great Mills, where you will find Cecil's Old Mill Arts & Crafts and the Christmas Country Store in **Cecil's General Store**. Both feature a wide variety of handmade items. You can buy homemade honey, baked goods, Christmas decorations, drawings, paintings and novelty items. More than 90 artisans display their one-of-a-kind creations, and there is often at least one working artist on hand. You can visit Friday, Saturday and Sunday from 10:00 A.M. to 5:00 P.M. from mid-March to December 24. In October, November and December the shops also open on Thursdays.

Directions: From Baltimore take Route 3 and Route 301 south to Route 5 at Waldorf. Turn left on Route 5 and go about 40 miles to Great Mills. For the Great Mill's crafts shops turn left on Route 471 and head up the road for just a short way. The stores will be across the street from each other. For the Patuxent Naval Air Test Center Museum return to Route 5 and go south to the next intersection, Route 246, and turn left. Take Route 246 to Route 237 and turn left. Route 237 will take you to Route 235, where you will turn right. Just before the navy base (at the light with the Mister Donut) turn left onto Shangri-la Drive, which will take you onto the museum parking lot. You do not want to go through the base gate because the museum is enclosed by a fence and cannot be reached once you are on the base. For the Harry Lundeberg School of Seamanship turn right off Route 5 at Callaway (just north of Great Mills) onto Route 249. The entrance to the school is on the left in Piney Point.

Point Lookout State Park

Fort Lincoln and Fiddler Crabs

From a summer resort to a Civil War prison camp and then back to a recreational retreat—that's the story of **Point Lookout**. In the early 1860s, on the southernmost tip of Maryland's western shore, there was a beach hotel, roughly 100 cottages, a large wharf and a lighthouse.

The onset of the Civil War signaled the end of an era for the Point Lookout resort. The U.S. government leased it for use as an army hospital, and the first Union army patients arrived on August 17, 1862. During the winter of 1863 some Confederate prisoners were sent here, primarily southern Marylanders accused of helping the rebel cause.

After the Battle of Gettysburg, in July 1863, a prison camp was built at Point Lookout to hold 10,000 Confederate prisoners of war. By the following summer double that many were crowded into this camp. A year later, in June 1865, the last prisoners left. With a total of 52,264 Confederates imprisoned here, this was the largest prison camp of the Civil War. For a time, Point Lookout had more rebel soldiers than General Lee had in his army.

The overcrowded conditions took their toll. Filth bred disease and the men alternately froze and baked. More than 3,500 prisoners died. One survivor wrote, "If it were not for hope how could we live in a place like this?"

One of the ironies for these Confederate prisoners was that many of their guards were former slaves. There were even masters who found their own slaves now in a position of authority over them. As one prisoner remarked, "The bottom rail's on top now."

The Union soldiers and guards who worked at the prison were stationed at Fort Lincoln, built on the banks of the Potomac River between 1864 and 1865. The fort's earthworks were reinforced by a wooden wall, and there was a guardhouse, enlisted men's barracks and two officers' quarters. Today if you walk up from the park's swimming beach along the historic trail, you can see the remains of Fort Lincoln. The earthworks are original, and part of the wooden walk and the walled entrance walk have been rebuilt. The guardhouse has been rebuilt and furnished and is open daily. New floors and chimneys mark the officers' quarters, while a chimney and foundations indicate the enlisted men's barracks. From the fort's southeast corner you can see a section of the prison stockade fence just 150 yards away. It too has been rebuilt, although not from chestnut trees, which were used for the original, but are no longer abundant in this area.

To get a better idea of how Fort Lincoln looked during the Civil War, stop at the Visitor Center Museum, where a complete model is displayed and audio-visual exhibits highlight prison camp life. An additional presentation points out the recreational options available at Point Lookout State Park.

The Visitor Center also has live specimens of animal life at the park: Eastern box turtles, black rat snakes and fiddler crabs. Check with the park naturalist or park historians about guided hikes, canoe trips, seafood cooking demonstrations, Civil War weapons demonstrations, nature craft, Junior Ranger programs and special events (call (301)872-5688).

From the Visitor Center you can take either the Fiddler Crab Alley Nature Trail (a sign warns that you should expect wet feet along its marshy path) or Periwinkle Point Nature Trail, which is only slightly drier. This marshy terrain means that there are mosquitoes, so bring bug repellent.

Many visitors come to Point Lookout not for history but for the excellent fishing along the park's three miles of sandy beaches, where the Potomac River empties into the Chesapeake Bay. Anglers also fish from the causeway. They sit beside their cars with their poles in the bay waters. This part of St. Mary's County is considered one of the ten best fishing areas in the United States. Croakers, blues, flounder and Norfolk spot are all found here, as are crabs, oysters and soft shell clams. Boats can be rented at the park marina or you can try your luck from the shore. Many fishermen enjoy camping at the park. One hundred and forty-three campsites are available; of these, 26 sites have full hookups.

Point Lookout State Park is open 8:00 A.M. to sunset, but the Visitor Center is only open Wednesday through Saturday from 10:00 A.M. to 6:00 P.M. and Sunday 10:00 A.M. to 5:00 P.M. from mid-June until Labor Day. During the months of May, early June and September the Visitor Center is open on weekends only.

Directions: Point Lookout is located 60 miles south of Waldorf at the southern end of Route 5.

St. Clement's Island—Potomac River Museum

Arrowheads and Atlatls

If it has been a while since you've visited the **St. Clement's Island—Potomac River Museum**, you won't recognize it now. The old clapboard house that was its home has been torn down and been replaced by a new weathered-wood museum overlooking the Potomac River.

This is the place to discover what's been happening along the Potomac since prehistoric man traversed these shores. Exhibits trace the history of man's interaction with the river back to the Paleolithic (or Old Stone) Period, from 10,000 B.C. until 8000 B.C. The first people who ventured into what was at that time a vast tundra resembling Siberia were tracking large herds of game. The mastodons and other large prey had migrated to this Maryland area from the midwest. The first of the museum's arrowheads are Clovis Point arrowheads. It is remarkable that the slight-statured prehistoric people hunted such giant game with these crude weapons. In addition to the arrowheads the museum exhibits the different materials from which arrowheads were made and the style changes in the different periods: Dalton, Le Croy, Kirk, Otter Creek, Morrow Mountain, Guilford Courthouse, Piscataway and Brewerton Eared.

It's worth mentioning that while all arrowheads are projectile points, not all projectile points are arrowheads. They were also used for atlatl, or throwing sticks. Other projectile points were used as spear, dart and javelin points. The exhibit of atlatls and axes explains that axes were multipurpose tools used for both hunting and felling trees.

In the Archaic Period, 9000 to 1000 B.C., the Chesapeake Bay began to be formed. The large herds that had grazed the land began to dwindle and die. The prehistoric people living here began making axes and other wooden working implements in addition to projectile points.

The museum next covers the Woodland period, which represented the renaissance of aboriginal culture in this area. From this period you will see a small human effigy found along the banks of the Port Tobacco River. The Eastern Woodland Indians wore amulets and pendants, examples of which are shown with their pottery.

In a windowed alcove overlooking the river, the boats and tools of Maryland watermen tell yet another story about life along the river. Quotes from James Michener's novel *Chesapeake* fill the wall beneath a gunning skiff. As Michener explains, "You don't point the gun, you point the skiff. And when you get seventy, eighty ducks in range, you put a lot of pressure on the trigger and. . ."

Since the first Maryland settlers landed just offshore at **St. Clement's Island**, the museum also covers Colonial ceramics, pipe bowls, tobacco culture and religious art. To get closer in touch with these 17th-century settlers, you can take the museum-operated boat to St. Clement's Island. Boats depart from Colton Point for the 20-minute trip from late May to late June on Saturday and Sunday from noon to 4:00 P.M. From July through

September they also run on Thursday and Friday from 10:00 A.M. to 3:00 P.M. Call (301)769-2222 to confirm the schedule.

It was at St. Clement's Island that the English first landed when they came to settle the Maryland colony. The *Ark* and the *Dove* (see selection) sailed up the Potomac River to St. Clement's in March 1634. It had been a rough four-month crossing. The ships lost sight of one another during a violent storm, so it was with great thanksgiving that they celebrated their safe arrival.

A large cross commemorates the mass of thanksgiving offered by Father Andrew White. While the settlers were still on St. Clement's Island, Royal Governor Leonard Calvert issued a proclamation formally taking possession of "Terre Mariae." Historic markers explain the events on this island during Maryland's earliest days. Picnic tables, barbecue grills, restrooms and two new piers have been added on the island.

The museum is open from May 30 to September, Monday through Friday from 9:00 A.M. to 5:00 P.M. and on weekends from noon to 4:00 P.M. From October through the end of March the hours are Wednesday through Sunday from noon to 4:00 P.M. In April and May hours are Monday through Friday 9:00 A.M. to 4:00 P.M. and weekends from noon to 4:00 P.M.

Directions: From Baltimore take Route 3/301 south to the intersection with Route 5 in Waldorf. Travel south on Route 5 about 25 miles and turn right on Route 242 to Colton's Point.

Sotterley

Old World Feud Recalled in
Spectacular Setting

A 500-year-old rivalry and a reckless roll of dice are both part of the story behind **Sotterley,** an 18th-century working plantation in Hollywood, Maryland.

The families Plater and Satterlee were English political rivals in 1471, when King Edward IV confiscated the original Sotterley Hall estate from the Satterlees and gave it to the Platers. In 1717, when later Platers established this American colonial plantation, they named it for the home their ancestors had been given. Alas, in 1822 George Plater V gambled the whole property away in a dice game. The Satterlees gained some measure of revenge for the king's theft when a descendant, Herbert Satterlee, purchased the plantation in 1910. Herbert Satterlee was the son-in-law of J.P. Morgan.

The brilliant red parlor where the notorious dice game occurred offers visitors still more drama. A narrow, hidden staircase leads from the parlor to an upstairs bedroom, otherwise accessible only by the bedroom next to it. It's easy to weave that staircase into a romantic scenario. The parlor also contains a secret compartment that was used to hide messages carried by a network of Confederate sympathizers. Although Maryland was a Union state, many southern Marylanders supported the South. During the Civil War the Briscoe family lived at Sotterley, and three of their sons served in the Confederate army.

The secret staircase may not have served romance. During the Plater residency when plantations along the water were frequent victims of marauding pirates, the staircase may have been used for hiding. A story is told about one time when pirates did stop. The pirates chose early morning thinking the men would be at work in the fields. Unluckily for them a hunt breakfast was in progress, and the gentlemen riders routed the pirates, leaving two attackers fatally wounded. It is said the slain pirates were buried in the field at Sotterley between the house and the river.

The large drawing room has the elegance we expect from the best of the southern plantations. Indeed, it is included in Helen Comstock's "100 Most Beautiful Rooms in America." The Great Hall, as it is called, was exquisitely carved by Richard Boulton, an indentured carpenter. Architectural experts consider the shell alcoves he carved on each side of the ornate fireplace to be some of the finest work ever done for an 18th-century house.

Boulton also carved the delicate tracery of the mahogany Chinese Chippendale staircase. It's said that his indenture expired when he had only a small bit of moulding on the stairs left to be carved. To this day it is still not finished.

In the library you'll see a rare jail Agra rug. Queen Victoria ordered Muslim prisoners—jailed because they wouldn't handle cartridges they believed to be greased with pig fat—to weave these rugs. The rugs are highly prized for their singular origin and limited number. Another rare find is the painting of George Washington floating on a cloud. His head is encircled with a halo, and the angels that surround him all bear Washington's visage.

The dining room, copied from Brighton pavilion, enchants all visitors; antique buffs especially rhapsodize over the partners' desk. Those who enjoy an actual taste of the past may want to purchase a smoked ham from Sotterley's smokehouse. Garden fanciers should stroll through the restored 18th-century garden; it is particularly attractive in the spring when the lilacs bloom.

Sotterley still has a number of dependencies, including a gate house now furnished to represent an old-fashioned schoolhouse and one remaining cabin from a row of slave cabins along the rolling road leading to Sotterley's dock. This plantation was a port of entry into the colony, and tobacco from Sotterley and nearby plantations was loaded at the wharf.

Sotterley is open daily 11:00 A.M. to 5:00 P.M., June through September. The last tour is given at 4:00 P.M. You can make an appointment, (301)373-2280, to visit during April, May, October and November. Groups can also arrange a luncheon on the verandah or a picnic on the lawn.

Directions: From Baltimore take Route 3 and Route 301 south to Route 5. Turn left on Route 5 at Waldorf and go 20 miles to the fork of Route 5 and Route 235. Follow Route 235 about 10 miles to Hollywood and make a left turn onto Route 245. Take Route 245 three miles to Sotterley.

CHARLES COUNTY

Dr. Samuel A. Mudd House

Whose Name Will Be Mud(d)?

For many of the descendants of Dr. Samuel A. Mudd, clearing the family name has been a crusade. None has worked more tirelessly than Mudd's youngest granddaughter, Louise Mudd Arehart. She is president of the Dr. Samuel A. Mudd Society; through her efforts Dr. Mudd's St. Catherine plantation farmhouse has been successfully restored. The building looks today as it did on April 15, 1865, when history rode to the door and forever changed the lives of Dr. Mudd and his family.

The drama began at Ford's Theatre the preceding night when John Wilkes Booth shot President Lincoln. Booth fractured his leg when he leapt to the stage to make his escape. The injured Booth and his accomplice David Herold rode out of the capital and made their way into Southern Maryland. The two men stopped at Mary Surratt's Tavern (see selection). Booth's leg was causing problems; they decided to get medical help and set out for Dr. Mudd's farm further south. Booth had traveled through this part of Maryland before, ostensibly to buy land and horses (and indeed one of the horses the two were riding as they made ther escape was purchased by Booth from Dr. Mudd's neighbor), but also to enlist support from the region's Southern sympathizers for various plots and plans that were constantly being made. On one of Booth's visits he had met and dined with Dr. Mudd; their paths had crossed again in Washington. Booth and Herold arrived at Mudd's door at 4:00 A.M. Easter Saturday morning.

Herold dismounted and roused the Mudd household. Dr. Mudd had been out late with a patient, but Mrs. Mudd awakened him rather than answer the knock. She was afraid it might be floaters, or free blacks, who were often found in this state that bordered the Confederacy. Herold gave Dr. Mudd false names (Tyler and Tyson) as the doctor helped the wounded Booth into the house. According to some reports Booth, an actor, had disguised himself with a false beard. Herold and Dr. Mudd helped Booth to the red velvet couch in the parlor (this historic piece of furniture has just recently been returned to the house by a Mudd descendant) so that the doctor could examine his leg. Dr. Mudd then moved Booth to an upstairs bedroom, cut off the boot and set the leg. The boot was tossed under the bed and forgotten (it would later be used as evidence).

Later Saturday morning Dr. Mudd and Herold set out to find a carriage for the two travelers to use on the rest of their journey; when none could be found Herold and Booth set off on horseback between 2:00 and 4:00 P.M. As they left, Mrs. Mudd got a look at Booth's face, which, heretofore, he had kept hidden. She remarked to the doctor that he appeared to be wearing a disguise. This is how the Mudds explained why they did not recognize a man who had been a guest in their home.

Dr. Mudd, who claimed not to have known of the assassination of the President when he ministered to Booth, was nonetheless convicted by a military court of aiding and harboring an escaping fugitive. He was found innocent of charges that he was involved in the conspiracy to assassinate Lincoln. Mudd was sent to Fort Jefferson Prison in the Dry Tortugas off Key West, Florida.

Dr. Mudd served part of his sentence in chains after an escape attempt. But when a yellow fever epidemic decimated the prison population and the prison doctor died, Mudd was unshackled and began treating his fellow prisoners. Shortly after the end of the epidemic he was pardoned by President Andrew Johnson for his humanitarian work. Dr. Mudd returned to his Maryland farm, and then toured the country lecturing on yellow fever. (He had contracted and survived the disease while at Fort Jefferson Prison.) Dr. Mudd died of pneumonia 13 years after his release from prison.

The Mudd house is filled with furniture and mementos, each piece prompting the costumed docents to tell another story about Dr. Mudd's experiences and the family's travail when the Federal troops camped around the house. History comes to life at this out-of-the-way farmhouse, where the clock seems to have stopped in 1865.

The **Dr. Samuel A. Mudd House** is open Saturday and Sunday afternoons from noon to 4:00 P.M. from late March to late November. Admission is charged.

Directions: From Washington Beltway (I-95) Exit 7 take Route 5 south to Waldorf. Two miles south of Waldorf turn left on Route 382 and go three miles to Route 232. Bear right onto Route 232 for one-tenth of a mile; the Mudd House will be on the right.

Port Tobacco

The Town Time Almost Forgot

Upon entering the reconstructed 1819 Port Tobacco Courthouse you'll see a copy of the map John Smith drew when he sailed up the Potomac River in 1608. The Indian village of Potopaco is marked by Smith on land that subsequently became the town of **Port Tobacco**, the first County Seat of Charles County.

The English had started settling this area as early as 1634, which makes the town one of the oldest continuous settlements in the U.S. Four years later Father Andrew White arrived to convert the Potopaco Indians. He Christianized the Indian village and wrote religious catechisms in the Indian dialect. White also wrote a grammar and dictionary that was printed on one of the first presses in America. This early text was discovered years later in an archive in Rome, Italy.

The **Charles County Museum**, located on the second floor of the Port Tobacco Courthouse, has exhibits detailing the history of the Charles County area. This is not the first courthouse built on this site. In 1727, at the direction of the Maryland Assembly, a courthouse was built at Port Tobacco, then officially known as Chandlers Town. The assembly changed the name to Charles Town, but inhabitants continued to call the village Port Tobacco, or versions of that, like Portafacco, Potobac, Potobag and Port-tobattoo. The more popular unofficial name was impossible to dislodge because the town was indeed a port from which tobacco was sent from the colonies to England. Until the Revolutionary War, Port Tobacco was the second largest river port in Maryland, after St. Mary's.

The courthouse, which was built between 1727 and 1729 at a cost of 2,000 pounds of tobacco, was destroyed by a severe windstorm in 1808. In 1819 the brick courthouse you see today was built, though a fire in 1892 destroyed the center section. Because of its historical significance to the county, it was restored between 1965 and 1973.

At the time of the fire the area around the courthouse was bustling. The town had 20 shops, approximately 70 homes, two newspapers, three hotels and numerous businesses. One of the hotels, the Brawner Hotel, was the Federal Field Headquarters for the manhunt launched to find Lincoln's assassin John Wilkes Booth. The Federal investigator, detective William Williams, offered Southern sympathizer Thomas Jones a staggering $100,000 for information leading to Booth's capture. Jones, who did indeed know the assassin's whereabouts, would not betray Booth.

"The Story of Port Tobacco," a 30-minute slide presentation giving the highlights of Port Tobacco's long history, is shown at the courthouse. It illustrates the significance of the restored homes on Courthouse Square, such as the 1765 Chimney House and the 1732 Stag Hall.

Directions: From Washington Beltway (I-95) Exit 7 take Route 5 south to Waldorf, then take U.S. 301 south to La Plata. Turn right on Route 6 in La Plata. Continue three miles on Route 6 to the junction with Chapel Point Road and bear left. You'll see Murphy's Store at this junction. Take Chapel Point Road for one-half mile to Commerce Street and the Port Tobacco Restored Area and Courthouse.

Smallwood State Park

Home of Washington's Friend and Look-Alike

William Smallwood entered the Continental Army as a Colonel in January 1776. By October of that year he was a Brigadier General and by 1780 he was a Major General, the highest ranking Marylander in George Washington's command.

We know little about the private life of this busy public man. He was a bachelor who lived on a 5,000-acre plantation, part of his parents' holdings. He called his tidewater home Mattawoman Plantation; today it is known as Smallwood's Retreat.

Despite the peaceful sound of its names, the plantation served as an active meeting spot for political and military leaders. Smallwood and his neighbors across the river, George Mason of Gunston Hall and George Washington of Mount Vernon, would meet at their respective homes to talk of independence from England.

Smallwood was involved in the Revolutionary struggle from the earliest days. When Washington had to retreat after the Battle of Long Island, Smallwood's troops, the Maryland Line, protected his flanks and saved them all from annihilation. Smallwood was wounded at the Battle of White Plains but did not relinquish his command. It was this brave action that led to his promotion to Brigadier General. After keeping the southern wing of the Continental Army from disintegration following the bitterly fought Battle of Camden (South Carolina), Smallwood was formally commended for his bravery and promoted to Major General.

Smallwood's friendship with Washington did not end when the war ended. Both were members of the Masonic Lodge of Alexandria. Smallwood was also active in the newly formed Protestant Episcopal Church. When Washington came to southern Maryland, he and Smallwood often attended Old Durham Parish Church, built in 1732. Markers at this church indicate their attendance. The church is off Route 425 and open to visitors.

William Smallwood, friend and lookalike of George Washington's, was the highest ranking Marylander in Washington's command. Smallwood's Retreat has been completely rebuilt.

After the Revolution, Smallwood helped form the Society of the Cincinnati for Former Continental Army officers. Smallwood also resumed a political career interrupted by the war. He had represented Charles County in the Colonial Assembly during the 1760s and 1770s. In 1785, he was elected Governor of Maryland and served three one-year terms.

This distinguished Marylander is buried on the front lawn of his plantation. When he died there was no will and the property was divided and sold. The house continued to be occupied for approximately 100 years after Smallwood's death. It fell on hard times though, and its last known use was as a storage barn for grain and hay. Only remnants of three walls and the foundation remained when the Smallwood Foundation was established to restore the general's retreat.

The fully rebuilt house is open for free tours, conducted by docents in colonial garb, on weekends and holidays from Memorial Day to Labor Day, noon to 5:00 P.M. Seven rooms have been furnished with 18th-century pieces similar to those Smallwood might have owned. Only three chairs in the dining room are original; they were made in Annapolis by John Shaw. In the Great Room there is a copy of a portrait of William Smallwood in his military uniform. It is surprising to see how much he resembles George Washington.

One curious feature of the house's design is the warming room, built off the dining room. The servants had to bring all the food through the dining room to the warming room before they started serving the meal. Then, because there was no exit door, they had to stay in the warming room until the meal was finished.

The layout of the downstairs rooms was determined by the debris patterns in the foundation. No such clues were available for the upstairs, so it was designed by conjecture. There is a guest bedroom, a gentleman's large bed chamber and a dressing room. The tour ends in the restored out-kitchen. After your tour be sure to see the herb and vegetable gardens. Throughout the year Smallwood hosts special events—garden parties, candlelight tours, military encampments and craft demonstrations (see Calendar of Events).

Located on Mattawoman Creek, a tributary of the Potomac River, Smallwood Park also has delightfully situated waterside picnic tables. There are boats for rent and guided nature walks, plus canoe trips for which reservations are needed. For information on guided walks and special events and canoe reservations call (301)743-7613.

Directions: From Baltimore take Route 3 and Route 301 south to La Plata (eight miles south of Waldorf) and turn right on Route 225. Continue west to the "T" intersection with Route 224 and turn left. Proceed down Route 224 for about six miles to park entrance on the right at Sweden Point Road.

Maryland's Upper Chesapeake

CECIL COUNTY

Mount Harmon Plantation and Chesapeake and Delaware Canal Museum

See World's End from Widow's Walk

Maps refer to land the second Lord Baltimore granted Godfrey Harmon in 1651 as World's End. Around 1730 William Ward built an elegant five-bay Georgian mansion here, on a knoll surrounded by the creeks and inlets of the Sassafras River. **Mount Harmon Plantation at World's End**, as the manor house was called, was a typical colonial frontier plantation.

In the early 1960s Mrs. Harry Clark Boden IV restored the interior of Mount Harmon to its 18th-century appearance. She filled the rooms with English, Irish and American period furnishings, including some lovely Chippendale and Hepplewhite pieces. It is, however, the portrait of Lady Arabella Stuart that captivates visitors. The painting is done on what looks like an accordian-pleated board, the angled surfaces allowing the painter to capture three different views. When seen from the left it is a traditional portrait of Lady Arabella. If you look straight at the picture, she appears to be behind bars, as indeed she once was. The painting becomes macabre when viewed from the right—all you see is her skeleton. It is a disquieting and unusual work of art.

The entranceway wallpaper, crafted in Hong Kong in a silver tea-box pattern, creates one of the most attractive areas in the house. The Oriental motif continues up the opulent Chinese Chippendale staircase. Each of the 21 railing panels leading to the third floor has a different pattern. Visitors are encouraged to tackle the few extra steps beyond the staircase to the widow's walk, an opportunity permitted in few old homes.

And what a view there is from this height! Looking in one direction you'll see part of the winding two-mile approach lane; in places the road is a veritable tunnel through the dense Osage orange trees. Between the house and the Sassafras River is the boxwood and wisteria garden. The bird's-eye view lets you appreciate the serpentine brick wall that encloses this garden.

Mount Harmon Plantation at World's End was built around 1730 on a knoll overlooking Sassafras River. The view from its widow's walk will take your breath away if the stairway doesn't.

You'll also see the outkitchen, which can be toured after the house, and the tobacco prize house at the river's edge.

Mount Harmon is now owned by the Natural Lands Trust, Inc., a land conservation organization. The entire estate is a wildlife and nature preserve. There are cleared trails winding through the forest along McGill Creek and the Sassafras River. Nature lovers will welcome the chance to see the American lotus, which rarely grows wild in Maryland. This lotus is the largest wild-flower found in the United States. The American bald eagle, also rare, nests in this area and is often seen at Mount Harmon.

Mount Harmon is open for tours April through October on Tuesday and Thursday from 10:00 A.M. to 3:00 P.M. and on Sunday 1:00 to 4:00 P.M. from mid-May through October. Admission is charged.

On your way to Mount Harmon, immediately after crossing the Canal Bridge at Chesapeake City, turn left for the **Chesapeake and Delaware Canal Museum**. It's well worth a stop. A six-minute audio-visual program introduces visitors to the C&D Canal. The canal opened on October 17, 1829. Crossing the Delmarva Peninsula to connect the Cheapeake Bay with the Delaware River, it cuts 300 miles of passage between these two bodies of water by eliminating the voyage around Cape Charles. Today the C&D Canal is one of the world's busiest canals, with thousands of vessels a year taking this shortcut.

A working model at the museum demonstrates how the canal's lift lock works. There are also models of vessels that have plyed the canal. The most colorful ship represented is James Adams's floating theater, which once brought entertainment to Chesapeake City and other towns along the canal. There is also a model of a canal barge, a pipeline dredge and various Chesapeake Bay sailing craft. Those interested in the mechanical operation of the canal locks will be fascinated by the two steam engines and the cypress-wood lift wheel in the Old Lock Pump House.

The C&D Canal Museum, on Second Street at Bethel Road, is open at no charge daily 8:00 A.M. to 4:00 P.M. and Sunday 10:00 A.M. to 6:00 P.M. Chesapeake City has a number of specialty shops and restaurants. The Bayard House, at Bohemia Avenue and the C&D Canal, is a restored Federal-style tavern and inn. The Inn at the Canal is a bed and breakfast with six guest rooms in an old Victorian house (call (301)885-5995). Italian food is featured at The Tap Room, on the corner of Second and Bohemia. Home-made ice cream and fudge are tempting after-meal treats at Susan's Sweets, at Third and Bohemia.

Directions: From Baltimore take I-95 north and exit on Route 279, which joins Route 213 at Elkton. For Mount Harmon Plantation take Route 213 south to Cecilton and turn right on Route 282. After 2.5 miles take a left on Grove Neck Road. Signs will indicate Mount Harmon entrance on the left.

Upper Bay Museum and Elk Neck State Park

Ducks. . .Duck!

On the upper Chesapeake Bay, both commercial and recreational hunters enjoy the bounty of the Susquehanna Flats. Five rivers join the Bay here: the Susquehanna, North East, Elk, Sassafras and Bohemia.

You can practically smell the cordite at the **Upper Bay Museum**. A wide range of hunting paraphernalia has been preserved here, including an extensive collection of duck decoys, sculling oars, gunning lights and old boats. Where else could you learn about sneakboating, body booting, sinkboxes and all types of decoys?

Both the body booting and the sinkbox were designed to let a hunter take a position within a group of decoys and lure the unsuspecting birds in for the kill. According to volunteers at the Upper Bay Museum, it gets plenty cold standing neck deep in the water even with body booting.

The sinkbox, now outlawed, also provided visual protection and offered a bit more comfort. The sinkbox surrounded a coffin-like boat with a wood-and-canvas-covered deck on which there were 20 to 30 wing decoys, some of cast iron to weigh down the sinkbox. It was outlawed in 1934 because the combination of hunters, pollution and lack of nesting areas had decimated the canvasback population.

Other boats are displayed at the museum. One building has a wide assortment of outboard motors and old bushwacking boats. In the main museum you'll see a punt-gun skiff with an absolutely enormous gun, two railbird skiffs, a Susquehanna River sportsfishing boat and a one-log canoe.

The museum, on the North East Creek and the North East River, used to be a fish-packing house. One section has been turned into a replica of a decoy maker's shop. Most of the equipment, furnishings and half-completed decoys were transplanted from Horace Graham's shop in Charlestown. As you peer into the shop, you'll see the gently flowing North East Creek out the far window.

There is a real goose named Charlie that has been adopted by the museum volunteers, who spend $25 a month on feed to keep him happy. Look for Charlie's portrait hanging beside the cases of wooden decoys.

The Upper Bay Museum is open at no charge on Sundays from 10:00 A.M. to 4:00 P.M., Memorial Day to Labor Day. Donations are welcomed.

Continuing down Route 272 past the Upper Bay Museum, you'll reach **Elk Neck State Park**. The park is bounded by the

238

Elk River, North East River and the Chesapeake Bay. The scenic Turkey Point nature trail takes you to land's end. It is one of four blazed trails that together cover eight miles.

This land was once traversed by the powerful Susquehannock Indians who impressed Captain John Smith, the first white man to visit the headlands of the Chesapeake Bay. He wrote of the friendly reception they gave him in the record of his 1608 journey.

Like the Indians, current visitors enjoy the bounty of Bay and rivers. Fishing and crabbing are popular park activities. Boaters can launch their craft at the park, and boats are available to rent. There is a large swimming beach on the North East River with lifeguards and a bathhouse. The park has 300 camper units for tents and trailers as well as nine four-room housekeeping cabins. For information on camping and cabins call (301)287-5333.

Directions: From Baltimore take I-95 north to the exit for the town of North East, also marked Route 272 south. For the Upper Bay Museum turn right on Walnut Street in North East. For Elk Neck State Park continue south on Route 272 to the park.

KENT COUNTY

Chestertown

Braver than Boston

Every school child knows the story—the American colonists of Boston were incensed about the high tax England imposed on tea. A tumultuous meeting on December 16, 1773, led to decisive action. Under cover of darkness, 40 to 50 radicals, disguised as Indians, crept aboard three British ships and dumped 342 chests of tea into the Boston harbor.

Few school children, even in Maryland, realize there was a second tea party, more courageous and closer to home. Like their Boston counterparts, the people of **Chestertown** were angered by the tea tax. On May 23, 1774, in broad daylight, the irate townsfolk rowed out to the brigantine *Geddes* and dumped not just tea but crew members as well into the Chester River. This Maryland "tea party" is re-enacted each year on the Saturday before Memorial Day. It's part of a day-long festival that includes a parade, historical vignettes, music, crafts and escorted walking tours.

The May celebration is an ideal time to get acquainted with Chestertown, but some visitors prefer it when the streets are empty and only the ghosts of the past share the old brick sidewalks. A "Walking Tour of Old Chester Town" brochure, available in most of the shops along High Street, provides information on the historic district and the town's lovely Georgian and Federal houses. Many of these houses were built before the Revolution.

Chestertown, when it was one of Maryland's most prosperous ports, was a major stop between Philadelphia and Virginia. Cargo from around the world passed through the 1746 Customs House. It is one of the largest surviving custom houses built in the 13 original colonies. It's just one of 28 locations marked on your tour map.

Of the private homes only the **Geddes-Piper House** at 101 Church Street is open to the public (May to October, on weekends from 1:00 to 4:00 P.M.). The three-and-a-half–story Philadelphia-style townhouse was the home of William Geddes, the Collector of Customs for the Port of Chester Town. It was his ship that his neighbors boarded and offloaded so unceremoniously in 1774. Tea not only contributed to Geddes' livelihood but to the decor of his home. His lovely collection of teapots is proudly displayed.

The 18th-century **Buck-Bacchus Store** is open May through October on Saturdays from 1:00 to 4:00 P.M. During colonial days many in-town establishments were both home and business and this restoration reflects that duality. There is an 18th-century living area and a 19th-century general store.

If you find yourself wishing you could see the interior of the town's lovely old homes, plan to return during September for the annual Candlelight Tour. This is the only time some of these private residences can be toured.

Try to arrange your day so that you're in Chestertown at tea time (3:00 to 5:00 daily), and you can partake of a delightful colonial experience at the White Swan Tavern. This is an establishment that George Washington once patronized. It's now a bed and breakfast inn with five 18th-century rooms. For reservations call (301)778-2300. One of the guest bedrooms was the one-room dwelling of the first owner of the property, John Lovegrove, the "Shoemaker of Chestertown." The property was enlarged by subsequent owners and served as a tavern betwen 1803 and 1853.

Reflecting turn-of-the-century style is the newly restored Imperial Hotel, which was built on High Street in 1903. Its 12 bedrooms and dining room are furnished in Victorian froufrou. If you are not staying overnight, try at least to have a meal here. The menu features American and French cuisine, and the wine cellar is so extensive that overnight guests may pre-arrange a cellar tour during their stay. For reservations call (301)778-5000.

Chestertown does not have the shopping options of Annapolis or Ellicott City, but there are a few shops to explore.

The Maryland Tea Party, which followed the Boston Tea Party by five months and bears the distinction of having been brought off in broad daylight, is re-enacted each year in Chestertown.

Directions: From Baltimore take Route 2 south to Route 50. Head east across the Bay Bridge. When Route 301 splits off Route 50, head north on Route 301 until it intersects with Route 213. Turn left on Route 213 for Chestertown.

Eastern Neck National Wildlife Refuge and Remington Farms

Splendor in the Grass and Sky

An interesting comparison between public and private wildlife management areas is offered by the geographical proximity of Eastern Neck National Wildlife Refuge and Remington Farms. These are both "no frills" wildlife exposures: There are no visitor centers, no slick exhibits and displays—just the splendor of nature.

241

The opportunity to see the largest concentration of wintering Canada geese in the world is one you shouldn't miss. At **Eastern Neck National Wildlife Refuge** and the nearby Blackwater National Wildlife Refuge (see selection) you'll see the striking Canadas and other waterfowl in their natural habitat. The best season to visit is winter, or late fall, when the birds have arrived for their seasonal respite from the northern chill. Fortuitously, the marsh terrain does not change with the seasons, the marsh grasses winter over, and you will see approximately the same vista summer and winter, though the sky may be gray, not blue, in winter. The best time of day to visit is either dawn or dusk, though most daytrippers find dusk a more convenient hour. When the sun rises or sets, the thousands of geese can be seen in flight. The sight and sound of these magnificent birds on the wing is truly a wilderness adventure.

It would be worth the drive if the Canada geese were the only attraction, but you'll also see flocks of white whistling swans who migrate here from as far north as Alaska. Snow geese are a common sight, both the white with black wingtips and the blue-gray birds with white heads and necks. Although the duck population has declined, they are still plentiful.

Eastern Neck is on the east side of the Chesapeake Bay at the mouth of the Chester River. Except for the Ingleside Recreation Area, which is closed October through April, this 2,285-acre refuge is open year-round at no charge during daylight hours. There are six miles of roads and self-guided nature trails through the woodland and marsh. Boardwalks, decks and an observation tower allow visitor access to the marsh area. You'll want to bring binoculars so that you can get a close look from the observation tower. The birds start arriving as early as October and leave by April.

On a pleasant winter's day the woodland nature trail may yield unexpected surprises; through the sparse undergrowth of winter you are apt to see a Delmarva fox squirrel, one of an endangered species. This squirrel can be identified by its white belly and feet. You may also spot a whitetail deer, raccoon, opossum, muskrat or woodchuck.

If you visit Eastern Neck during the late spring or summer, you can try your luck at crabbing. If you don't want to go to the trouble of bringing your own boat, try wading out with a net and a bushel basket. Old hands recommend that you balance your basket in an inner tube; this will leave both hands free for netting. Blue crabs are caught as early as May, but July is the best month for crabbing.

Less than ten miles away is **Remington Farms,** a privately sponsored refuge operated by the Remington Arms Company. This 3,300-acre retreat is open to the public at no charge daily from dawn to dusk. The self-guided driving tour is open to the public February 1 to October 15. During hunting season, mid-October through January, only the waterfowl sanctuary pond is open. The sound of gunfire from nearby hunters may prove disconcerting to nature lovers. As many as 20,000 ducks have been counted wintering at Remington Farms.

This sanctuary was established to improve the natural habitat so that both farming and hunting can coexist with the wildlife. Part of this land once belonged to airplane magnate Glenn Martin. It is now farmed, and the corn helps feed the more than 20,000 Canada geese who spend the winter at Remington Farms. The birds are attracted by the proximity of feed and by the sanctuary's fresh water ponds.

Directions: From Baltimore take Route 2 south to Route 50 and cross the Chesapeake Bay Bridge. When it veers off from Route 50, take Route 301. Follow Route 301 north to the intersection with Route 213. Turn left on Route 213 and take Route 213 into Chestertown. When you intersect with Route 20 turn left. Remington Farms will be on your left about ten miles down Route 20. For Eastern Neck National Wildlife Refuge continue on Route 20 to Rock Hall and then take Route 445 eight miles south to the island refuge.

QUEEN ANNE COUNTY

Tuckahoe State Park

Tucked Away

Have you ever been to a "swamp brunch," or on a "Barking Up the Right Tree" guided walk? These are two innovative nature programs offered at **Tuckahoe State Park**. This park hosts a swamp brunch on some of its short canoe trips. It also schedules all-day canoe trips down Tuckahoe Creek.

Tuckahoe Creek, which runs through the park, is the county line between Queen Anne's and Caroline Counties. Tuckahoe Park's 3,500 acres include a 60-acre lake, wooded swampland and a 500-acre arboretum. The latter, **Adkins Arboretum**, is an ideal place to identify the trees, plants and shrubs of Maryland. You will indeed learn how to "bark up the right tree." Three miles of loop trails lead through examples of the three growing regions of Maryland: Western, Central and Eastern Shore. Plantings representing the first two regions, respectively, are already well under way and the third is in the planning stage.

Many of the trees along the arboretum trails are labeled. Growing in the western portion are forests of white pine, hemlock, yellow poplar, spruce and fir. In the central section are shortleaf and Virginia pine, sweet gum, yellow poplar, black gum and basket oak. Plans call for loblolly pine, pond pine, Atlantic white cedar and cypress to be planted along the third loop. Nature lovers will want to monitor the progress of this comprehensive arboretum.

Located seven miles west of Denton, the park offers 71 campsites for tent and trailer camping. Campers and daytrippers can fish the lake from the shore, rent canoes, or launch their own boats from the shore or from a ramp. A tidal fishing license is needed to fish the creek south of the dam and a non-tidal license is needed for lake fishing.

Although fishing is permitted, there is no swimming in the lake. Even wading is forbidden. You may, however, have a picnic beneath the pines as you overlook the scenic lake. Trails give hikers a chance to wander along the shoreline. The park has a physical fitness trail, a self-guided nature trail and the Piney Branch Trail. Hunting is permitted in season, roughly mid-October to mid-February, in designated areas.

The park is open daily during daylight hours, although certain sections, such as the campgrounds area, are closed in late fall and winter. A Visitor Center has a calendar of park activities and special events.

Near Tuckahoe in Centreville there are two old homes open on summer Fridays. They depend on volunteers, however, and therefore are not always open on schedule. Centreville was Queen Anne's county seat in 1782. The Court House, circa 1791, is the oldest in the state still in continuous use. In front of the courthouse is a statue of Queen Anne. The Taylor House on S. Commerce Street (Route 213) is considered the oldest original house in Centreville. The lot, the second to be purchased in town, was bought in 1792. The house is now furnished with period pieces and is open on a limited basis on Fridays during the summer months from 12:30 to 3:30 P.M. It is advisable to call ahead, (301)758-1208. Across the street is Wright's Chance, which is open during the same hours (call (301)758-0658 to verify). This old plantation house was moved into town in 1964. Wright's Chance was listed as an "old dwelling" in a 1744 survey; its four rooms and nursery are furnished with period pieces.

Directions: From Baltimore take Route 2 south to Route 50. Take Route 50 east across the Bay Bridge. At Wye Mills bear left on Route 404 and then follow Tuckahoe State Park signs. Centreville is located off Route 301 on Route 213.

TALBOT COUNTY

Chesapeake Bay Maritime Museum

All Quiet on the Eastern Shore

The shipbuilding heritage of St. Michaels goes back to colonial days. There is a marvelous, but perhaps apocryphal, story about how this quaint town managed to survive unscathed the second American-British confrontation. Before dawn on August 10, 1813, the British navy anchored offshore and began firing at St. Michaels. Residents hung lanterns high in the trees, thus tricking the British into overshooting the town, which thereafter called itself The Town That Fooled the British.

For more St. Michaels, as well as Chesapeake Bay, history visit the multi-dimensional **Chesapeake Bay Maritime Museum.** It's a 16-acre complex that includes an 1879 lighthouse, a small boat exhibit, bell tower, bandstand, aquarium and several museum outbuildings.

Few can resist heading directly to the stilt-legged Hooper Strait Lighthouse. This is one of only three remaining "cottage" lighthouses. Great screw pile supports almost literally screwed these lighthouses into the muddy Bay bottom. The lighthouse's spartan furnishings remind visitors that even these watermen who never fished lived a rugged life tending the warning lights. The lightkeeper's family could spend only two weeks a year at the lighthouse, although the keeper did get periodic leave.

From the top of the lighthouse you'll have a sweeping view of the Bay and harbor. Every day, unless weather makes the Bay unnavigable, oystermen, crabbers and fishermen sail in and out. One skipjack that is no longer part of the work fleet is the *Rosie Parks*, now a museum exhibit. In the boat shop craftsmen work to restore and repair the museum's fleet of historic workboats. St. Michaels builders are credited with crafting the first Baltimore Clipper and the first racing log canoe. The techniques and tools of boat building are explained, and finished products can be seen at the nearby small boat shed, which has yachts, workboats and hunting skiffs.

You can move from hunters' boats to their guns and decoys on display in the Waterfowling Building. In the autumn the shores around St. Michaels are crowded with the migrating fowl so painstakingly duplicated by decoy carvers. Children who obey the exhibits' "Do Not Touch" signs can be rewarded with time to climb on the iron Chesapeake Bay retriever just outside on the porch.

Visitors to the Chesapeake Bay Maritime Museum have a chance to visit quaint country inns such as the Robert Morris Inn in Oxford, Talbot County.

Sportsmen not only hunt, they also fish these waters, and for a look at what they are likely to catch, visit the museum's aquarium. The fish were all caught by the museum's staff.

To put everything you've seen in perspective stop at the museum's Chesapeake Bay Building. It traces life back to the formation of the Bay during the last Ice Age. In the prehistoric period this region was part of the valley of the Susquehanna River, but as the glaciers melted it became a "drowned river." The story continues with the advent of precolonial Indians who fished and traveled this region. The Bay's role in the American Revolution, War of 1812 and Civil War is reviewed, as is the life of the watermen who've worked the Bay for centuries.

Currently under construction is a Waterman's Village, which will re-create everyday life on the Bay. There will be a steamboat landing and a collection of antique steam and gas engines. Craftsmen will demonstrate such skills as blacksmithing, sailmaking, trapmaking as well as operating a steam-powered sawmill.

The Chesapeake Bay Maritime Museum is open daily during the summer from 10:00 A.M. to 5:00 P.M. and summer Saturdays until 7:00 P.M. During the spring and fall seasons the museum is open 10:00 A.M. to 4:00 P.M. From January to mid-March it is open on weekends only. Closed Christmas and New Year's Day. Admission is charged.

Be sure to save time to stroll the quiet streets of St. Michaels. Along Talbot Street you'll find an assortment of boutiques, antique shops, specialty stores plus a deli and the town saloon. The harbor area boasts three popular restaurants—the Crab Claw, Longfellows and the Town Dock. There are also several bed and breakfast spots in town for overnight stays.

Directions: From Baltimore take Route 2 south to Route 50, cross the Chesapeake Bay Bridge and continue on Route 50 to Easton. From Easton take Route 33 west to St. Michaels. In St. Michaels turn right on Mill Street for the museum located at the end of the street at Navy Point.

CAROLINE COUNTY

Martinak State Park

Roadside R&R

Baltimore and Washington area residents heading for the Atlantic beaches have seen signs for **Martinak State Park** along the way. And many have stopped to discover the charms of this picturesque 100-acre park on the Eastern Shore. It's an ideal spot for a highway pull-off. Picnic tables beneath shady oaks on the banks of the Choptank River make this a cool lunchtime oasis even on a hot, muggy summer day.

Quite a number of those who have stopped to picnic here return for a longer stay in one of the 60 campsites that can be rented on a nightly or weekly basis. The weekend campfire programs recall the Indians who once camped here. Historians know that in 1669 the Choptanks, a subtribe of the Algonquins, had a reservation down river near Secretary. They suspect there was a village on the high ground within this park.

The Indians came for the excellent fishing here, and so do many modern visitors. A fishing license is required in the tidal waters of the Choptank River and Watts Creek. The park has a boat pier and a launching ramp for easy access to the water. Don't let the nearby wreckage of an old pungy, a turn-of-the-century sailing vessel, scare you—these waters are quite calm.

Children will enjoy the playground. But this is not the spot to let your pet out for a run; pets are not permitted at Martinak.

Martinak State Park is open for 24-hour camping from the first weekend in April through the last weekend in October. Daytime use continues year-round.

Directions: From Baltimore take Route 2 south to Route 50. Take Route 50 east across the Bay Bridge, then turn east on Route 404 to Denton. Martinak State Park is two miles south of Denton off Route 404 on Deep Shore Road.

Maryland's Southern Eastern Shore

DORCHESTER COUNTY

Blackwater National Wildlife Refuge

Take a Gander

If you enjoy National Geographic television specials, you'll love the experience of being part of the natural world at **Blackwater National Wildlife Refuge**. In fact, camera buffs can bring equipment and shoot their own nature film complete with sound effects—the honking and the rustle of wings as thousands of geese arrive and depart. The sound could be mistaken for the boisterous enthusiasm of a crowd at a football game. In late November there may be as many as 50,000 Canada geese at Blackwater. The five-mile scenic Wildlife Drive will give you a close look at these substantial birds—they can weigh as much as ten pounds. You might want to bring binoculars for birdwatching from the refuge's observation tower or along the Wildlife Drive, which you can hike, bike or drive.

The striking Canadas mate for life, and only if a partner dies will one occasionally take a new mate. Most of these geese nest during the summer at James Bay in Canada, but some pairs nest at Blackwater. In the spring you may see strings of five to eight goslings being closely supervised by their parents. Canada geese form a close-knit family; they are social birds and fly in large V-formations with older birds alternating the lead.

The waterfowl population at Blackwater also includes whistling swans, snow and blue geese, and 20 varieties of ducks. This refuge was established in 1932 as a home for migratory ducks, but its popularity with the geese has overshadowed the duck population.

Two endangered species are nurtured at Blackwater. The large, gray Delmarva Peninsula fox squirrel, unique to Maryland's Eastern Shore, is found in the refuge's woodland area. Its numbers have declined with the elimination of local forests. You are most likely to spot these foragers on the Woods Trail. The trail also gives you a chance to see varieties of birds different from those spotted elsewhere in the refuge. Here you'll see towhees, woodpeckers, brown-headed nuthatches and other forest birds.

A Great Blue Heron stands guard at the Blackwater National
Wildlife Refuge. As many as 50,000 Canada geese winter here.
Their sound can be mistaken for a football crowd.

The other endangered species, the bald eagle, nests here. The eagle nesting spots are protected from man's encroachment, but if you see a large pile of sticks and twigs at the top of a tree, you'll likely have spotted an eagle's nest. In spring, if you watch patiently, you may see one of the mature eagles returning with food for the young.

You can explore Blackwater National Wildlife Refuge from dawn to dusk. The Visitor Center is open 7:30 A.M. to 4:00 P.M. Monday through Friday and 9:00 A.M. to 5:00 P.M. on Saturday and Sunday. Closed on weekends during June, July and August, on Christmas Day and on all Federal holidays. If you have time, continue into southern Dorchester County, drive across scenic Narrow Ferry Bridge, which opened in 1980, and on to **Hoopers Island**. Here you'll see picturesque fishing villages: Honga, Fishing Creek and Hoopersville. A number of seafood packing houses operate in these waterfront towns where fishing, oystering and crabbing are a way of life.

Directions: From Baltimore take Route 2 south to Route 50. Cross the Bay Bridge and continue east on Route 50 another 45 miles to Cambridge, then go right on Route 16 to Church Creek. At Church Creek take Route 335 south for four miles and turn left on Key Wallace to the Visitor Center.

Cambridge Historic District and Brannock Maritime Museum

Historical View of the Bay

James Michener visited **Cambridge** while researching Maryland's Eastern Shore for his novel Chesapeake. He was captivated by High Street, as are all visitors who discover the stately mansions along this tree-lined street. In the spring the delicate blossoms of the Bradford pear trees top off the charm.

In almost any Cambridge shop or restaurant you can pick up a walking tour guide. It provides the historic and architectural background of the homes, churches and businesses in the historic district. Most of the district was built in the 19th century, but next door to Christ Church is Josiah Bayly's law office, built in 1796. It's the oldest continuously used business office in Maryland. Be sure to take the time to go inside Christ Church. The Rose Window, crafted in London, is a sparkling gem. The church also has some not-to-be-missed Tiffany windows. A church has stood here since 1693, although the present structure was not erected until 1883. Buried in the church cemetery are early settlers, Revolutionary War heroes and several Maryland governors.

At the end of High Street there is a town park overlooking the yacht basin and busy harbor. Picnic tables and benches make this an ideal spot for a midday break. If you prefer to dine in a restaurant, just off High Street on Commerce is Clayton's on the Creek, a waterside eatery with both indoor and outdoor dining. The seafood is fresh daily and Clayton's is popular with both natives and visitors.

For an overview of Cambridge's maritime heritage, visit **Brannock Maritime Museum**. You'll learn all about the Maryland Oyster Navy and its commanders. It had no military affiliation; it was simply the colloquial name for the Chesapeake Bay oyster fleet.

Cambridge was home to both ship sailors and ship builders. This was once an important shipbuilding center. Legend has it the ship that pursued Moby Dick was built in Cambridge. The museum has photographs of the whaling vessels built here, as well as models of other ships.

The first steamboat in the Bay, the *S.S. Chesapeake*, was launched here by Captain Trippe, a builder. The museum has photographs of all but one of the steamboats that made Cambridge a port of call.

Early maritime history is recalled through navigational tools that date back to the 1700s. The museum showcases the career of Matthew Fontain Maury, the father of oceanography. There is also a library for research on maritime history and the Chesapeake Bay. The Brannock Maritime Museum, at 210 Talbot Street, is open on weekends from 1:00 to 4:00 P.M.

Directions: From Baltimore take Route 2 south to Route 50. Cross the Bay Bridge and go about 45 miles to Cambridge. After you cross the Choptank River Bridge into Cambridge proper, turn right on Maryland Avenue and cross over Cambridge Creek. Bear right for High Street. Park and explore High Street and the historic district on foot. For the museum, take High Street down to the Choptank River and turn left on Water Street and then left again on Talbot Avenue.

Dorchester Heritage Museum and Spocott Windmill

Winner by a Neck

Dorchester County's Neck District is bounded by the Choptank and Little Choptank Rivers, which are all but connected by the finger-like creeks that crisscross the land between them. You're rarely out of sight of water as you drive the quiet back roads, all of which dead-end at water's edge. Scenic appeal is only part of the reason to head east from Cambridge into the Neck District for a self-guided tour. If you arrive on a weekend you can explore the **Dorchester Heritage Museum**.

The museum is located on what was once the estate of Francis DuPont. He bequeathed the land to the city of Cambridge, and the city then gave it to the University of Maryland to use for Environmental and Estuarine Studies. High school students became involved and enlisted community support for preserving the history of the county. The result of their efforts is the Dorchester County Museum, housed in an old airplane hangar.

Early aviation is one of the major themes here. The hangar sits beside one of the country's best grass-stripped runways. Each May, on the weekend prior to Memorial Day, the museum sponsors an Antique Aircraft Fly-In. This annual festival gives visitors a chance to see vintage aircraft in action, plus talk to the owners who have lovingly restored these classic planes. There are also aviation exhibits inside the museum.

Another focus of the museum is local archeology. One room displays some of the 30,000 artifacts volunteers and museum staffers have excavated from 17th- and 18th-century sites on the museum grounds. The first house on the "Horne" site was built around 1670. It burned to the ground in 1700. The ruins were cleared and a second house built, but it too was destroyed by fire around 1770. The remains of these two tragedies have yielded rich details about upper-middle-class family life during the colonial period. If you are interested in volunteering to help at the dig, call (301)228-5530 on weekends or (301)228-1899 during the week.

Other museum exhibits feature tools and household items of the region's watermen and farmers. In Dorchester County the same family names appear generation after generation, and many of these long-time residents have contributed memorabilia. The Dorchester Heritage Museum on Horn Point Road is open 1:00 to 4:30 P.M. on weekends from mid-April through October. There is no charge for admission.

After your visit to the museum, head back down Horn Point Road, then turn right at Lovers Lane, the first road to the right. At the intersection with Route 343 turn right; in two miles you'll see the distinctive **Spocott Windmill** on your left.

This is Maryland's only existing post windmill for grinding grain. The mill was built in 1850 by John Anthony LeCompte Radcliff, as part of a self-contained community that included sawmills, blacksmith shops and shipyards. The windmill that you will see was reconstructed in 1971 using millstones and other parts of the original, blown down during the blizzard of 1888.

A one-room schoolhouse, circa 1868, also stands with the windmill on the greensward along the marshy banks of the Little Choptank River. These are among the most picturesque sites along the Neck District Tour. If you continue your drive along the "neck" you will pass several charming community churches. Once you've completed your visit to this Eastern Shore region, simply reverse direction and head back to Cambridge.

Directions: From Baltimore take Route 2 south to Route 50 east. Cross the Chesapeake Bay Bridge and go about 45 miles to Cambridge. After you cross the Choptank River Bridge as you come into Cambridge, turn right on Route 343 for the Neck District.

Meredith House and Neild Museum

Maryland Lore

The 18th-century Georgian-style **Meredith House**, overlooking the Choptank River in Cambridge, is known as the house of chimneys. John Woolford built this Flemish-bond-brick plantation house with three chimneys in 1760. It is now the home of the Dorchester County Historical Society. Docents entertain visitors with stories about the early county residents whose portraits grace the dining room walls. You'll learn about Anne Francis Tilghman, whose smile suggests the Mona Lisa. Her son, Trench Tilghman, was the only aide George Washington retained throughout the Revolutionary War. Another portrait is of Mary Richardson LeCompte, daughter of one of the early Huguenot families in Dorchester County.

Antique buffs will love the Chippendale, Hepplewhite and Sheraton period furniture in the downstairs rooms. Younger visitors will want to linger upstairs with the doll collection— shelves, baby buggies, high chairs and cradles all hold period dolls. History buffs may learn about Maryland in the Dorchester County Room. Six Maryland governors came from this county: Hicks, Henry, Lloyd, Harrington and both Charles and Philip Lee Goldsboro. A seventh, Thomas King Carroll, while not born in Dorchester, is buried here in Old Trinity Church near Church Creek.

On the third floor of the Meredith House there are two country bedrooms. Spool beds, rag rugs, lace night shirts and two old quilts bring back the bygone years. The splendid Star of Bethlehem quilt was made in 1762; its colors are felicitously arranged and still surprisingly vibrant.

Adjacent to the Meredith House is the **Neild Museum**, filled with artifacts from the past. The collection represents early American life along the river, in the home and on the farm. You'll see shipbuilding tools, an old dugout canoe and several ship models. Farm tools include an 1831 McCormick Reaper, an 1820 Fanning mill, which was used with a threshing machine, and a life-size horse model that once stood in front of Philips Hardware Store displaying the latest in harnesses.

One exhibit focuses on Annie Oakley, who, with her husband Colonel Frank Butler, settled along the Choptank River (at 28 Bellevue Street). Oakley chose this location, declaring it was the most beautiful she had discovered on her travels with Buffalo Bill's Wild West show. After your museum visit, take Cambridge's Scenic Drive past their house. They built a modest place; it's said that Oakley had lived out of trunks so much of her life she forgot to include closets in her house and they had to be added. When you drive past, notice the sloping roof. Legend has it that the slant was added so that Little Miss Sure Shot, as Oakley was called, could step out her bedroom window and shoot passing wildfowl. Locals tell the story of the time Butler went out in his skiff to retrieve some of her birds. He was smoking, a habit she detested, so she took aim and shot the offending cigarette from his mouth.

The Meredith House and Neild Museum are open on Fridays from 9:30 A.M. to 4:30 P.M. and at other times by appointment. Call (301)228-7953. On the grounds between these two attractions you'll see an 18th-century smokehouse and colonial herb garden.

Directions: From Baltimore take Route 2 south to Route 50 east. Cross the Bay Bridge and follow Route 50 to Cambridge. Once you cross the Choptank River Bridge into Cambridge turn left on Maryland Avenue (that's at the first traffic light after crossing the bridge). Turn left off Maryland Avenue onto Le-Grange Avenue for the Meredith House.

WICOMICO COUNTY

Poplar Hill Mansion and Pemberton Hall

Newtown Is an Old Town

Do you like gingerbread—not the kind you eat, but the architectural type of the Victorian era? If so, then you'll like Newtown, too. Fish-scaled towers, conical turrets, elaborately balustraded porches, bay windows, a gabled pavilion, mullioned transoms and colored leaded windows ornament the houses of Salisbury's Newtown Historic District. East Isabella Street and East William Street, both off Poplar Avenue, have the greatest concentration of houses with these ornate features. A walking tour guide describes the architectural details of 27 homes in this district. To obtain a copy write the Convention and Visitors Bureau, Glen Avenue Extended, Salisbury, MD 21801.

In 1886 a fire raged through Salisbury, destroying many residential communities. Newtown, like a phoenix, rose from the ashes. It was the first neighborhood to be rebuilt. Within this historic district is **Poplar Hill Mansion**, which survived the fire and is the oldest house in Salisbury.

Records are sketchy about just who built Poplar Hill, and when. Current thinking is that this 19th-century country Georgian-style mansion was begun around 1805 by a Dr. John Huston. The land was first owned by Major Levin Handy, who came to the Eastern Shore from Rhode Island. Major Handy acquired a sizeable acreage in Maryland, but financial problems forced him to sell 228½ acres at public auction on March 31, 1804. The land on which Poplar Hill stands was purchased by Peter Dashiell who later transferred it to his brother-in-law, Dr. Huston.

The front door of Poplar Hill is flanked with fluted pilasters and crowned with a broken pediment arch and a fan-shaped window. Splendid bulls-eye windows grace the east and west peak roof lines. The interior has the original heart pine floors, handcarved cornices and chair rails. Tours are given of Poplar Hill Mansion, at 117 Elizabeth Street, on Sundays from 1:00 to 4:00 P.M. Donations are welcome.

Another Handy, Colonel Isaac Handy, built an 18th-century house on the Wicomico River near what is now Salisbury (formerly Handy's Landing). This 1741 gambrel-roofed plantation house, **Pemberton Hall**, is in the process of being restored. Although it is incomplete and furnished with only a few pieces, you are welcome to visit Sundays from 2:00 to 4:00 P.M. from the third Sunday in May through September. Pemberton Hall is part of the 61-acre Pemberton Historical Park. There are three nature trails to explore, and ambitious plans are underway to re-create an 18th-century barn to house the Wicomico Historical Society's collections.

Directions: From Baltimore take Route 2 south to Route 50 east. Follow Route 50 across the Bay Bridge approximately 80 miles to Salisbury. For Pemberton Historical Park turn right on Route 349 west and then make an immediate left onto Pemberton Drive. Continue two miles to Pemberton Historical Park entrance on the left. For Poplar Hill turn left off Route 50 on North Division Street. Continue past East William and East Isabella streets to Elizabeth Street. Poplar Hill Mansion is on the corner of Poplar Hill Avenue.

Wildfowl Art Museum and Salisbury Zoo

Compare the Decoy with the Live Bird

Seeing is not believing, certainly at first glance, at the Ward Foundation's **North American Wildfowl Art Museum** at Salisbury State College. The woodcarvings exhibited here are so realistic, right down to the wispy delicacy of a single feather, they seem ready to take wing.

The transition from functional decoys to decorative wildfowl carvings was led in the mid-1920s by Crisfield, Maryland, carvers Steve and Lem Ward (see Crisfield selection). The Ward Foundation, formed to preserve and perpetuate the art of the handmade decoy, was named in their honor and memory. Their Sackertown Road decoy shop in Crisfield is re-created at the museum, and a television news clip is presented, featuring Lem Ward carving and reciting poetry. It is a moving, personal look at this rugged pioneer.

The best way to explore the Wildfowl Art Museum is from top to bottom. Pick up a self-guiding tour brochure and climb to the balcony. The decoy story begins with an Indian reed-and-feather decoy found in Lovelock Cave, Nevada, and dating from 1000 A.D. The first European settlers also crafted decoys, but they used wood remnants and driftwood for their working materials. Accompanying the display on early decoys and the next display on pre–Civil War decoys are hunting rifles—a flintlock shotgun and a breech-loading shotgun.

In the late 1800s and early 1900s there was a tremendous demand for wildfowl by restaurants across the country. Market hunting became a big business and special boats were constructed to increase the number of birds bagged. You'll see an example of a sinkbox (also displayed at the Upper Bay Museum, see selection). This boat, resembling a coffin, had wooden and canvas wings on which 20 to 30 decoys were mounted. When in use the sinkbox was surrounded by 200 to 300 floating decoys completely camouflaging the hunter. A similar "icebox" was used in winter. Another camouflaged craft you'll see is a sneakbox, a floating blind that was surrounded by scores of decoys.

Market hunting ended with the passage of the 1918 Migratory Bird Act prohibiting the sale of wildfowl for food. Although this much-needed law saved the birds, it was a blow to hunters, who lost their livelihood. It was at this time that many who, heretofore, had made only working decoys began to carve decorative pieces to help make ends meet.

Personal style became more apparent with decorative decoys, but there had always been regional differences in the hunting decoys. The next section of the museum displays styles originating from 14 geographic regions. Two are from the Maryland area—Crisfield and the Susquehanna Flats—and two are from Virginia—the Back Bay and the Eastern Shore.

It is in the downstairs gallery that the art of carving is displayed. Since 1971 the Ward Foundation has hosted an annual World Championship Wildfowl Carving Competition. The $65,000 in prize money and the chance to compete against fellow craftsmen attract carvers from all over the world. There are four main categories: Decorative Pairs, Decorative Miniatures, Decorative Lifesize and Natural Finish Sculptures. The World Class winners in these competitions provide the nucleus of the museum's collection.

One interesting display features three variations of a Canada goose. The Canada by Hans Bolte has fine feather details, the one by William Burns features the wood grain and transparent paint, and Lem Ward's pose and features are highly stylized. Lem's Canada goose is only one of many decoys made by the Ward brothers. Incidentally, they started out earning 50 cents per piece in 1918 but eventually commanded upwards of $2,000 each.

The Wildfowl Art Museum is open Tuesday through Saturday 10:00 A.M. to 5:00 P.M. and Sunday 1:00 to 5:00 P.M. Closed Mondays and holidays. Donations are encouraged.

Nearby **Salisbury Zoo** is "one of the finest small zoos in North America," according to Dr. Theodore Reed, Director Emeritus of The National Zoo in Washington, D.C. Here you'll find many of the same wildfowl captured so realistically at the Wildfowl Art Museum. But you'll also see more exotic species: brilliant blue peacocks, bright yellow sun conures, and orange-beaked toucans as well as guanacos, capybaras and jaguars. The more than 400 mammals, birds and reptiles share naturalistic enclosures, and many of the birds seem to have the run of the park. This is an inviting and relaxing zoo to explore.

Less than five minutes off Route 50, the Salisbury Zoo and an adjacent picnic area and playground make an ideal stop for beach-bound families. There is no charge to visit the zoo, which is open daily, except Christmas and Thanksgiving, from 8:00 A.M. From Memorial Day to Labor Day the zoo closes at 7:30 P.M.; at other times it closes at 4:30 P.M.

Directions: From Baltimore take Route 2 south to Route 50. Follow Route 50 east across the Bay Bridge 80 miles to Salisbury. From Route 50 turn right on Route 13 south and proceed to College Avenue, where you turn right. The Wildfowl Art Museum is in Holloway Hall, next to the Salisbury State College Admissions Office at College and Camden Avenues. A sign with a duck indicates the turn. For the Salisbury Zoo return to Route 13 and head north until you reach East Main Street. Turn right on East Main and then right again on Snow Hill Road. Then take the first left onto South Park Avenue. After you pass the picnic and playground area, you'll find the zoo entrance on your left. To reach Salisbury Zoo directly from Route 50, turn right on Civic Avenue and follow the zoo signs.

SOMERSET COUNTY

Crisfield

Islands in the Sun

It is certainly worth taking a daytrip that includes the "best crab cakes in the world" for lunch. Such noted publications as *The Washington Post, The New York Times, People Magazine* and *Southern Living* have raved about the crab cakes at Capt's Galley Restaurant on the Tangier Sound waterfront in **Crisfield**.

Just about everything in this picturesque southern Eastern Shore community is on the waterfront. While in town you can visit the **J. Millard Tawes Museum**, which commemorates the two-term governor (1959–67) born in Crisfield on April 8, 1894. The museum displays the papers, pictures and memorabilia of Governor Tawes, whose 45 years of public service spanned a period of enormous growth and change in the United States. Inaugural gowns worn by the governor's wife, the former Helen Avalynne Gibson, are also shown.

Another Crisfield native, Dr. Sarah Peyton, is also remembered in the Tawes Museum. She was one of the first women physicians at the School of Medicine at Johns Hopkins. Included in this display is her father's 1890s prescription counter.

The museum has exhibits tracing the history of the region back to the Indians who once camped along these shores. The work of the region's current residents, the watermen, is covered too. Many visitors come to the area during the hunting season. Decoy making is a fine art in these parts. The museum has re-created the decoy carving workshop of Len and Steven Ward (see Wildfowl Art Museum selection). There are splendid examples of this regional craft on display.

The J. Millard Tawes Museum, which overlooks Somers Cove Marina, is open May 30 to September 30 daily from 10:00 A.M. to 5:00 P.M. From October through November and from March through May, hours are Tuesday through Saturday from 10:00 A.M. to 4:00 P.M. The museum is closed December through February. A nominal admission is charged.

At the marina just outside the museum, charter boats depart daily during the summer months for **Smith Island**. This is the

Nearly everything in Crisfield happens on the waterfront. Called the "Seafood Capital of the World," Crisfield also lays claim to the world's best crab cakes.

largest inhabited offshore island in the Chesapeake Bay. The boat trip is roughly 12 miles across Tangier Sound from Crisfield and passes the 5,000-acre Glenn L. Martin Wildlife Sanctuary. The island was charted by John Smith in 1608 and settled in 1657. English accents still can be heard in the islanders' speech, and the names of the early settlers still can be found—Bradshaw, Evans, Tyler and Marshall.

The island has three villages—Ewell, Tylertown and Rhodes Point—and though the various charter boats dock at different communities, you'll have plenty of time on any of the trips to explore the eight-mile long, four-mile wide island. One of the pleasures of this outing is the opportunity to eat at the island's family-style restaurants. The Harbor Side Restaurant, Bayside Inn, Frances Kitchen's and Ruke's Seafood Deck are all popular with visitors. If you prefer you can bring a picnic lunch and dine alfresco.

Charter boats leave Crisfield at 12:30 and return at about 5:15 to 5:30 P.M. You can call or write Capt. Alan Tyler, Rhodes Point, MD 21858, (301)425-2771, or Capt. Larry, or Capt. Terry, Laird at (301)425-4471 and (301)425-5931. You can also book full and half-day sportsfishing trips aboard charter boats from Somers Cover Marina (call (301)336-0710).

If you want to enjoy an island adventure but don't have enough time for a voyage to Smith Island, head over to **Janes Island State Park**, just 1½ miles outside Crisfield. The park's Hodson Area, on the mainland, has log cabins that can be rented, campgrounds, a marina and a picnic area. Across Annemessex Sound, reachable only by boat, is the park's island area. During the summer months you can rent boats at the marina or join a pontoon party to cross to the island's trails and beaches. This area is also popular with fishermen and hunters.

Directions: From Baltimore take Route 2 south to Route 50. Take Route 50 across the Bay Bridge to Salisbury. At Salisbury take Route 13 south for roughly 15 miles to Route 413. Make a right on Route 413 and head down to Crisfield.

Eastern Shore Early Americana Museum

Imagine the Smithsonian's Attic

Covered wagon jacks, a tattoo machine, a jigsaw puzzle cutter, slot machines, toy trains and cow horn cutters. . .a Salisbury hearse, a surrey with the fringe on top, bone-meal grinders, door hinges, old irons; an addressograph. . .feather pluckers, pea hullers, stump pullers, corn shellers. . .parcel-post fresh egg shippers, cherry seeders, cream separators. . .a barber's chair and a shoe-shine chair. . .a rickshaw and a pony cart, a bowling ball shiner, a broom-making device. . .eel gigs, model airplanes, Christmas decorations, Avon products, political buttons, oyster tonging forks. . .an Erector set ferris wheel and a loom. All this and more, and more, and more fill the **Eastern Shore Early Americana Museum**.

It's impossible to estimate the number of items Lawrence Burgess has collected in his Marion Station museum. When queried, Burgess just chuckles and counters with "What's an item?" There are literally millions of old things that this enthusiastic collector has spent 30 years gathering at farm auctions. He is still buying by the boxfull. He never discards, just groups his items by use. Burgess's collection is displayed in a converted two-story poultry broiler house. Visitors wander bemusedly down the 300-foot long corridors between displays as Mr. Burgess points out the oddities of his eclectic assortment.

You'll envision bygone days when you spot items that you, or your grandparents, once used. You'll marvel at the specialization of the early 19th-century tools. The museum provides an overview of the progress of technology in the home, on the farm, in fishing and in various trades. Probably the ideal visiting pair at this museum would be a grandparent with grandchild; it's the best place imaginable to talk about the "good old days." But no matter what your age, there is something—or a lot of some-things—to fascinate you.

In addition to the main collection, there is a second building with the merchandise from four old country stores. All were once neighborhood gathering spots in their Eastern shore communi-ties. The glass counters are filled with items you're not likely to find today: men's stiff celluloid shirt collars still in their original boxes, "Roll Your Own" Bull Durham tobacco, and boxes of slate pencils. And you're not going to find prices like those posted in this old store: Coca Cola is advertised at 5 cents, stamps at 3 cents.

The museum is open year-round and there is a nominal ad-mission charge. To be sure someone is on hand to escort you, it is best to call ahead, (301)623-8324. The buildings are not heated, so visitors are advised to dress warmly during the winter months.

Directions: From Baltimore take Route 2 south to Route 50 and then go east. At Salisbury take Route 13 south to the intersection with Route 413. Go right on Route 413, then make a left on Old Westover Road to Hudsons Corner and the Eastern Shore Early Americana Museum.

Teackle Mansion and Princess Anne

Somebody Forgot the Stairs

Littleton Dennis Teackle was a Virginian and a friend of the illustrious triumvirate—Jefferson, Madison and Monroe. He made his mark on Maryland's lower Eastern Shore, however.

Teackle and his wife, Elizabeth Upshur, purchased the 18-acre Beckford Grant in Somerset County between 1795 and 1800. The **Teackle Mansion** was patterned on a Scottish manor house. The center section was built in 1800 and the wings added in 1803. Teackle did not conceal his staircase as Thomas Jefferson did, for esthetic reasons, at Monticello. According to legend, Teackle simply overlooked the need for stairs when he designed his man-sion. Thus, the "hidden" staircase had to be squeezed into the narrow space between the walls of the central section and the wing.

Littleton Dennis Teackle was a builder in many ways. He es-tablished the Maryland public school system, the first public school system in the nation, and in 1826 was appointed Com-missioner of his brainchild. He also established the first public commercial bank in America in Princess Anne and was instrumental in getting the first commercial banking laws of Maryland passed.

At the request of President Jefferson, Teackle provided lumber for the "gunboat" fleet, the floating defense network needed to enforce the mercantile blockade against Britain. Teackle's shipping interests, alas, brought him financial ruin. The Barbary Pirates pillaged Teackle's merchant fleet in the Mediterranean and caused him to lose not only his ships, but his home. The account of the family's bankruptcy is given in George Alfred Townsend's 1884 novel, *The Entailed Hat*, which also includes information on the Nassawango Iron Furnace (see Furnace Town selection and also see Gathland selection for more on Townsend).

The Teackle Mansion is filled with period furnishings. In the drawing room you'll see a portrait of Mrs. Teackle. The ornate mirror over the fireplace is from the Ogle House in Annapolis. You'll notice there are mirrored windows along the hall wall. One explanation for these mirrors is that Mr. Teackle enjoyed watching the reflection of boats plying the Manokin River. Another story is that Mrs. Teackle liked to see her garden from both the real and false windows. The most likely explanation is that the mirrors reflected light, making the room brighter.

From the drawing room you'll go on to the south wing of the mansion; the north wing is owned by the Somerset County Historical Society and is open only on special occasions. In the south wing there is a small sitting room, or retiring room as it was called, a dining room and the old kitchen. The kitchen's restoration was enhanced in 1974 when workers exploring behind one of the walls uncovered a seven-foot fireplace and beehive oven that had been walled up for over a century.

The second floor has museum rooms; one room is filled with children's toys and fashion accessories, while another is a repository of Somerset County and Maryland State history books and memorabilia. There is also a Victorian sitting room and bedchamber filled with the heavy furniture of that era. The house can be toured Sunday afternoons from 2:00 to 4:00 P.M. and at other times by appointment. Call (301)651-1705.

After touring Teackle Mansion you may want to stroll around **Princess Anne**. Littleton Dennis Teackle and his wife are buried in the St. Andrew's Episcopal Churchyard on Church Street. On Somerset Avenue you can stop for lunch or dinner (or even stay overnight) at the Washington Hotel, built in 1744. The hotel retains anachronistic touches like the separate ladies' and gentlemen's staircases. Like so many early American towns, Princess Anne was ravaged by fire; but some lovely colonial and Federal homes have survived. Each year during Princess Anne Days, the second weekend in October, a number of these private homes are open to the public.

Directions: From Baltimore take Route 2 south to Route 50. Continue on Route 50 to Salisbury, then take Route 13 south to Princess Anne.

WORCESTER COUNTY AND OCEAN CITY

Assateague Island

Not Far from the Madding Crowd

Even longtime beach buffs get confused when questioned about Assateague Island. Is it in Maryland or Virginia? Is it a national or state park? Where is it in relation to Chincoteague Island?

Here are some answers: Assateague is a 37-mile-long barrier island that has its northern two-thirds in Maryland and its southern third in Virginia; no road connects the two sections. In fact, much of the island is accessible only by boat or on foot. Assateague shelters the smaller Chincoteague Island located west of the Virginia portion in the Chincoteague Bay. As you cross the bridge from the Maryland mainland, you'll immediately see the state park. Most of the island, however, is part of the National Wildlife Refuge even though it is on Assateague Island.

The barren, unsettled island is constantly shifting. The fragile dunes, anchored by equally fragile grasses, protect the low-lying bay side portion of the island. Those who despair at the body-to-body throng around Ocean City delight in the endless stretches of relatively empty sand here. Because the human population is so carefully controlled by limited roadway access, the animal population is plentiful. The best-known four-legged inhabitants are the wild ponies. Reputedly descended from survivors of a wrecked Spanish galleon, they more likely come from stock grazed by settlers. You're also likely to see a variety of birds in the small, marshy island meadows.

For many it is the denizens of the sea, not the land, that provide the inducement—fisherman flock to the island. Surf casting, clamming and crabbing are all popular.

The two-mile Maryland state park on Assateague has bathhouses and campsites open most of the year. Food service and protected beaches are available summer only. Just to the south is a National Park Service beach, which is open for day use. You can camp in a primitive campground year-round. Just before you cross the Sinepuxent Bridge onto the island there is a Visitor Center where you can see an aquarium and a natural history film and where you can familiarize yourself with happenings on Assateague. You can pick up a map and brochure showing the various park areas on the island. Visitor Center hours are 8:30 A.M. to 5:00 P.M.

Assateague Island, the 37-mile-long barrier island that has its northern two-thirds in Maryland and its southern third in Virginia, is home to the wild, free-roaming ponies.

Directions: From Baltimore take Route 2 south to Route 50. Follow Route 50 to the outskirts of Ocean City. Turn right on Route 611 to the Visitor Center and the Sinepuxent Bridge over to Assateague.

Furnace Town

Huff and Puff

The south had plantations worked by slave labor, while the north had industrial villages worked by laborers who were virtual serfs on feudal-like estates. Just a few miles from Snow Hill, you can visit a re-created 19th-century industrial town that was run in this manner. The Nassawango Iron Furnace was in operation from 1832 to 1847. Step back in time at this remarkably intact historical site.

Bog ore was discovered along the Nassawango Creek as early as 1789. But 40 years passed before the Maryland General Assembly, in 1829, granted a charter to the Maryland Iron Company, after which the company acquired 5,000 acres of forest and swamp land around the creek. Originally it built a cold blast furnace but switched between 1834 and 1837 to the hot blast technique developed in Scotland. It is this hot blast furnace you'll see today and that calls up mental pictures of the miners, sawyers, colliers, molders, firemen, carters, draymen and bargemen who were living and working in **Furnace Town** in its heyday.

Originally the ore was thought to be a higher grade than it actually was, thus the furnace was never as profitable as anticipated. The bog ore was obtained beneath the creek waters by miners using picks, shovels and rakes. Ore was then carried to the shore in flat-bottom boats. It was smelted day and night in the 35-foot-high furnace.

The furnace is recognized by historical experts as one of the finest examples of its kind in the country. It offers insights into how the smelting process worked. Because the trough, in which the molten ore was cooled after it had passed through the casting hearth, looked to some people like a sow with piglets, this cast iron came to be called pig iron. The entire iron-making process is explained at the Furnace Town Visitor Center. Be sure to stop there before you see the furance; it will give you an appreciation and understanding of what you'll be seeing. Other buildings at Furnace Town incude a country store selling local handicrafts, a blacksmith shop, smokehouse, broom house, 19th-century print shop and the Old Nazareth Church, circa 1874.

A fictional account of the decline of the Nassawango Iron Furnace is included in George Alfred Townsend's novel *The Entailed Hat* (see Gathland State Park). The book, published in 1884, is out of print but can be obtained through the Maryland public library system.

The Nassawango Creek and Swamp come under the jurisdiction of the Nature Conservancy. If you have the time, take the nature trail that begins at the furnace site. The trail is particularly enjoyable in the spring when the wildflowers are in bloom. It is always a mecca for bird lovers.

Furnace Town hosts many festivals throughout the spring, summer and fall. Living history is an integral part of these special events (see Calendar).

Furnace Town is open Tuesday through Sunday from 11:00 A.M. to 5:00 P.M. Admission is charged.

Directions: From Baltimore take Route 2 south to Route 50. Take Route 50 east about 90 miles to Salisbury, then take Route 12 south about 16 miles to Old Furnace Road. Turn right at the highway sign for Furnace Town.

Julia A. Purnell Museum and Snow Hill

An Old Town That Loved an Old Woman

The story of the founding of Snow Hill's **Julia A. Purnell Museum** is guaranteed to warm a mother's heart. William Z. Purnell was justly proud of the needlework his mother, Julia Lecompte Purnell, created. He felt it was all the more remarkable since she didn't take up fine stitching until she was 86. She started her new hobby after a fall confined her to a wheelchair. Miss Julia lived to be 100; she was born in 1843 and died in 1943. During the last 15 years of her life she produced nearly 3,000 needlework pieces. A fraction of these are framed and displayed at the museum.

William Purnell and the town residents were not the only ones to recognize Miss Julia's accomplishments. After ten years of needleworking, she sent her work to the Philadelphia Hobby Show and won both a First Prize and the Grand Prize. Two years later, when she was just shy of 100, she was inducted into the Hobby Hall of Fame of America.

Miss Julia's creations, however, are only a small part of the museum's collection. The museum also covers the history of **Snow Hill** and this part of Maryland from the days of the Indians through the Victorian era. The story of the Pocomoke River region unfolds chronologically beginning with the Nanticoke Indian arrowheads and other artifacts. Next come the hand-hewn utensils and tools from the colonial period. You'll see such oddities as a Johnny cake board, handmade wooden pitchers, a foot warmer with a built-in lamp, a mangle and a mustard dipper. Handmades soon gave way to trade goods, for by 1690 Snow Hill was a Royal Port with a lively trade linking it to other regions.

Like the rest of the country, Snow Hill was divided by the Civil War. In fact, dissidents sought refuge in the tangled forest along the banks of the Pocomoke River. Runaway slaves also found sanctuary here. The museum has reminders of the slave trade, such as the 1852 slave allowance list. You'll see that slaves were given white bread on Sundays. They were fed meagerly and their size was measured by a slave stick, like the one displayed, before they were auctioned at the Snow Hill Courthouse.

One of the major Snow Hill events of the late 1800s was the Great Fire of 1893 (an earlier fire in 1834 had consumed 40 homes, 8 stores and 2 hotels). Newspaper stories tell of the town's difficulties in 1893. Fire buckets and grenade bottles are reminders of citizen involvement in fire fighting. Other exhibits deal with agriculture and trade tools. There are carpenters' tools, tanners' fleshing knives, weights and measures to check store scales, and both a Snow Hill dentist's and doctor's tools.

A selection of lighting devices ranges from pitch pipes to electricity. There are lighter knots (torches made from pine knots and used at outdoor meetings), sperm oil lamps, a baker's lamps and even a courting lamp. The latter enabled the girl's father to measure out the oil in keeping with the desirability of the suitor. If the gentleman did not seem promising, a modest amount of oil would insure an early end to the evening.

The Victorian era is brought to life with a re-creation of Miss Julia's sewing room. There is also a collection of old gowns and accessories—lace mitts, hair combs and a courting mirror. Everything in the museum was donated by friends and relatives of the Purnells and by Snow Hill residents.

Be sure to pick up a Snow Hill Walking Tour map and stroll the tree-lined streets. There are some 100 buildings in Snow Hill that were built before 1877. The tour map gives brief descriptions of 50 of these old structures—homes, churches, government buildings and also a one-room schoolhouse.

While you're exploring, take time out to enjoy lunch, dinner or an overnight stay at the Snow Hill Inn, built circa 1790. This inn has seven bedrooms furnished with period pieces. The restaurant offers regional cuisine. Call (301)632-2102 for accommodations or reservations. If you plan a weekend visit, you should make lunch or dinner reservations ahead; this is a popular spot.

Directions: From Baltimore take Route 2 south to Route 50. Go east 90 miles on Route 50 to Salisbury, then take Route 12 south to Snow Hill.

Ocean City Life Saving Station Museum

The Place to Go Overboard

There's nothing worse than the beach in the rain, right? In Ocean City you can wile away a cloudy afternoon at the **Ocean City Life Saving Station Museum** opposite the Inlet Village specialty shops at the south end of the boardwalk.

This museum explores both the history of the Life Saving Service and Ocean City's boardwalk attractions. Most visitors have never heard of the Life Saving Service, forerunner of today's Coast Guard. The service was formed in 1848, but it wasn't until December 25, 1878, that the first Ocean City Life Saving Station opened. It was one of a series of stations along the country's 10,000-mile coastline. The picturesque building in which the museum is located was built in 1891 to replace the small original station.

The museum's boat room contains apparatus used for sea rescues. The largest piece is the fully restored surf rescue boat from Caffey's Inlet Station in North Carolina. Visitors are also fascinated by the surfcar, or life car. Into this small, 11- by 4-foot claustrophobic contraption four people could be squeezed, if necessary. Speed was essential in saving passengers from wrecked vessels. The breeches buoy, which you will see in old photographs, could handle only one survivor at a time. Surfcars were necessary because ships ladened with immigrants frequently ran aground along the Atlantic coast off Ocean City. To appreciate the rescue service in action, there is a short film about the rescue of the crew of the *Olaf Bergh*, a Norwegian freighter that was hugging the shore in fear of German submarines and foundered off Ocean City (around 94th Street). A faded photograph shows the Norwegian consul watching as a survivor is brought to shore in the breeches buoy.

The collection of life-saving equipment is reputed to be the largest in the country. It includes old uniforms, photographs, boats and other equipment. The museum exhibits shift from sea rescue to sea salvage with a collection of articles recovered from shipwrecks. The assorted bottles and rusted artifacts are not likely to inspire you to don a wet suit and start searchng for treasure.

Sailors were apt to spend their off hours at sea tying complex knots; and visitors who have thought of macramé as a relatively new craft will be surprised to see the 50 different sailor's knots on the museum's knot board. There is also a substantial shell collection that might encourage you to start combing the beaches.

Out on the beach you certainly won't see the swimsuits collected here. They date from the turn of the century and include rental suits. Beach trips were so infrequent that families simply rented swimwear for the day. These vintage outfits were hardly figure-flattering. Take, for example, the 80-year-old suit made from ten yards of heavy wool. The collection exhibits progress gradually from bloomers to bikinis. If you are tempted to chuckle at these far-from-fetching suits, you can chime in with Laughing Sal, a mannequin remnant of Jester's Funhouse. Sal, a busty, oversize lady whose laugh once echoed down the boardwalk, bows and waves her arms while cackling uproariously. Hers is no fleeting fame: she was immortalized in John Barth's *Lost in the Funhouse* stories. He wrote of her laugh, "You couldn't hear it without laughing yourself." Push her button and see if you agree.

Laughing Sal is not the only exhibit that brings back the good old days. There is a model collection of 12 formerly well-known boardwalk hotels, some of which still stand. The models, which include a miniature grocery store, pharmacy and even the museum, are exact to the smallest detail. You can even see Lilliputian people strolling along the boardwalk (none wear slogan-covered T-shirts).

The Ocean City Life Saving Station Museum is open June through September from 11:00 A.M. to 10:00 P.M. daily. In May and October the museum is open daily from 11:00 A.M. to 4:00 P.M. and November through April it is open on weekends only from noon to 4:00 P.M. A nominal admission is charged.

Directions: Take Route 2 south to Route 50 and go east to Ocean City (about 120 miles). The museum is located at the south end of the boardwalk.

Pocomoke River State Park

Two-Firs

Both sides of the Pocomoke River are included within the 13,000 acre **Pocomoke River State Park** and State Forest. On one bank you'll find Milburn Landing State Park (370 acres) and four miles north on the opposite side, Shad Landing State Park (545 acres).

The Pocomoke River winds through the cypress swamps and primitive forests of Maryland's lower Eastern shore. The river has both scenic and historical appeal. Captain John Smith explored the Pocomoke River around 1608. Although the swamp proved an impenetrable barrier to colonial settlement, the river did carry trade vessels to and from Snow Hill. Years later, Civil War deserters and escaping slaves sought haven along the Pocomoke River and its tributaries.

These days the Pocomoke belongs to wildlife; you'll hear the splash of jumping bass, the amazingly diverse bird calls and the croaking of the ubiquitous frogs. The Pocomoke River area supports more bird species than almost any other in the Atlantic inland area. Rare prothonotary warblers and elusive pileated woodpeckers can be sighted in this birdwatcher's paradise. Each park area has a nature trail to bring visitors into close proximity with the park's bird population.

At Milburn Landing the one-mile, self-guided Bald Cypress Nature Trail winds through three different forest areas. In a once-cultivated area, loblolly pines grow where corn was harvested. Gradually the pines will be replaced with the second type of growth, the hardwood forest. Hardwoods include red maple, American hornbeam, dogwood, oak and sweetgum. The third area is the bald cypress swamp.

Across the river at Shad Landing you can explore the ¾-mile Trail of Change. This 45-minute hike will give you a chance to observe the changes taking place in the Pocomoke Forest. Over the years both nature and man's use of this area have changed. The trail was once a road used by shad fisherman, who brought their catch in at the river landing. Along the trail there were scattered homesites, now reclaimed by the forest. Man's impact can also be observed in the nonindigenous vegetation you'll see. There are a prickly pear cactus, black walnut and Norway maple, all added by long-ago residents.

The bald cypress swamp, primordial in its appearance, is a natural world like that found in the Dismal and Okefenokee swamps. This is the northernmost limit of the bald cypress (see Battle Creek Cypress Swamp sanctuary selection). To learn more about the wetlands, visit the Nature Center at Shad Landing. There you'll see hands-on exhibits focusing on the flora and fauna of the park. The park is open Memorial Day weekend and then daily during the summer months. Guided canoe trips are organized during the summer. Call ahead—(301)632-2566—to register for these naturalist-led Pocomoke River trips.

Boat docks and launching ramps are at both park areas. Shad Landing also has a marina where you can rent canoes and rowboats. Those with their own boats can rent one of the 23 marina boat slips. They all have water and electrical hookups.

Both parks offer picnicking and fishing (including a Fish for Fun pond for youngsters at Shad Landing). Shad Landing also has a Marina Commissary Store, a swimming pool, athletic fields and camping. The Park Office is open 8:00 A.M. to 4:30 P.M. off season and 8:00 A.M. to midnight in season. No pets are allowed in the park.

Directions: From Baltimore take Route 2 south to Route 50. Take Route 50 east about 90 miles to Salisbury. Then take Route 12 south 20 miles to Snow Hill. At Snow Hill turn right on Route 394 and right again on Route 113; this will lead to Shad Landing. For Milburn Landing from Route 12, proceed one mile north on Route 354.

Pick Your Own Produce

Dozens of Maryland farmers open their orchards and fields to those who enjoy picking fresh fruits and vegetables. Many of these farms are featured in my book *Beauty & Bounty: One-Day Nature Trips in and Around Washington, D.C.* A free brochure, compiled by the Maryland Roadside Marketing Association in cooperation with the Cooperative Extension Service and the Division of Agricultural Development and entitled *Pick Your Own & Direct Farm Markets in Maryland*, provides a county-by-county guide to picking produce, with a handy chart on harvest dates. This brochure is available at county libraries and extension offices, or by sending a self-addressed, stamped envelope with your request to the Division of Marketing, Maryland Department of Agriculture, Parole Plaza Office Building, Annapolis, Maryland 21401.

Maryland Calendar of Events

The exact date of an event often varies from year to year. For general planning, each month has been divided into three parts: Early (1st–9th); Mid (10th–19th); and Late (20th–31st). Event phone numbers may change in such cases, contact county tourism office. All Maryland phone numbers have a 301 area code.

JANUARY

Late:

Baltimore Convention Center, Baltimore. *Chesapeake Bay Boat Show.* 561-1140.

FEBRUARY

Mid:

Boordy Vineyards, Hydes. *Valentine's Day Celebration.* 592-5015.
Mary Surratt House, Clinton. *Antique Valentine Display.* 868-1121.

MARCH

Mid:

Wisp Ski Area, McHenry. *Winterfest.* 334-1948.
Cunningham Falls State Park, Thurmont. *Maple Syrup Demonstration.* 271-7374.
London Town Publik House, Edgewater. *Tavern Days.* 956-4900.

Late:

Historic St. Mary's City. *Maryland Days.* 862-0990 or 862-0960.
Brookside Gardens, Wheaton. *Spring Flower Display.* 949-8230.

APRIL

Early:

Historic St. Mary's City. *Tavern Night, Farthing Ordinary.* 862-0960.

Mid:

London Town Publik House & Gardens, Edgewater. *Daffodil Show.* 956-4900.
Brunswick Museum, Brunswick. *History Days.* 834-7100.
National Colonial Farm, Accokeek. *Farm Day.* 283-2113.
Mary Surratt House, Clinton. *John Wilkes Booth Escape Tour.* 868-1121.
National Capital Trolley Museum, Wheaton. *Trolley Car Spectacular.* 384-9797.
Sandy Point State Park, Annapolis. *Sandy Point Boat Show.* 268-8828.
Antietam Battlefield, Sharpsburg. *Easter Sunrise Service.* 432-5124.

Late:

Furnace Town, Snow Hill. *Fish 'n Fowl Day.* 632-2032.

Ocean City Convention Center. *Wildfowl Carving Competition, Ward Foundation.* 742-4988.

London Town Publik House & Garden, Edgewater. *Horticulture Day.* 956-4900.

Mary Surratt House, Clinton. *Civil War Encampment.* 868-1121.

Statewide. *Maryland House and Garden Pilgrimage.* 269-2686.

MAY

Early:

Martinak State Park, Denton. *Martinak Day.* 479-1619 or 479-1623.

Ellicott City. *May Arts Festival.* 992-2483.

Howard County Fairgrounds. *Maryland Sheep & Wool Festival.* 823-4037.

Fire Museum of Maryland, Lutherville. *Steam Sunday.* 321-7500.

Costen House, Pocomoke City. *May Day.* 957-1738.

Montpelier Mansion Grounds, Laurel. *Montpelier Spring Festival.* 776-2805.

Shriver Homestead, Union Mills. *Flower and Plant Market.* 848-2288.

Mid:

Smallwood State Park, Marbury. *Military Muster.* 743-7613.

Furnace Town, Snow Hill. *Country Music Festival.* 632-2032.

Late:

Dorchester Heritage Museum, Horns Point. *Antique Fly-In.* 228-3234 or 228-3999.

Chestertown. *Tea Party Festival.* 778-0416.

William Paca Garden, Annapolis. *Rose & May Flowers Day.* 267-6656.

Carroll County Farm Museum, Westminster. *Memorial Day Celebration.* 848-9050.

Fort Frederick State Park, Big Pool. *Fort Frederick Rendezvous.* 842-2155.

Historic St. Mary's City. *Publik Times* (thru Sept.). 862-0990.

JUNE

Early:

Carroll County Farm Museum, Westminster. *Antique/Craft Fair & Farm Show.* 848-7775 or 876-2667.

Fort Frederick State Park, Big Pool. *Black Powder Shoot.* 842-2155.

Berrywine Plantations Winery, Mt. Airy. *Great Strawberry Wine Festival.* 662-8687.

Mary Surratt House, Clinton. *Victorian Wedding & Reception.* 868-1121.

Steppingstone Museum, Havre de Grace. *Highland Games.* 939-2299.
Clara Barton House, Glen Echo. *Turn-of-the-Century Sunday Afternoons.* 492-6245.

Mid:

Fort McHenry, Baltimore. *National Flag Day Celebration.* 563-FLAG.
Patterson Park & Museum, St. Leonard. *Children's Day.* 586-0050.
Carroll County Farm Museum, Westminster. *Deer Creek Fiddler's Convention.* 848-7775 or 876-2667.

Late:

Historic St. Mary's City. *Grand Militia Muster/Charter Days.* 862-0990 or 862-0960.
Steppingstone Museum, Havre de Grace. *Old Fashioned Game Day.* 939-2299.
Cypress Park, Pocomoke City. *Pocomoke Cypress Festival.* 957-1919.
Fort Frederick State Park, Big Pool. *Military Field Days.* 842-2155.

JULY

Early:

Cloisters Children's Museum, Brooklandville. *Indian Summer.* 823-2550.
Inner Harbor, Baltimore. *July 4th Fanfare.* 837-INFO.
Allen Pond Park, Bowie. *Independence Day Celebration.* 262-6220.
Washington Monument State Park, Middletown. *July 4th Fireworks.* 432-8065.
Carroll County Farm Museum, Westminster. *Old Fashioned Fourth.* 848-7775 or 876-2667.
Grantsville. *Penn Alps Summerfest & Quilt Show.* 334-1948.

Mid:

Smallwood State Park, Marbury. *Garden Party.* 743-7613.
Cecil's Old Mill & General Store, Great Mills. *Cecil Appreciation Days.* 994-1510.
Furnace Town, Snow Hill. *Militia Day.* 632-2032.
B&O RR Station Museum, Ellicott City. *Christmas in July.* 461-1944.
Carroll County Farm Museum, Westminster. *Heritage Day-Ethnic Festival.* 848-7775 or 876-2667.
Fort Frederick State Park, Big Pool. *French & Indian War Days.* 842-2155.

Late:

Lilypons Water Gardens, Lilypons. *Lotus Blossom Festival.* 874-5133.
St. Clement's Island, Colton Point. *Blessing of the Fleet.* 884-2144.
Kimmey House, Westminster. *Ice Cream Sundae Sunday.* 848-6494.

AUGUST

Early:

Union Mills Homestead Park, Union Mills. *Old Fashioned Corn Roast Festival.* 848-2288.

Furnace Town, Snow Hill. *Old Fashioned Camp Meeting.* 632-2032.

Historic St. Mary's City. *Tidewater Archeology Weekend.* 862-0990 or 862-0960.

Hager House, Hagerstown. *Jonathan Hager Frontier Craft Days.* 790-3200.

Mary Surratt House, Clinton. *Tea Time.* 868-1121.

Mid:

Berrywine Plantations, Mt. Airy. *Winery Festival & Bluegrass Jamboree.* 662-8687.

Late:

North Branch C&O Canal Park, Cumberland. *C&O Canal Boat Festival.* 777-7563.

Crownsville. *Maryland Renaissance Festival.* 266-7304.

Fort Frederick State Park, Big Pool. *French & Indian War Days.* 842-2155.

Steppingstone Museum, Havre de Grace. *Civil War Re-enactment Demonstration.* 939-2299.

State Fairgrounds, Timonium. *Maryland State Fair.* 252-0200.

SEPTEMBER

Early:

Point Lookout State Park. *Point Lookout State Park Bath Tub Races.* 872-5688.

Carroll County Farm Museum, Westminster. *Steam & Gas Round-Up.* 848-7775 or 876-2667.

Lilypons Water Garden, Lilypons. *Koi Festival.* 874-5133.

Brunswick Museum, Brunswick. *Railroad Day.* 834-7100.

Mid:

Fort McHenry, Baltimore. *Defender's Day.* 962-4290.

Sandy Point State Park, Annapolis. *Maryland Seafood Festival.* 268-7682.

Mary Surratt House, Clinton. *John Wilkes Booth Escape Route Tour.* 868-1121.

Historic St. Mary's City. *Maritime Heritage Festival.* 862-0960.

Smallwood State Park, Marbury. *Candlelight Tour & Encampment.* 743-7613.

Ellicott City. *County Fair & Antique Auction.* 992-2483.

Chestertown. *Candlelight Walking Tour.* 778-0416.

Shafer Park, Boonsboro. *Boonsboro Days.* 582-6969.

London Town Publik House & Gardens, Edgewater. *Grand Illumination*. 956-4900.

Chesapeake Bay Maritime Museum, St. Michaels. *Museum Days Members Weekend*. 745-2916.

Late:

Hampton National Historic Site, Baltimore. *Hampton Colonial Farm Day & Craft Fair*. 823-7054.

Pemberton Hall Park, Salisbury. *Pemberton Colonial Fair*. 546-3466.

Carroll County Farm Museum, Westminster. *Maryland Wine Festival*. 848-7775 or 876-2667.

National Capital Trolley Museum, Wheaton. *Trolley Car Extravaganza*. 384-9797.

Ocean City. *Sunfest*. 289-2800.

New Market. *New Market Days*. 831-6791.

Remington Farms, Chestertown. *National Hunting & Fishing Day*. 778-1565.

Fort Frederick State Park, Big Pool. *Governor's Invitational Firelock Match*. 842-2155.

Brunswick Museum, Brunswick. *Railroad Days*. 834-7100.

Steppingstone Museum, Havre de Grace. *Fall Harvest Days*. 939-2299.

Furnace Town, Snow Hill. *Fall Festival*. 632-2032.

Larriland Farm, Woodbine. *Fall Apple Festival*. 489-7034.

Kimmey House, Westminster. *Needlework Show*. 848-6494.

OCTOBER

Early:

Christmas Country Store, Great Mills. *Christmas Open House*. 884-4829.

Oakland. *Autumn Glory Festival*. 334-1948.

Chesapeake Bay Maritime Museum, St. Michaels. *Mid-Atlantic Small Craft Festival V*. 745-2916.

Ballestone Mansion, Essex. *Fall Festival*. 686-0043.

Chancellor's Point Natural History Area, Historic St. Mary's City. *Indian Culture Day*. 862-0960.

Furnace Town, Snow Hill. *Fall Festival*. 632-2032.

Wicomico Youth & Civic Center, Salisbury. *Wildfowl Carving & Art Exhibition*. 742-4988.

Schifferstadt, Frederick. *Oktoberfest*. 663-1611.

Mid:

Clearwater Nature Center at Cosca Regional Park, Clinton. *Nature Craft Festival*. 297-4575.

North Market Street, Frederick. *In the Street*. 694-1435.

Mary Surratt House, Clinton. *Victorian Craft Fair*. 868-1121.

Teakle Mansion, Princess Anne. *Olde Princess Anne Days*. 651-1705.

Calvert Marine Museum, Solomons. *Patuxent River Appreciation Days.* 326-2042.

Thurmont. *Catoctin Colorfest.* 271-4432.

Fort Frederick State Park, Big Pool. *Black Powder Shoot.* 842-2155.

St. Mary's County Fairgrounds, Leonardtown. *St. Mary's County Oyster Festival.* 373-5242.

Berrywine Plantations, Mt. Airy. *October Wine Festival.* 662-8687.

Carroll County Farm Museum, Westminster. *Fall Harvest Days.* 848-7775 or 876-2667.

Godiah Spray Plantation, Historic St. Mary's City. *Harvest Home Celebration.* 862-0960.

Fire Museum of Maryland, Lutherville. *Model Show.* 321-7500.

Late:

London Town Publik House & Gardens, Edgewater. *Needlework Show.* 956-4900.

Cloisters Children's Museum, Brooklandville. *Halloween Party & Parade.* 823-2550.

Washington College, Chestertown. *Chestertown Wildlife Show & Sale.* 778-1046.

B&O RR Station Museum, Ellicott City. *Haunted Railroad Station.* 461-1944.

Fort Frederick State Park, Big Pool. *Ghost Walk.* 842-2155.

Sandy Point State Park, Annapolis. *Chesapeake Appreciation Days Festival.* 647-4747.

NOVEMBER

Early:

Brookside Gardens, Wheaton. *Fall Chrysanthemum Show.* 949-8231.

Essex Community College, Essex. *Ethnic Heritage Festival.* 522-1216.

Mid:

Easton. *Waterfowl Festival.* 822-4567.

Chesapeake Bay Maritime Museum, St. Michaels. *Guns & Gunners of the Chesapeake.* 745-2916.

B&O RR Station Museum, Ellicott City. *Treasury of Trains.* 461-1944.

Mary Surratt House, Clinton. *Victorian Collectors' Show.* 868-1121.

Late:

Brunswick Museum, Brunswick. *Victorian Christmas.* 834-7100.

Carroll County Farm Museum, Westminster. *Christmas Open House.* (thru early Dec.) 848-7775 or 876-2667.

Brome-Howard House, Historic St. Mary's City. *Christmas Shopping Fair.* 862-0960.

Schifferstadt, Frederick. *Holiday Open House.* 663-1611.

Market Street, Pocomoke City. *Pocomoke City Christmas Parade.* 957-1919.

DECEMBER

Early:

Kimmey House, Westminster. *Victorian Tea.* 848-6494.

Annapolis. *Christmas in Annapolis.* 268-8687.

Downtown Frederick. *Christmas in Frederick.* 694-1435.

Ballestone Mansion, Essex. *Ballestone's Holly Tour.* 686-0043.

State House, Historic St. Mary's City. *Christmas Madrigal Evenings.* 862-0960.

Ladew Topiary Garden, Monkton. *Christmas at an English Country House.* 557-9466.

Courtyard Museum, Baltimore. *Candlelight Evening.* 396-3523.

Brunswick Museum, Brunswick. *Victorian Christmas.* 834-7100.

London Town Publik House & Gardens, Edgewater. *Child's Colonial Christmas.* 956-7100.

Heritage Society Museum, Essex. *Christmas Tour.* 574-934.

Carroll County Farm Museum. *Christmas Open House–Christmas in the Country.* 848-7775 or 876-2667.

Mount Clare Mansion, Baltimore. *Colonial Christmas.* 837-3262.

Belair Mansion. *City Holiday Tree Lighting Program.* 262-6200.

Historical Society of Carroll County, Westminster. *Victorian Christmas Tea.* 848-6494.

History House, Cumberland. *History House Victorian Christmas Tours.* 777-8678.

Annapolis. *Candlelight Pub Crawl.* 263-5401.

Montpelier Mansion, Laurel. *Candlelight Tours.* 779-2011.

Mid:

Historic Havre de Grace. *Candlelight Tour.* 939-3947 or 939-2686.

Smallwood State Park, Marbury. *Candlelight Tour.* 743-7613.

Cloisters Children's Museum, Brooklandville. *Candlelight Tour.* 823-2550.

London Town Publik House & Gardens, Edgewater. *Christmas Candlelight Tour.* 956-4900.

State Circle, Annapolis. *State House by Candlelight.* 269-3400.

Union Mills Homestead Park, Union Mills. *Poinsettia & Greens Sales.* 848-2288.

Mary Surratt House, Clinton. *Victorian Christmas by Candlelight.* 868-1121.

Beall-Dawson House, Rockville. *Holiday Open House.* 762-1492.

Brookside Gardens at Wheaton Regional Park, Wheaton. *Brookside Gardens Christmas Show.* 949-8231.

Hagerstown. *Christmas at the Miller House.* 797-8782.

William Paca House, Annapolis. *Christmas at the William Paca House.* 267-8149.

Chestertown. *Historic Chestertown Christmas Tour.* 778-0866.

Vienna. *Luminaries.* 376-3275.

B&O RR Station Museum, Ellicott City. *Old Fashioned Christmas Gardens.* 461-1944.

Late:

Fire Museum of Maryland, Lutherville. *Christmas Opening.* 321-7500.
Inner Harbor, Baltimore. *New Year's Extravaganza.* 837-INFO.

INDEX

TO HELP YOU PLAN AND ENJOY YOUR TRAVEL IN THE MID-ATLANTIC AREA

THE WALKER WASHINGTON GUIDE   **$6.95**
The sixth edition of the "Guide's guide to Washington,"
completely revised by Katharine Walker, builds on a 25-year
reputation as the top general guide to the capital. Its 320
pages are packed with museums, galleries, hotels, restaurants,
theaters, shops, churches, as well as sites. Beautiful maps and
photos. Indispensable.

**ADVENTURE VACATIONS IN
FIVE MID-ATLANTIC STATES**   **$9.95**
This all-season guide to making the most of free time in PA,
MD, VA, WV and NC features hiking, biking, cross-country
skiing, trail riding, sailing and canoeing; also archeological
digs, mystery weekends, craft and specialty workshops, and
lending a hand and elder-hosteling. Tips on planning, costs,
equipment and special attractions included.

WASHINGTON ONE-DAY TRIP BOOK   **$7.95**
101 fascinating excursions within a day's drive of the capital
beltway—out and back before bedtime. The trips are arranged
by seasons and accompanied by calendars of special events,
map and notes on facilities for the handicapped.

PHILADELPHIA ONE-DAY TRIP BOOK   **$8.95**
And you thought Independence Hall and the Liberty Bell were all
Philadelphia had to offer? Norman Rockwell Museum, Pottsgrove
Mansion, Daniel Boone Homestead, Covered Bridges and Amish
Farms are among 101 exciting one-day trips featured.

ONE-DAY TRIPS THROUGH HISTORY   **$9.95**
Describes 200 historic sites within 150 miles of the nation's
capital where our forebears lived, dramatic events occurred
and America's roots took hold. Sites are arranged chronologically starting with pre-history.

THE VIRGINIA ONE-DAY TRIP BOOK   **$8.95**
Jane Ockershausen Smith, one of the most experienced travel
writers in the Mid-Atlantic area, admits to being surprised by
the wealth of things to see and do in the Old Dominion. With
101 sites divided into seven geographic regions, this is the
perfect guide for anyone who is anywhere in Virginia.

Also:

Florida One-Day Trips (from Orlando). What to do after you've done Disney. **$5.95**

Call it Delmarvalous. How to talk, cook and "feel to hum" on the Delaware, Maryland and Virginia peninsula. **$7.95**

Going Places With Children. More Than 400 things for kids to see and do in Washington, D.C. **$5.95**

Footnote Washington. Tracking the engaging, humorous and surprising bypaths of capital history by one of the city's most popular broadcasters. **$8.95**

Mr. Lincoln's City. An illustrated guide to the Civil War sites of Washington, as readable as it is informative. **$14.95**

Walking Tours of Old Washington and Alexandria. $100,000 might buy you the original Paul Hogarth watercolors reproduced here in full color, but then you'd be missing the engaging text and the convenience of taking it all along as you step back into the distinguished heritage preserved in our Capital's finest old buildings. Usable art; exquisite gift. **$24.95**

Order Blank for all EPM books described here. Mail with check to:

EPM Publications, Inc.
Box 490, McLean, VA 22101

Title	Quantity	Price	Amount	Shipping
The Maryland One-Day Trip Book		$10.95		$2.00 each book

Subtotal	
Virginia residents, add 4½% **tax**	
Shipping	

Name _____

Street _____

City _____ **State** _____ **Zip** _____

Total	

Remember to enclose names, addresses and enclosure cards for gift purchases.
Please note that prices are subject to change. Thank you.

About the Author

Jane Ockershausen Smith of Bowie, Maryland, is perhaps the most active travel writer covering the Mid-Atlantic. She is the regional contributor for National Geographic *Traveler* and travel editor of *Go* magazine, and writes a feature column for *AAA World*. Her byline is seen frequently in the *Journal* Newspapers, and her articles have appeared in *The Baltimore Sun, The Washington Post, The Washington Times, Washingtonian, Mid-Atlantic Country, The Buffalo News, The Chicago Tribune, The Oregonian* and *The Dallas Times Herald*. A member of the Society of American Travel Writers and the American Society of Journalists and Authors, Ms. Smith is also the author of five previous One-Day Trip books.

J. AUGUST SMITH